PENGUIN NON-FICTION

800,000,000 The Real China

Ross Terrill was born in Melbourne in 1938
and educated at Melbourne and Harvard
Universities. A China scholar and a political
scientist, he is Associate Professor of
Government at Harvard University. Author of
R. H. Tawney and His Times and co-author
of *China and Ourselves* and *China Profile* he
has written many articles on the Far East in the
American *New Republic* and *Atlantic Monthly*
and publications in Australia and Japan. A
visitor to China in 1964, 1971, and 1973, Dr
Terrill is writing a new book on life and work
in five Chinese cities, entitled *Flowers on an
Iron Tree.*

Ross Terrill

800,000,000
The Real China

Penguin Books

Penguin Books Ltd,
Harmondsworth, Middlesex, England
Penguin Books Australia Ltd,
Ringwood, Victoria, Australia
Penguin Book (N.Z.) Ltd,
182–190 Wairau Road, Auckland 10, New Zealand

First published in the U.S.A. 1972
Published in Great Britain by Heinemann 1972
Published in Penguin Books 1975

Copyright © Ross Terrill, 1971, 1972, 1975

Made and printed in Great Britain by
Richard Clay (The Chaucer Press) Ltd
Bungay, Suffolk
Set in Linotype Baskerville

Contents

Acknowledgements

For their kind assistance, my thanks to:

Hosts in China who did not let my impatience sap their keenness to help me see and learn, among them: Chou Nan, Liu Ju-ts'ai, Ma Yu-chen, T'ang Ming-chao, P'eng Hua, Chou P'ei-yuan, Chou I-liang.

Friends scattered abroad who lit or smoothed my path: Wilfred Burchett, who knows today's East Asia better than any of his countrymen; Paul Lin and Lee Tsung-ying, patriots in *diaspora*; Etienne Manac'h, lively mind and spirit as well as diplomat; Stephen Fitzgerald, scholar, drinker, best of travelling companions; Jack Gregory, historian of China, who first turned my gaze to the China coast; Margaret Flory and co-workers in the United Presbyterian Church; Chao Fu-san, whom I did not see in 1971 but often thought about.

Colleagues at Harvard's East Asian Research Center who make it a happy place to work in; especially the high standards, encouragement, and conversation of Ben Schwartz, John Fairbank, and Jim Thomson.

R.T.

Harvard University
December 1971

Some Terms and Names

catty   half a kilogram
C.C.P.   Chinese Communist party
Chi P'eng-fei   Foreign Minister
Lao Tzu   Taoist philosopher-recluse of some 2,500 years ago
Liberation   Chinese term for 1949 revolution
loess   dusty yellow-red soil in parts of north and north-west China
Lu Hsun   left-wing writer and social critic (1881–1936) admired by Mao
Luxingshe   (pronounced 'Loo-shing-sheh') China Travel Service
May 4 Movement   nationalistic cultural and political upsurge started by students in 1919
May 7 school   correctional school, mixing labour and study, for professionals in need of 'remoulding'
May 16 organization   extreme leftist network of the Cultural Revolution period, now attacked for having used violence and opposed Mao
mou   one sixth of an acre
Pai Hsiang-kuo   Foreign Trade Minister
P.L.A.   People's Liberation Army – the Chinese army
Revolutionary Committee   unit of administration in China since the Cultural Revolution, from the province level to that of individual factories and communes
ta tzu pao   wall poster written in large characters
yuan (Y)   Chinese monetary unit, about 17p

1 To China

A heat haze sits over Hong Kong harbour on a bright
June morning. The taxi draws up at Kowloon railway
station. For several years, I have looked at this building
the way a discontented East German looks at the Branden-
burg Gate in Berlin: an enticing, infuriating doorway to
a world much desired but hard to enter. But this morning
the Victorian brick station was delightfully inviting. For
in my pocket was a Chinese visa and a train ticket to
Canton.

In my imagination, the train was history's conveyor
belt, rolling, not ninety miles to Canton, but from one
universe to another. In fact, the train was its usual workaday self. It was loaded with housewives, workmen heading for the New Territories, vendors with beer and cigarettes, youths going out to Shatin for a swim. For these
people the train was a 'local', boring as a subway ride
in Manhattan. For a few others – politicians from the
Komeito (Clean Government party) of Japan, an Indian
diplomat, myself – it was an international train, bound
for a land which even today exudes mystery. These bored
and worldly carriages also contained a certain excitement.

South China reclines green and gold beneath the hot
morning sun, as we approach the border village of Lo Wu.
Peasants are in lunchtime circulation, wearing broad
hats, carrying bundles. Chickens scratch placidly at the
foot of a banyan tree. Boys call a greeting from a railside
path, appealingly unawed by proximity to this frontier,
which is not only political but almost moral and philo-
sophical. The line of demarcation is a footbridge. Walk-

ing across it, I look high into the green mountains. On the highest peak is a frontier guardhouse with glass windows. Behind me, the aggressive vendors, the gaudy clothes, the Coca-Cola. Ahead, a world which is sterner in its political imperatives, but which in human terms may be a simpler and more relaxed world.

There really *are* 'two Chinas'. Not 'Taiwan' and the 'Mainland', but rather the *image* we have of China in the United States, and the *reality* of China. Our press talks of China as power struggles and bombs and numbers. But here is China as rice and heat, glue and vaccinations, babies crying, old men playing chess. Last week, China was for me a matter of embassies and letters and magazines arriving by post. This morning, it has become a matter of trains and tea, Chinese beds, telephone numbers, weariness. There is a purging, utterly simple wonder about actually chugging mile by mile into China. The cardboard figures of a frozen scenario start to breathe and sweat and make a noise. From San Francisco to Singapore and beyond, you find pockets of Chinese society. But only in China do you see this civilization in its present power and in its ancient and beautiful cradle, and begin to sense how much the Chinese people and nation may mean in the pattern of future decades.

On the Chinese side, in the township of Shumchun, the traveller enters a building which is combined railway station, customs house, and hotel. The colour red impinges at once, as at a carnival. Political texts and admonitions light up the corridors and salons like labelled pillar-boxes. The frontier formalities are as sparse as the surrounding propaganda is luxuriant. Luggage is not examined. The questions of the border officials are not technical. The health man is first and he has been briefed. Before looking at my papers he asks with a smile, 'Have you come from America or Australia this time?' The next official is a People's Liberation Army man and he has only one question: 'Where did you learn *p'u-t'ung hua* [standard Chinese]?' Then I am ushered into a waiting room until lunch is served and the train for Canton is ready to depart.

The room gives onto a whitewashed balcony, covered with grapevines, and through the brilliant green leaves you see the red soil and curved hills of Kwangtung. In the foreground are two huge signboards, red and white with political exhortations, as if to stir the midday lassitude. One is about world-wide unity against imperialism. The other is about the economic tasks necessary to the building of socialism. Peasant China meanders gently by, amiable and placid in a time-honoured daily round. Political China stridently addresses it from a printed board, which seems stiff and impersonal among the chickens and the children.

Mao adorns the interior of the building as Jesus adorns a church. But that morning in Shumchun, the 'cult' struck me with a meaning it had never had before. I doubt I can convey it. This 'image' is Mao Tse-tung, *the Chinese politician*, not some fictional device, half bogey, half god. To see these pictures in China is to be less shocked by the cult than to see them on the printed page far from China. This is not our country, or a country we can easily understand, but the country of Mao. He remarked two generations ago, 'We cannot even speak of socialism if we are robbed of a country in which to practise it.' He rose from obscurity and led it to dignity. He is one of these 800,000,000 people, and his life's work has transformed their life.

I became critical of the propaganda in China, as later pages show. But this morning at the frontier, it seemed to me that the cult of Mao is not *incredible*, as it seems outside China. It becomes odd when it encounters our world. On its own terms, within its own functioning political reality, it is less odd. And much of the gulf across which the cult of Mao seems odd, I felt, is not political, but cultural and linguistic. It is odd to us partly because we have no consciousness of Chinese social modes, and because we read the texts and slogans as sets of

English phrases, which is like imbibing wine as frozen ice-blocks.

Behind me in another room, lunch is being noisily and aromatically prepared. A girl with plaits and rosy cheeks (Miss Wang) pads in to fetch me, and we walk to the dining room past a banner which begins: 'The Nixon government is beset with troubles ...' Miss Wang is a plain girl, with kind eyes. A native of Shanghai, she finds Kwangtung too hot. She rails against Liu Shao-ch'i (purged former President of China) as she leads me to a table arrayed with chicken soup, shrimps, and boiled rice. Engagingly, she sits beside me as I eat, and, bubbling like a brook, instructs me in the concept *i-fen wei-erh*. It means 'one divides into two' and is a key notion of Chairman Mao, opposed to Liu Shao-ch'i's false, liberal, harmonic concept, *ho-erh wei-i*, 'two unites into one.' There are contradictions in *everything*, she warns me with odd persistence as I press on with my lunch; one always divides into two ...

Across the room are the Komeito party politicians, and the Indian diplomat, who, like me, has his separate table. The luggage of the Komeito men is plastered with Swissair tags and labels. Diplomatically, they have avoided travelling Japan Airlines (a company then in the doghouse with Peking, for it was flying to Taipei, and thus 'trading with Taiwan'). To advertise that, they have made themselves look like a P.R. team for Swissair. A group of Chinese officials dine at a circular table. All but one of them are from the north of China. They are tall and bony, their skins are light, and they slurp large plates of noodles. But one, whose arms are darker, is a southerner. Instead of noodles he eats boiled rice, which he replenishes constantly from a large vat on a bench near the table. Miss Wang, perhaps assured that she has made her point, leaves me to my cup of tea. The room is languid as diners sit back from their empty dishes and let the beer lull them toward somnolence. But a whistle pierces the calm; the train for Canton is ready to go.

I realized that day how long seven years can be. In 1964 I had ridden this train (in reverse direction). To ride it again was to recall what changes – in China, in China's relation to the world, in myself – have occurred since then. In China there has taken place the amazing up-heaval of the Cultural Revolution.

In China's relation to the world there has begun a mutation of historic proportions. The walls crumble; China can no longer be called 'cut off' from other peoples. But the mutual interaction that now commences is quite unlike that when China was 'opened' to the West after the Opium War. The flow of power and influence was – from the Opium War at least until the 1949 revolution – largely one way. China was the *object* of Western *impact*. But in 1971, it seemed to me, a new kind of interaction between China and the world was actively under way.

The direction of the flow of influence is no longer one way – upon China – but increasingly *from* China as well. China's actions, its ideas, its bomb, have become vital motifs of world history. To be sure, China's change from a passive to an active force in the world has been gradual, not sudden, and will yet be gradual. But Peking's new diplomacy since the Cultural Revolution, and her new ties especially with the United States and the United Nations, have greatly stressed and spurred the process. Senator Wherry, a tireless exponent of the notion that China should be the object of Western schemes, vowed in 1940, 'With God's help, we will lift Shanghai up and up, ever up, until it is just like Kansas City.' But the time has arrived when Kansas City is no more likely to be a model for Shanghai than is Shanghai to be a model for Kansas City (or Manila, or Bombay). This new, active importance of China I pondered as the train sped across the East River and on to Canton.

The traveller himself had also changed. I knew that I was more sceptical of the claims of any 'ism' or any political system than seven years before. No longer did there seem to be a sharp and compelling choice between capital-

ism and Communism. I liked neither. I was a *saboteur de
l'absolu*. I now felt it was possible that a civilized human
being ought to put certain private values above the public values of either. The day before leaving the United
States for China, I delivered to its publisher a book on
social democracy. Here was this traveller's creed. A socialism never frozen, but constantly tested by men's reason
and values; one which holds social justice in one hand
and liberty in the other; which pursues collective purposes, yet not against the opinions of ordinary people;
which rejects both the political tyranny of Stalinism and
the economic tyranny of unbridled capitalism.

There are four major routes into China (as well as those
from Rangoon, Hanoi and Pyongyang). The Trans-
Siberian railway carries you slowly across the Eurasian
landmass to Peking, from Moscow via Ulan Bator. Again
from Moscow, there are flights, on both Aeroflot and
China Airlines, via Irkutsk to Peking. This way I entered
China in 1964. In recent years, both Air France and P.I.A.
(Pakistan) have begun service to Shanghai. The French
come into China from Rangoon, the Pakistanis from
Dacca. Neither is permitted to fly to Peking; only in a
Chinese plane may a traveller to the capital cover the last
leg of this route. The flight to Shanghai is now the most
common one from Europe to China.

The fourth route was the one I followed in 1971: the
three-hour train trip from Hong Kong to Canton. Like
the route to Shanghai, it provides a way of travelling to
Peking in stages, which is how the Chinese long required
foreigners to approach their capital. The entry by train
is in some ways the best. The traveller savours the landscape and peasant life of China before he is swallowed by
that small part of the nation which is urban China.

The *real* vehicle for travelling into China is not a plane
or a train. It is a piece of paper. Three inches by five
inches, elegant in red and black ink, it is headed 'Entry
and Exit Visa' and stamped with the title and red flag of

the People's Republic of China. In 1964 my visa had been issued in Poland. Travelling in Europe, I had applied in the summer of 1964 for a Chinese visa in London, Paris, Moscow, Budapest, and Prague. The response was not yes and not no. Disappointed, I reached Warsaw, my last port of call in Europe before returning to Melbourne. I went to the Chinese Embassy, a fawn oblong block on Bonifraterska Street, but with hardly a flicker of hope. I asked to see the ambassador, as much to complain about the discouragement offered to an (arrogant) young man who wanted to see China, as to make yet one more plea for a visa.

Surprisingly, I was seriously received. A senior Chinese diplomat sipped his tea gravely as I made my pitch. I filled in no more application forms, as I had done five times in other Chinese Embassies, but just talked about my interest in China. I was ushered out of the marble lobby, a little flushed from an ardent performance. At eleven o'clock that night I was in bed at the Hotel Bristol. A phone call came from the Chinese Embassy. A visa awaited me; would I kindly come and get it at eight the next morning?

In 1971, word of the visa also came by a telephone call. Again, there had been applications, but again the green light did not seem to come as a response to those applications. In 1967 I wished to go once more to China. After making a request through the Chinese Embassy in Warsaw, I received from Peking in May 1967 a letter stating: 'We are pleased to inform you that we agree with your visit to China.' But the visit never occurred. Perhaps because of the Cultural Revolution, the actual arrangements were indefinitely delayed.

Amidst the diplomatic fluidity of the spring of 1971, I was in touch with Chinese officials on larger matters. Out of the blue on 31 May came a call from a Chinese source in Canada. Would I like to visit China? If so, I should leave within two weeks. Arrangements were to be made at the Chinese Embassy in Ottawa.

The button for number 1201 at the Juliana Apartments – a building on Bronson Avenue where the Chinese temporarily had their embassy – was so well worn that the number was now scarcely visible. Diplomats there were extremely helpful, though they had no information from Peking about the nature, timing, or duration of my visit to China. Only on the morning of receiving the visa did I fill out an application form. I asked why the visa was not stamped into the passport but provided on a separate piece of paper. 'Because China and Australia do not have diplomatic relations.' I pointed out that in 1964 the Chinese Embassy in Warsaw had stamped the visa in the passport. The official replied simply, 'The comrades in Warsaw made a mistake.'

The private citizen visiting China today will be received through one of three channels. If he is a tourist, Luxingshe, the China Travel Service, will arrange his entire journey. It may even meet him at the frontier, and escort him to the frontier when the visit is done, as the Chinese used to do with foreigners under the dynasties. Especially since the Cultural Revolution, the Chinese do not expect tourists to come merely to see the sights. Luxingshe assumes as a matter of course that tourists will wish to examine the industrial and agricultural life of China, and the programme is set up almost as a study tour.

Most visitors coming on cultural exchange will be dealt with by the Chinese People's Association for Friendship with Foreign Countries. This covers doctors in China at the invitation of China's medical authorities, sportsmen, personages from associations having friendly links with China. The third category is the visiting journalist. He will be handled by the Information Department of the Foreign Ministry. In all three cases the visitor follows a daily programme set up by the Chinese authorities after considering the visitor's requests.

I went to China as a 'journalist and scholar' and was received mainly by the Foreign Ministry. My association with the visit of the Australian Labour party delegation in July complicated this arrangement, since this delegation was received essentially by the Chinese government (acting through a semi-official arm of the Foreign Ministry, the People's Institute for Foreign Affairs). I also had contact with the Association for Friendship with Foreign Countries.

What can the visitor learn in China? The pages of this book are my answer. They contain not what I know about China, but what I found in China in the summer of 1971. I have not set my account on a pedestal of history, or stretched it across a frame of theory; history and theory are for another occasion. What is offered is an eyewitness report. The reader can assess for himself the credibility of the report, and give it whatever wider context he chooses. As for *ways* of learning about China on a visit, I found there were five.

One may hear responsible government officials speak at first hand on Chinese policies. Instances were meetings with the Premier, Chou En-lai, and with the Vice-President of the Standing Committee of the National People's Congress, Kuo Mo-jo. Second, the visitor may obtain concrete data at particular institutions on the basic level, as in days spent at factories, communes, hospitals. Third, there can occur discussions between the visitor and Chinese of training or interests similar to his own. An example was a session with a professor of Peking University about topics in history and politics of mutual concern. Fourth, one may talk with *anyone* about his or her views and conditions of life. Though my spoken Chinese is not fluent, I learned much this way, and the reader will find many a quotation from a casual conversation in a taxi or on the street. Fifth, the visitor can simply look around him. A land of 800,000,000 people is a fantastic theatre for the curious eye (and being able to read the signs and posters helps). Between political talks, I never tired of watching the grace and order and habit of Chinese social life.

To be frank, my weeks in China exceeded expectations. The 1964 visit, a brief one of only two weeks, had made sufficient impact to entice me into study of China and its language. The 1971 visit deepened my admiration for China and its people.

I happen to like the peace of the brightly coloured hills and valleys of China. The concrete turn of the Chinese mind. The poise and calm, the understatement and irony, the cheerfulness and modesty, of Chinese conduct. The excellence of Chinese cuisine and the conscientious spirit of a Chinese kitchen.

I happen to admire the cultural confidence of the Chinese, which pads them against the rougher consequences of history's crimes and chaos. The long and rich past, which seems, for the Chinese, to rob the present of its tyranny and the future of total uncertainty.

I happen, too, to be moved by the social gains of the Chinese revolution. In a magnificent way, it has healed the sick, fed the hungry, and given security to the ordinary man of China. It has rolled off the weight of exploitation whose excess of evils strained patience and altruism beyond all reason. It has followed the principle of the ancient classic, *The Great Learning*: 'To disperse wealth is to collect the people.' It has put a flash of pride in the Chinese eye.

Yet I make serious criticisms (as the Chinese make self-criticisms). Post-1949 China is by no means a new heaven and a new earth. Wrong turns have at times been made, in economic and other policies. Disputes occur at high levels and low. The position of intellectuals, it seems to me, is especially problematic. All this is not too surprising, given China's problems, and given the familiar flaws in the Communist view of society. The Chinese purse cannot match what the Chinese hand would like to grasp. The steamroller of exigency snuffs out ideals and spoils tidy plans in China as in other countries. Chinese spirits have unfulfilled yearnings like all others.

There is no substitute, in my view, for weighing up the

Chinese revolution sector by sector, on the scale of its on-going effect on the lives of the Chinese people. History grants no automatic victories, nor the blessing of permanence to any moment, however splendid. The Chinese have no destiny to do right what everyone has done wrong before. They are not borne upward by some pre-set cosmic escalator. The great social progress in China has been sweated for lap by lap. Any 'blanket' faith in the Chinese way of socialism as necessarily superior to all others would be misplaced. The Chinese are unlikely to succeed in all they are attempting. They can count big achievements; they cannot deny grave problems. I *hope* China may evolve a settled social and political system that serves all of the people.

In Canton I ran into an American clergyman friend and we talked of religion in China. He brushed off the closing of churches, temples, and mosques. 'Anyway,' he declared, 'I am interested not in the churches but in the revolution.' I saw his point, yet I felt uneasy. His remark somehow recalled the quip about de Gaulle. He loved France, but not the French. Is there such an overarching reality, the 'Chinese revolution'?

I can only weigh a revolution in the lives of the people affected. I cannot condemn the Communist revolution in China, yet claim to have compassion toward the poor, the sick, the maltreated. I cannot without qualification call it a 'liberation', if I think there is no reason why people should not read a Bible or pray in a temple if they wish. The revolution is food and good health; short-cropped hair and hard work; dunce caps and boarded-up churches; buses and aqueducts; educational opportunities and dignity.

In the end, it is respect for China that makes it necessary to criticize. Taking the challenge of China seriously – its power *and* its social values – I feel I must bring my own values into the picture when I report on China. This makes a visit to China a spiritual struggle. Big questions of value rise every day from the din of the factory and the dust of the commune. To write blandly about China and neglect these questions would not be to respect but to demean China, and to fail in solidarity with the people of China. The future is open and in our own hands, and the Chinese people and all other peoples are now drastically interlocked in facing it. We shall understand ourselves together, and make a livable future together, or not at all. Chairman Mao is ultimately right when he insists: 'The people, and the people alone, are the motive force in the making of world history.' We owe it to our common humanity, and to the children of the world, to turn a steady, critical eye on the land of the 800,000,000.

2   *Perspectives*

Shimmering mirage, a China is conjured in our minds by scraps of news and speculation. Devilishly well organized; neat and regimented; striding ahead to overtake Russia and America; clean, abstemious; an army of sexless puppets, their daily life an incarnation of the Thought of Mao Tse-tung. Absence from China feeds the mirage. Fear, buttressed by ignorance, hints that China is formidable, or awful, or awfully formidable. How cunning those Chinese are! Do they not constantly surprise us? Such sacrifice of indulgence today for glory tomorrow!

We can be like Voltaire, philosophic China-watcher of another age. Sitting in Paris, he spun a mental tapestry of China less from facts than from disenchantment with the Europe of his day. The picture of Confucius in his study was a totem; maybe our pictures of Mao are too. As if the Chinese millions were mere moving illustrations of a Concept. Walk-on actors in a Drama of Historical Optimism or a Drama of Historical Pessimism!

The actual world of sweat and cicadas, boiled rice and bicycles, is a bit more complex. After seven years, I was back again. Did the mirage lift for a moment? Instead of 'China', here were rivers and mountains, and people getting up, working, eating, singing, arguing, planning, going to bed. Not objects for investigation, but situations, in which I seemed to be involved only a little less than the people around me.

Of course a visit has its illusions, as does absence. You feel the human simplicities of China too acutely. You get talking to Shanghai citizens about bringing up children, to a professor in Peking about how he teaches modern history. As if you and they stood on the same ground, wrestling with the social problems of the 1970s and the human dilemmas of all time. That is illusory. For while we remain grouped in nation-states, as long as East Asia remains a place of collision between American substance and Chinese shadow, China *is* another world. Mao chairs them; Nixon presides over us. Our human solidarity is at the mercy of what they cook up between them. You leave Canton, cross the border at Shumchun, and China again becomes 'China'. One corner of the triangle of hope and terror, the United States, Russia, and China. Stage play of Communism, before the beaming portrait of Chairman Mao. Belly of real estate at the south-east tip of Eurasia, which fifty nuclear bombs could turn into charcoal and gas within a week.

But the separateness is not forever. The strangeness of China is not objective, like that of the platypus. Separateness and strangeness both stem from the past relationship between China and ourselves. Here there are changes; will soon be more. Countries' 'images' of each other can depart terribly from fact. U.S.–Chinese relations give rich illustration. Yet international politics and our human existence do play out a crazy dialectic. It means that visiting China has its bit of the future to reflect. 'Being there', like waking up at 3 a.m., gives its own special angle on the totality of things.

Being in China in 1971 means realizing that although in the United States Vietnam looms large on our mental screens, with China a big country behind Vietnam, in Peking Vietnam fades into one of many countries down beyond the Middle Kingdom's southern provinces. It means observing that chance and distraction fleck Chinese politics no less than ours; a Foreign Ministry official remarked, when Peking in late June did a long (and favourable) commentary on the Common Market, 'During the Cultural Revolution we rather neglected the Common Market; now we're catching up and getting our position straight.'

Being in China means fielding queries at a university in Sian about how we dealt, at Harvard in the spring of 1970, with the question of giving or not giving grades and exams to students who went on strike because of the invasion of Cambodia. It means finding propaganda less depressing when spoken than when one reads it from afar on the printed page, because people do not always mean what they say, and when they do mean it, do not always believe it. You read a tirade about the high tide of African revolution; then next day a Chinese diplomat who has worked in Africa remarks on the immaturity of African movements and their inability to make revolution as China made it. Paraphrasing the ancient writer Sun Tzu, he smiles: 'They don't know themselves and they don't know the enemy; that's the trouble.'*

To be there is to recall – did I need the reminder? – that Chinese cooking is not just a 'great cuisine of the world', but a daily joy to 800 million and *the* major factor in any calculation of bright and dark sides to the Chinese people's life in 1971. To hear a high official say, when speaking of Western leftists who stay away from Taiwan for reasons of conscience, 'They should go, see what the place is like. When foreign leftists come to Peking, I urge them not to stay away from Moscow, but to stop over there and look around.' 'Being there' means boredom and humour, clashes of personality, getting up at 5 a.m., finding time to read the newspaper, deciding between the ballet and the cinema for tonight's entertainment.

I suppose each man has his China, as his Rousseau. A visit does not do much to replace the subjective with the objective. But the subjective has its own scale of truth and falsehood. The visitor is a human being; what hits him?

Appealing imprecision. People wander around; daydream. They will, when marketing, or in conversation, let the world go by in search of the pearl of great price. They

---

* Sun Tzu wrote in *The Art of War*: 'Know the enemy, know yourself, and in a hundred battles you will win a hundred victories.'

don't mince like Japanese, but amble as men in secure possession of the earth under their feet. They will stand and stare at you, then win you with a grin if you look up in anxiety or irritation. Officials at banquets, faces pink with wine, lean head-in-hand across the table, forgetting their elbows in the excitement of a line of talk. Men on duty in trains, when every passenger has been served his tea and all is calm, turn down the radio and play poker, or draw the blinds, swing two seats together, and snooze in the peace of the afternoon sun. China is comprehensively organized, but not perfectly organized – certainly not to Japanese pitch. The ragged edges, the ragamuffin element, the expansive gesture, have happily not been organized out of existence.

Asia's heart. China has a staggering cultural self-confidence, and she is beholden to no one. In the timeless haze of Peking you realize that today's Bangkok, Saigon, Taipei, are not cities of Asia's Asia but of America's Asia. Here in the 'Forbidden City' is the real challenge to Western hegemony. Today but an embryonic challenge, partly of the spirit, tomorrow it will develop the sinews of a power challenge. The importance of China is being transmuted from symbol to actuality by the increasing powerlessness of the West in Asia. In China you feel a strength which comes from belief in oneself. America's Asia cannot match this kind of strength. But then America's Asia is China's periphery. And in Peking, China seems to South-east Asia as the garment to the hem.

China's touchy pride. I went to the East Room of the Great Hall of the People on 5 July with E. Gough Whitlam, leader of the Australian Labour party, for a late-night talk with Chou En-lai. Recounting China's bitter experience with Russia, the Old Tiger warned us against trusting *our* ally, the United States. His point was a passionate assertion of each country's right to run its own affairs. Whitlam said America had not treated Australia badly, as Russia had China. The Premier threw apart his arms. 'But they both want to control others.' He beat his wicker chair for emphasis. 'Our socialist country will not be controlled by anyone.'

Chou summed up what is evident up and down China: deep sensitivity about China's dignity as an independent power. It goes back to the humiliation of the Opium War, when Britain bullied a weak China into a falling-domino torrent of concessions. You are constantly reminded that 'those days are gone.' The East wind prevails over the West wind. China has stood up. She will not be controlled by others.

The past is very present. Halfway between Sian and Yenan, in the orange loess-country where Chinese civilization began, lies the market town of Huang Ling. I drove there to see the tomb of the Yellow Emperor, father of the Han people. My Chinese companions (who had suggested this visit) entered with awe the grey-green gardens, lit up by the red pillars of a temple of commemorative tablets to the Yellow Emperor. It was 7 a.m., and the gnarled trees, one said to date from the time of the Yellow Emperor (some five thousand years ago), were ghostly in the still, clear morning air.

My Communist companions gazed at the elegant inscription: 'Cradle of the Fatherland's Civilization'. One of them, a diplomat called Chou Nan, who does calligraphy with a brush daily and writes poems in the traditional style, quoted suitable lines by heart from the Chinese classics. The five Chinese clustered round the hoary tablets, as Mr Chou pointed out passages to his eager colleagues.

Not a single slogan or Mao quote is found near the mound in which the Father of China may (or may not) lie. 'It would be unsuitable here,' a Shensi provincial aide explained crisply. I looked around the site, well kept by the Communist government. Apart from the historical inscriptions, some in Kuo Mo-jo's rich hand, the only writing near by was a placard on an old grey tree: 'Protect the forest, fight fires.'

Mental unity. Chou En-lai urged me to study the essay

Peking put out to mark the fiftieth anniversary of the founding of the Chinese Communist party. 'As you are a professor in America and Australia, it can be reference material for you.' That essay was, in early July, a Bible in China.

Drivers read it. The girls in the elevator at the Peking Hotel read it, between passengers. The radio broadcasts it. Companions cite it. Hosts ask my reaction to it. In Shanghai it is no less omnipresent; the same in Nanking, in Wusih. Sometimes a visitor to Harvard might think students read only books by Harvard faculty. A parallel impression, magnified a thousandfold, I had in China. It is intellectual incest on a gargantuan scale. Information, opinion, comes down from the mountain of authority to the plateau of public consumption. The people all have this official information; they have no other. The whole country, from Canton to the north-east, from the east coast to Sinkiang, has at least a surface mental unity unmatched in China's history. (Just as the whole country has the chronological unity of being on Peking time.) There is a rule by phrase, a bond in headlines, a solidarity by syntax. In the beginning was the Word ...

To the visiting writer, information is like melons in the market. If it's available, you get it. If it's not, your hands are empty. There is nothing in between. No point in trying to get light on government policy from a Chinese who has not received it from above. When you get something, however, it is reliable. The system would surely delight an eighteenth-century *philosophe*; the 'Word' is sovereign. On the other hand, it is a nightmare for the diplomat who has to put something in the pouch every week. Mingling one night with foreigners in Peking, I recalled a remark of a French diplomat who served in China, then in the United States: 'In Peking we had too little information. In New York we had too much. In neither case did we know what was going on.'

Formidable children. Here is a French class at the Middle School attached to Peking Normal University.

The faces are pictures of concentration. The class screams in unison: *'Vive le parti communiste; Vive la solidarité des peuples du monde.'* I ask one pretty lass in a coloured blouse why she studies French. 'To further the world revolution.' The answer seems ridiculous, but the ardent hunger for knowledge behind it is not.

The Chinese nation is studying as if for some cosmic examination. The bookshops are stiff with schoolchildren reading and buying textbooks, a lot published in the last year. A laundry boy is wrestling with Marx's *The Class Struggles in France*. A taxi driver has a recent pamphlet, *Philosophy for Working Men*. Tots in Shanghai sport aprons sewn with characters: 'Love science, Love hygiene, Love labour.'

Nor do they stuff their minds and forget their bodies. Rise at six and you find Chinese young people exercising in parks, on the waterfront, on rooftops. They twist and spin, jerk and wheel, doing 'hard' exercises (forms of karate), 'soft' (forms of *t'ai-chi ch'uan*, the snakelike, rhythmic art), and countless improvisations of their own. Some do theatrical swordplay; many walk on their hands, first steadying their upturned legs against a wall.

In short, China's 300 million young schoolchildren seem a formidable prospect for tomorrow's China. True, research is in many spheres backward. True, present professional opportunities are cruelly limited. But generations of scientifically minded, intellectually hungry, fit, earnest youth will be a magnificent base for more sophisticated advances in the 1980s and 1990s.

Equality is dull. Stroll along the Whangpu River bank (the 'Bund') in the evening, and you think at first the heart has gone out of Shanghai. Red neon lights up the river's ripples, but every single sign is a slogan. The row of tall British buildings, Shanghai's greeting to the Western world across the water, are shabby, and many unused. The former British Consulate, its furry lawns stretching out toward the junction of Whangpu River with Soochow Creek, is just a sailor's club. Not one prostitute, hardly a car. Some blocks beyond, Great World, once a sparkling place of entertainment, is silent as a morgue.

Nor do the vast billboards have anything to quicken the pulse. Posters and commentaries tell the story, congress by congress, of fifty years of the Chinese Communist party. The ear cannot vary the story. 'Sailing the Seas Depends upon the Helmsman' fills the air. The vast Big Ben of a clock on the Customs House strikes the hour, but instead of a chime, it booms out a rusty rendering of 'The East Is Red'. Is this Shanghai, or have I come upon a May 7 school (rural place of mixed labour and study for those found in the Cultural Revolution to need 'remoulding') set amidst a cardboard replica of the great Chinese port?

The Shanghai Bund is nothing, yet it's many things that matter. Forget the images; attend to the people. Watch them in the light of a full, bright moon, heads to the breeze off the water – a nice change, after work, from the heat of their houses. They read, lick ice-creams. Lovers leave their bicycles against the rails and seek a dark spot in the park (two cents admission, full of unlighted nooks). Listen to their talk, some on haunches in groups, young couples discussing future plans, old men at chess, precocious boys who ask me about my country.

Here are people in bland possession of a sector where once they were little better than things. For the Western visitor the Bund is nothing. Yet the fact that *he* is nothing as he wanders unheeded proves that what was once a preserve where he felt his authority now belongs to the Chinese people. There exists an obvious, to some people moving, egalitarianism in the social relationships of these streets and parks. Of course it is 'dull' for the spender or the adventurer. Justice is not necessarily exciting, and it is the face of international and social justice which smiles behind the blandness of the Shanghai Bund.

3 Anatomy of a Visit

My visit, from fluttery-stomached entry to exhausted exit, spanned forty days. It took in seven major cities, as well as towns and rural pockets. When possible, I took a train or drove, in a Shanghai or Volga car: by road to Yenan, a train trip from Changsha to Canton. The long hops were generally by air, in British Viscount, large Ilyushin 18, or the grasshopper of an Ilyushin 14, in which you sit (at a giddy angle until take-off) without seat belts, beside panoramic oblong windows. This *hsiao fei-chi* (small plane), as the Chinese call it, roars angrily but flies low, and there are splendid views.

There below is the flat, geometric somnolence of Sian, ancient capital of China and now capital of Shensi province, specked with T'ang dynasty pagodas. Its boulevards are lined with six and eight rows of trees and punctuated with four massive Ch'ing dynasty gates, sentries to a civilization. Down here now, the swelling mountains between Hunan province and Kiangsi province, which we bounce across flying from Nanchang to Changsha. At their foot, a world of rivers, canals, ponds, shimmering dusty blue in the morning heat, watering a patchwork of rice and cotton fields now alive with harvest activity and new planting.

Many of the air passengers are government officials, as often as not military men. One day on a flight to Peking, I found myself next to an air-force officer. He had the window seat, but when he noticed my interest in the landscape he offered to switch with me. I declined, but shifted to the window seat one row back when it proved to be vacant. The air-force officer, vigilant for my convenience, saw that my view was now obstructed by the propellers. He again went to great lengths to persuade me to accept his seat, and thus get a better elevation on the rolling plains below.

The hostesses of China Airlines are cheerful and informal. On a four-and-a-half-hour flight from Canton to Peking, after eight hot hours of delay at White Cloud Airport, I fell asleep when the meal of fruit and biscuits was done. A hand banged my shoulder. *'Pu yao hsui chao le! Tao le, tao le!'* ('Stop sleeping, we're here!') But Miss Wang had a pretty smile as she handed me chewing gum with an inscription on the wrapper: 'China Airlines: Safety, Speed, Comfort, Convenience.' Dressed like labourers, their hair straight and short, these girls are nevertheless often pretty.

My Chinese companions – diplomats, officials of the Revolutionary Committee in each province, aides of Luxingshe, the China Travel Service – did not warm to comments on physical appearance. One night there was a dinner in Nanking given by the Foreign Affairs Section of the Revolutionary Committee. Chiang Kai-shek's old capital was living up to its reputation as one of China's 'three furnaces' (Chungking and Wuhan are the others). As a sweet wine called *huang chiu* spurred the theme of 'friendship between the Chinese and Australian peoples', I remarked upon the good looks of the hostess on that day's Shanghai–Nanking flight. My host looked with concentration at his 'fish mandarin'. 'It is not the physical side but the thought which counts,' he pointed out. So I re-phrased my sentiment and won all-round approval: 'The thought of today's hostess seemed, from whatever angle you viewed it, admirable and inspiring.'

The hotels are comfortable and they have excellent service. They can be hot in summer, especially in the south, for there is no air conditioning. (In the cavernous oven called the Tung Fang Hotel at Canton, each room has a thermometer, as if to taunt the midsummer visitor with a measure of his misery.) In Peking I first stayed at the Hsin

Ch'iao, a functional hotel bordering the Legation Quarter; later, when Mr Whitlam arrived, at the luxurious Peking Hotel.

At the Hsin Ch'iao in 1964, I faced the courtyard, and early each morning could watch the hotel employees doing the rhythmic *t'ai-chi ch'uan* exercises. This time I overlook a hospital, which has written on it no nameplate but simply: 'Proletariat of the World Unite!' My bathroom towels have sewn into them the characters: 'Serve the People!' In Canton, the taps had the English markings for hot and cold, but here (and in all other cities) they have only Chinese characters. I mention at the service desk that I would like a radio. Within minutes there appears a set, the size of a TV, which I rent for a tiny fee. The room has a tall ceiling and a marble floor. Two large armchairs are covered with fawn linen and antimacassars. The china lamps have delicate silk shades. On the desk is a steel-nibbed pen and a bottle of ink.

The window is my TV set, and I often sit absorbed beside it. Now, a platoon of P.L.A. (People's Liberation Army) men running by at the double early in the morning. Now, tiny tots singing political songs as they march past. Shoppers with laden baskets. Girls and youths chatting in groups. And, endlessly, the bells of a thousand bicycles. Together with the cicadas and the morning sun, they ensure early rising. Opposite my bed is a picture of the mighty Nanking Bridge. I lie – without bedclothes, like a fish upon the mattress – in the first rays of the sun, and the light is reflected brilliantly from the silken red flags atop the bridge; a rosy beam to summon me to a new day.

The Peking Hotel (normally for official or semi-official guests) is older, with handsome, creaking wooden floors. Its staff, many of whom remember the hotel when it was under French management, are trained to a high pitch. The special delight of this hotel is the view from its vast, ornate windowsills. You see the bones of the city of Peking as Marco Polo saw them. Seven hundred years ago he noted: 'The streets are so straight and wide that you can see right along them from end to end and from one gate to the other. And up and down the city there are beautiful palaces, and many and great hostelries ... The whole city is arranged in squares just like a chessboard.' It is still like that.

The great Ch'angan boulevard runs across the city, set about with rows of trees. Bicycles swarm by, ringing their bells as if in irritation. Amidst their silver tangle, like carp among the minnows, cruise red and white buses. Sometimes two are hooked together with folding canvas connections, giving a caterpillar effect.

To one side of the boulevard lies the Tien An Men square. Symmetrically, the Great Hall of the People faces two vast museums, and the Monument to the People's Heroes stands in the square's centre. To the other side of the Ch'angan, there nest the purple walls and orange tiles of the former Imperial Palace (Forbidden City). The tower of the central post office rises behind the red pillars and green ridges of the compounds that flank the Palace. To the south, the Ch'ien Men gate stands, grey and solid sentry over the heart of official Peking.

The Peace Hotel in Shanghai is one of the world's best. It no longer echoes to the sound of titillating entertainment, as it did in pre-Liberation days. But for comfort, service, and one form of the 'peace' promised by its name, few hotels can match it. On my first stay, the room was so large that two elephantine white couches seemed lost within it. A separate 'massage alcove' was attached, and a blackwood robing room in which the lights went out automatically, by stages, two minutes after being switched on. Fresh peaches and cakes lay about the tables.

On my second stay – after returning from a trip to Nanking and Wusih – they put me in a room completely panelled in oak squares, and pink with a fairyland of lanterns in the traditional Chinese style. The bed is turned into an arena by a rose-tinged mirror spread across the opposite wall. A bronze mirror of human height guards the entrance hall of the suite. The various closets are lined with mirrors and cunningly concealed lights. Many of the hotel staff are suave Shanghai types who speak some English or French, for whom the Peace Hotel seems almost a world in itself.

From the hotel rooms, you see the Bund (waterfront) and its row of British buildings. Next door is a former hotel that looks just like the Y.M.C.A. in Great Russell Street, London. The same bleak grey concrete, the same ledges under the windows, the same railing with little pillars two floors from the top of the building, the same tower keeping watch at one corner of the roof.

I look down upon an orgasm of physical exercise along the curved public spaces of the waterfront. Girls spring up with handstands on the benches which line the Whangpu River. A boy in a tangerine-coloured shirt whirls his arms at lightning speed. Old men with soft limbs do *t'ai-chi ch'uan* sequences, their eyes staring intently out into space, their breathing carefully controlled. Little boys lie on their backs, legs moving in all directions with an almost boneless suppleness. A girl in bright aqua slacks and a pink blouse has her left leg on a railing; as she twists to one side and the other her plaits swirl like angry snakes. Experienced exponents of all these forms can be seen instructing beginners, and a crowd clusters around each teacher and his pupils.

Specializing on foreign-policy and education issues did not prevent visits to factories and communes; to hospitals – to see how Chinese medicine and Western medicine fit together; literary and historical spots; and the beautiful village in Hunan where Mao Tse-tung was born and raised, full of memories and mosquitoes. Impossible to miss performances of the 'revolutionary operas and ballets' – eight new excellent if not very varied dramas, of universal household familiarity in China today.

Summertime makes a vast difference in visiting China. People sit languidly outside their houses, eating and even sleeping in the open air. Opportunity to observe social life, and talk informally (in winter, folk go inside to their stove or *k'ang* – combination stove-and-bed in northern peasant homes – and the air of community conviviality is gone). Scant clothing thickens the air of sensuality, which is anyway seldom absent from Chinese life. Few men wore more than shorts and singlet in Shanghai, Changsha, and Canton – different in Peking – and the brassière, though widely available in shops, was not, it seemed, in frequent use.

I wandered into parks. Nowhere better to watch and chat with people as they lounge around, roller-skate, play chess or *wei ch'i* ('Go'), boat, and swim. Elaborate parks, such as Peihai in Peking, have been closed since the Cultural Revolution. But not ordinary ones, such as the vast People's Park around Lake Hsuan Wu in Nanking. Here I wanted to swim, and this led to over-careful preparations for my safety and comfort.

A car went on ahead to select a secluded spot. Irritated, I remarked as I got ready to dive in that it was not safe to swim alone. Alas, a casual sentence, uttered only to re-inforce dissatisfaction at not being able to mingle with other swimmers, brought fresh complications. A motor-boat was summoned from the far shores of the lake. While Chinese companions watched from the bank, the boat circled this poor swimmer, spitting out oil and fumes. How to protect me from my protector? I said I wanted to ride in the boat. Before anyone could say no, I sprang in and joined four young fishermen in a trip around the lake. Now I could swim where others swam, chat with people without feeling like an exhibit. A trivial incident, no doubt, yet one case of many where the line between 'well-cared-for' and 'isolated' seemed a little too fine.

In Shanghai I came across a very different park, opposite the former British Consulate, which is now the Shanghai Seamen's Club. It is a secluded garden, full of amorous couples. By night the pink glow from neon signs that dot the waterfront provides almost its only light. I stand at the gate, where you must buy a ticket to enter (two cents). A group of boys materialize around me and one of them suddenly says, 'Go in, go in!'

Inside, I find an air of quiet concentration. After my eyes become accustomed to the gloom, I judge that some two thirds of the throng on the low stone seats and along the winding gravel paths are couples. Conversation is subdued, and now and then it is drowned by a ship's foghorn from across the silky ripples of the Whangpu. Most of the couples hold hands; many have arms around each other; some are entangled in yet other ways. A girl sits beside a rockery, while four or five men try, with mixtures of shyness and aggression, to coax her from her sulky reticence. In places, you can make out the outline of human forms only by the white shirts. Close your ears to the language, and you could be in a park in any large Asian city.

Strolling to another corner of the park, I blink with discomfort at a bright light fixed above a board to which newspapers are pinned. A large crowd gathers round that day's edition of the Shanghai paper *Wen Hui Pao*. They are reading two cool and factual articles about the United States. One is a straightforward piece about Long Island. The other is an historical survey of how the original thirteen states expanded to the present fifty. Neither article contains propaganda or mentions the name of Chairman Mao.

Were there serious restraints on the visitor? Formal restrictions exist. No photos from the air, nor at certain industrial areas (such as the docks looking north from central Shanghai). Among the provinces closed to nearly all foreigners is Szechwan, whose mountains and rivers and spicy cuisine I would like to have savoured. A query about a visit to Amoy brought this response: 'How could you go there? It's opposite Taiwan. Your safety could not be guaranteed.' Then with a smile which conveyed no great fear of Chiang Kai-shek's forces: 'Why, you might be shelled by the Kuomintang!'

Generalized control stems from the practicalities of a visit. Rarely does the visitor select which factory, school, commune he will see. Taxi stands are few, so personal mobility is limited. The Peking Hotel, though a palace in its way, is also a prison, since there is no taxi rank outside; you must phone and state your destination. Somehow, my Luxingshe aide always knew when I came into a hotel (even when I did so alone). For no sooner was I in the room than he would phone to discuss the next part of my programme.

Yet many things I did in perfect freedom. Two legs and some knowledge of Chinese are wings indeed in the cities. Few people closed up on a simple talk; some opened like a rose. Professional men dined alone with me in Peking restaurants. I strolled in on families at random in a Shanghai apartment block. As for officials, they allowed visits to some places which were not yet open to anyone, foreigner or Chinese: former residences in Peking and Shanghai of the great Lu Hsun (a leading twentieth-century writer of stories and poems, much admired by Mao); an array of Han, Chou, and T'ang treasures unearthed during the Cultural Revolution. And at the Chinese border there were few formalities. I brought out unexposed film, tape recordings, and notebooks – but the border officials didn't know, because neither going in nor coming out was there any baggage examination of any kind.

One day I meandered with Stephen Fitzgerald, an Australian scholar, in Foochow Street, central Shanghai, looking for its renowned secondhand bookshops. None remain. Some are turned to other uses (the former Foreign Literature Bookshop is selling textiles); some are open only for new books on the ground floor, closed on the second floor which (I suppose) holds the secondhand books. But nearby was a *lu-kuan*, a simple Chinese hotel where foreigners never stay. We looked in, were welcomed, given fruit punch, and chatted with guests and staff. Over the inside of the doorway, in fresh red characters, there was a warning. 'When leaving watch out for your purses and money.' That should not be a surprise, for there is theft in China like everywhere else – though less than in most places. Bicycles are often padlocked in the street, and houses, so far as I could see, are generally locked.

Foochow Street is scarred on one side with earthworks. Air-raid shelters are being painstakingly built, often with intricate underground links between them. The finished shelter is well concealed – a small door leads down from certain shops which are well known in the neighbourhood. Among the well-stocked, well-patronized food shops the pastries look good, and we go into a small place to buy some. The shopkeeper, a genial and worldly Shanghai-type of sixty-seven, tells me he graduated in commerce from a Shanghai university in 1927. Until Liberation, he owned a tea shop a few blocks away. It must be hard to adjust, I say, from being an owner to being a shop assistant. 'Not really,' he replies, gazing out into the street, 'given all the circumstances.' What are the circumstances, I wonder? 'The change in society. Look outside the shop, at the people, what they wear; ask them who they work for.' He turns back inside the shop and pauses. 'It's a big change; exploitation has gone – my change from owning a tea shop, you have to see it in that context.' My pastries are wrapped up. But anything with flour in it is rationed. 'Where are your coupons?' the old man inquires, his face long in mock desolation. Of course I have none, but he lets me off as a 'friend from across the seas'.

Further down the street is a billboard with a vast world map in bright colours. Captions on the various countries show the 'excellent situation' for revolution that seems, in the Chinese view, to prevail almost everywhere. A young man stares intently at the heading: 'People of all the world unite and put down American aggressors and all their running dogs.' The map is conveniently placed at a bus stop. A news-stand on the pavement does good business, especially in technical magazines – and that is a sign of the times in China. A new one has recently appeared, *Scientific Experimentation,* with popularized articles on the contribution science can make to society. I buy its first three issues, and some recent fiction – but am refused Shanghai newspapers (see page 50).

Turning back toward the hotel, we pass a Protestant church – its closed gates bearing the banner 'Carry through the Cultural Revolution to the end' – and then come upon a municipal 'cultural and scientific library and reading room'. Step off the crowded street, and you find at once an air of quiet concentration. At battered wooden tables, young and old pore over books, magazines, and newspapers. Again mostly technical stuff. Although a studious man is reading *Hung Ch'i* (*Red Flag,* the monthly theory journal of the Party), and some have Marx or Lenin, no one at the tables I circle is reading Mao. At the counter I ask for the famous historical novel *Dream of the Red Chamber.* The lady seems pleased to be asked – but, no, she does not have it. Lu Hsun? 'We have almost all of his works; which would you like?' But few are reading fiction.

Getting nearer to the waterfront, the streets are lined with people, and more arrive each minute in trucks, to be marched in columns of two, then spread out three-deep along the road. The bell on the old British Customs House strikes five; most of the crowd seem to have come direct from work. We draw near and find no air of excitement. But why are they here? People readily answer the question. 'We are here to welcome foreign guests to Shanghai.' We rack our brains and recall that a French Parliamentary delegation is in China and that a Korean group is due in Shanghai soon. But our curiosity is not shared by the welcomers themselves. None of a dozen or so asked know who is coming or seem to care. 'It's just foreign friends,' one girl sums up with a trace of impatience.

Soon the fussy marshals have got everyone in line and

black limousines glide into view. The crowd stiffens into ceremonial festivity, faces beam with joy, hands clap vigorously. We dash into the Peace Hotel, climb to the eighth floor, and watch the scene from the dining room. A panorama of international friendship! The limousines, looking long and flat from high up, creep slowly enough for the elated faces of the foreign guests to be visible – they seem moved indeed by the reception. It was the Koreans – we found out that night at the ballet *Whitehaired Girl*, which they also attended – but I suppose the afternoon throng didn't know that any more than we did.

Sometimes a change of schedule threw amusing light on the ways of Chinese hosts. With the Australian group, I was in the resort town of Wusih, to drink up the tranquillity of Lake T'ai and the hills around it (rich in mulberry trees). A visit to a peach orchard was planned, but one of the Australians had a special interest in handicrafts and wanted to see the famous clay moulding of Wusih. Hastily, it was arranged that we should go to the Clay and Plaster Figures Factory.

In the reception room, brightly painted soldiers with fierce expressions stare down at us from glass cases. Some artists and cadres are here to brief us. We all sit down, and the vice-chairman of the factory's Revolutionary Committee clears his throat to begin. But he pauses, and turns to the Foreign Ministry official who is travelling with us. I am close to both and hear his whispered query: 'Who are they?' The Ministry man hisses back 'Australian Labour party.' The vice-chairman inquiries again: 'Friends?' The Ministry man returns: 'Yes, you can say so.' The vice-chairman then turns back to the table, smiles broadly, and begins in a loud voice: 'Friends, we are very happy ...'

Walking around Peking brings endless fascination. I would wander in the Wang Fu Ching street, a shopping area just east of the Forbidden City. Here is the Eastern

Bazaar, where you may rummage for jade and stone carvings, ivory, lacquerware, or gauze lanterns. The Wang Fu Ching department store is the biggest in Peking, though modest in size (and in its prices) by American standards. People move among the bright displays with shopping lists and bags. There is a commercial spirit in the air, but no one rushes.

Only in the fur section are there many slogans or quotations on the walls. Perhaps people who buy furs stand most in need of political exhortation! I inspect the excellent furs and am assisted by an old man with a moustache who says he has worked in Peking shops for forty-five years. You see an abacus here and there, but cash registers are more numerous in this modern store. Beside each one sits the inevitable flask of tea. The salesmen are not at all apathetic – as might be expected in a state-owned store – but eager to persuade the customer of the quality of the wares. Mr Liu, my Luxingshe aide, and I pause to buy a fruit drink, and watch this informal, prosperous tableau of urban China.

Afterwards I go across the street to the Hsinhua bookshop, then to order the making of an ivory seal (with my name in Chinese characters) at a small old-fashioned shop where the abacus is used, the light is dim, and the service is courtly. A few blocks away, I find an air-raid shelter under construction. A double-brick tunnel leads down and sideways from one end of a literature shop. Half the shop is closed during the construction. When the tunnel is finished, its entrance will not be easily visible from the street.

The foreigner who feels pressured by crowds, or by the uniform 'Chineseness' around him, has only to look above him. The sky is the same, man's common bond. Yet is there not something unique about the Peking sky, or the North China sky? It is a pale, high sky. By contrast, the sky of South China seems a low-hanging, deeply coloured sky. Quite a different atmosphere results. The northern sky affords a sense of spaciousness and calm that you do not find in the south. Climate reinforces the feeling. The stability of the northern days makes men equable. There seems to be a compact between the people and the heavens, which puts human beings in the timeless realm of the cosmos. In the south, any moment may produce a downpour. Men must switch abruptly with nature's mood. The Cantonese temperament is more florid. Feelings are more intense, as the colour of the sky is more intense; less remote, as the low-hanging sky is less remote.

Another walk took me to the Pai T'a Szu (White Dagoba Temple) in Peking's western section. This temple, which no longer functions, was originally built in 1096, and in its present form dates from 1457. Behind it is a white dagoba rising majestically above residential surroundings. Its upper part is like the tip of an auger with a series of graceful rings. Above this sits a massive plate, hung around its edge with bells, which looks like the head-dress of some heavenly being.

I had come to the dagoba after visiting the near-by former home of the writer Lu Heun. Every *hu t'ung* (lane) is full of children at play. It is late afternoon and older folk are doing household chores or relaxing on canvas chairs. Slogans on the walls – put up during the Cultural Revolution – are now very faded. In a neighbourhood tea shop, old men and boys play Chinese chess in silent concentration. The scene is relaxed, but not somnolent as a similar scene would be in much of (non-Confucian) Asia. A basic web of organization undergirds the peace of the afternoon. People have the air of being about their business, even when their business is not work.

The houses are low and old and grey. Around a group of them runs a wall, with a door from the street every few yards, leading into secluded courtyards where green foliage sprouts against the grey. The roofs are in grey tile and there are gables. Now and then a gate is ornamented with stone lions or other beasts. Pink mimosas along the streets bring to life the dull walls and gates. Often I asked

43

Chinese – generally officials – whether they personally prefer the traditional Chinese house with its courtyard, or the modern apartment house. Always the answer was the same, always it was animated. Of *course* the courtyard house is better. You have the marvellous well of light which a courtyard gives; and you have privacy.

Later I view the area from a taller building. These traditional Chinese houses look like flocks of grey cattle standing silently together. Beyond them, amidst the trees, there gathers the orange profusion, layer after layer, of the glazed tile roofs of the pavilions and palaces in the Forbidden City. In the sunset rays, there is an effortless peacefulness about the scene. The past is heavy and not to be ignored, but it does not seem to intimidate the Chinese of today. It only lends a historical, almost a cosmic, calm.

A friendly tension existed between the authorities and myself. Some things they apparently thought I did to excess ('mingling'). Ruses were found to limit my mingling. At intermissions of a ballet or acrobatic show, I would be whisked to the luxury of a side room, to sit in boredom with my companions. Yet they did not make mingling impossible. At a Shanghai concert, I declined to enter the side room, smoked in the foyer, and watched an amusing and vigorous struggle by a hundred people to get tickets for the next performance. And often there was banter about my waywardness. 'Mr Terrill, we have to protect you; please go by car.' 'But Mr Wang, China is the "safest country on earth", I'm going to walk.' Walk I did, and no hard feelings resulted.

The overnight trip to the delightful Ts'ung Hua hot springs near Canton was typical. It is a valley of tranquillity. Also a sensitive place. Leaders come to take rest and the waters. Kuo Mo-jo, after a tough time during the Cultural Revolution, came here to recover. A major army base nestles in the near-by hills. Both aspects – aesthetic, military – tickle the ear at 5.30 a.m. The air is rent not

by 'Sailing the Seas Depends upon the Helmsman' or
'The East Is Red' (China's two inescapable political
songs), but – long live Chairman Mao! – by a faultless
trumpet rendering of reveille! No need here for a political message to nerve the soul at dawn.

Necessarily there are restraints. The scenery lures me for
a walk. Yesterday's typhoon has left things fresh and
beaten. Winds still bend the fine bamboos deeply to one
side. A severed tree-portion leaps crazily along the river's
broad white sandbank. A stone bridge squats comfortably
across the blue-yellow waters. Higher up is a towering
waterfall in jostling whiteness. 'Like ten thousand horses
galloping,' wrote a T'ang poet. But wherever I walk,
there is a People's Liberation Army man with boyish
grin and fixed bayonet. 'Back the other way.' Well, it is
a sensitive area, and they did not have to bring me here.
There was, in sum, an openness and a practical root to
nearly all the restraints that met me in China.

4 Seven Years Later

I wondered about differences from 1964. Of course the military are more prominent. Army men in baggy green uniforms, with a red star on the cap. Navy men, the same thing in blue-grey; you could mistake it for pyjamas. Air force, blue trousers with green jacket. Curiously, police uniform is the same as air force – with one variation. The policeman's cap has a red circle, not a red star like the cap of the three services.

At White Cloud Airport in Canton, during long hours of waiting for a storm to clear, most of the passengers were military men. Indeed, the delay's consolation was a chance to chat nimbly with Chinese generals. Earthy, amiable, informal men. With a Szechwanese officer, I talk as we drink tea from porcelain mugs. The face is leathery, eyes deep-set, smile disarming. Trousers rolled up to the knee – but he rolls them down as I sit beside him. His floppy uniform bears no insignia of rank – these were abolished in 1965 – but I think he may be a general. Two aides are with him (their sandals are not the usual plastic, but leather). His wristwatch is not inexpensive. I ask him why clothes in China are so loose and big. Are these shapeless garments, I muse, designed to mask the human form and keep passion at a distance? His answer is different. 'Tight clothes are no good for working in; loose clothes are.' Stationed in Fukien, his business in life is to keep prepared against Chiang Kai-shek. His views on Chiang are not angry, just totally scornful. Yes, he said without zeal, China is stronger since the Cultural Revolution. More roused, he explained how Szechwan is much prettier than Kwangtung.

But what really stirred him was an Iraqi Airlines jet which zoomed into the tranquil haze of the afternoon. With his colleagues (and nearly everyone else in the terminal), he went outside to watch it land. China in 1971 has no jets on commercial service (though it possesses Tridents, and has just bought six more). P.I.A. (Pakistan) is the only airline which lands passenger jets at White Cloud; the Iraqi plane was a 'special', containing ministers. To watch a big jet is quite something to a Chinese. Even to a general. 'Not bad,' he grinned as he sank back on a couch and reached for his tea.

Not only do you see many military, you meet a lot in institutions. When the Cultural Revolution reached its pitch of factionalism, People's Liberation Army men went into factories and schools. Mostly, they are still there – as politically reliable managers. The (P.L.A.) Chairman of the Revolutionary Committee at the Peking Petroleum Refinery had, he told me, never been to school. He learned all he knew in the 'great school' of the army. Yet he now administered a factory with ten thousand workers. Another P.L.A. officer, a tough, cheery man who confessed his total ignorance of medicine, was head of a Peking (Chinese-Medicine) hospital. His first act on coming to the hospital, others told me, was to spur all personnel to more devoted service by offering his own body for experimentation. Acupuncture needles were put three to four inches into him in a test to find the root of certain nerves. It was his way of living up to Mao's idea that the whole nation should 'learn from the P.L.A.'.

A third P.L.A. officer, the new Minister of Foreign Trade, I met with Mr Whitlam. (Six of the eight ministers then identified were military men.) Pai Hsiang-kuo is a practical man, who showed a detailed grasp of Australia's trade position. In the business talks, the word 'capitalism' was never uttered, nor Mao's name. Gentle in manner, yet strong in argument, Pai appeared for the sessions in army uniform, without mark of rank, and left his cap on throughout. (Even at our meeting with Chou

En-lai, which he attended but without speaking, he never took his cap off.) None of this military presence was evident seven years ago. Indeed, I can't remember a single conversation with a military man on the 1964 visit.

I found cultural life far more politicized. In 1964, I talked with the director of the Peking Library (which has some seven million volumes) and browsed in his library. I went to church services in Canton and Peking, and interviewed Chao Fu-san, a leader of Chinese Protestantism (his barbs against Russian divines and the World Council of Churches caused reverberations in church circles of various countries). This kind of thing was, in 1971, out of the question. Public libraries, and museums too, are closed. Churches are boarded up, empty, and chequered with political slogans. National religious organizations are 'suspended', while religious workers undergo an indefinite phase of 'struggle, criticism, and transformation'. Chao Fu-san is 'not available'. In 1971, you simply do not find, as you could in 1964, segments of social and intellectual life around which the tentacles of politics have not curled.

The politicization has its visual testimony. Cities are striped red and white with slogans and quotations. It is hard to locate buildings, for during the Cultural Revolution their nameplates were mostly replaced with a (more or less appropriate) slogan. The Industrial Exhibition in Canton has on it simply: 'Long Live Our Great Leader Mao Tse-tung.' Since it is not the only big building which displays that irreproachable sentiment, the newcomer cannot easily find his way around. On Chinese commercial planes the large red characters read: 'Long Life to Our Great Leader Mao Tse-tung.' Less noticeable, in smaller black characters, is the airline's name: 'China Airlines'. Even garden plots have been ingeniously planted in the shape of characters expressing a political message; the flowers in their beds must bend and sprout to uphold Chairman Mao!

Reaching Canton, I was hit by this political gaudiness.

It looked as if the left wing of the Signwriters Union had taken over China! But the impact is a double one, and the second aspect is as striking as the first. The city is plastered with banners and posters. *But they are faded.* They date from 1966 to 1968. There has been no apparent move to refurbish them. So Canton has a face of shabby militancy. Not having been there since 1964, I was struck by the plastering. Yet an Australian scholar (Stephen Fitzgerald) who had visited in 1968 was more struck by how much it has faded. The slogans are much less obtrusive in the life of the cities, he remarked, than three years ago.

One might welcome the fading of banners, as Fitzgerald did, because of the new political moderation it signifies. Aesthetically, however, it gives Canton a shabby, run-down look – like a city after a bad flood. Parks I had enjoyed in 1964 were now scrawny and overgrown. The beautiful grounds of the Sun Yat Sen University had not recently seen a hoe or a mower. The Cultural Park, a diverting place for Cantonese, is less well cared for. So is Shameen, the shaded haven isle which in colonial days gave secluded comfort to the British and French.

The Cultural Revolution, of course, accounts for this neglect. The former political boss in Canton, T'ao Chu, was attacked in 1967 for spending too much time and energy on prettifying Canton. He wanted, said his detractors, to impress foreign businessmen arriving for the Canton Fair, and the Hong Kong folk who come to visit their families. It was, Red Guards reasoned, a wrong use of time and resources.

But the greatest change since 1964 is a heightened sense of citizenship on the part of ordinary people. I am not saying people's minds are full of Mao's Thought – who knows what is in their minds? The point is not about political orthodoxy, but about sense of involvement. The lady from whose roadside stall I buy tea in Nanking knows which four provinces still have not established new Party Committees. Shopkeepers in Shanghai venture comment on world affairs. Singers and dancers in Yenan had been to Peking during the Cultural Revolution, and now have fresh interest in the capital and what goes on there. They quoted to me an adage of their province: *'ko shan, ko ho, pu ko yin'* ('separated by mountains, by rivers, but not from the voice of Peking'). It had, they said, a new meaning for them.

Drivers and Luxingshe aides showed no timidity or subservience – in 1964 there had been some. One morning in Canton my driver launched into a discussion of how intellectuals should behave. I don't know if he had me in mind when he spoke of the uselessness of theoretical knowledge divorced from practice. 'Some intellectuals are hopeless,' he observed, 'electrical engineers who can't replace a fuse.' A Luxingshe aide in the north was no less forthright. Often he would proffer political views. They were straight from the *People's Daily*; yet the illustrations were his own.

One afternoon at the Tomb of Sun Yat-sen in Nanking, a small argument flickered (there were several arguments in Nanking; the air seemed tense for some reason). It concerned 'local' newspapers – the Chinese use the word 'local' (*ti-fang*) to apply to almost all papers other than the *People's Daily*. The day before, in Shanghai, I had tried to buy the *Wen Hui Pao*, a Shanghai paper. Six times at six news-stands I was refused it. 'Foreigners', it was explained, 'may not buy local newspapers.' Well, at the Tomb in Nanking, an official happened to remark, in the course of a conversation about freedom in China, that a foreigner could buy 'anything he likes.' I refuted him with the Shanghai example – perhaps too vigorously. My Luxingshe aide, the junior man in the group, turned to me: 'Mr Terrill, you will learn more if you are modest.' In 1964 I did not find such refreshing forthrightness.

There were other differences. Service frills had been cut here and there. No beer on the planes now. In 1964, I had drunk my way across the Gobi Desert on the plane from Irkutsk to Peking, with the dusty-flavoured Tsingtao beer. In Peking, you can no longer dial from your hotel room for weather forecasts, theatre tickets, or subscriptions to magazines. Yet for the Chinese themselves, variety of consumer goods may be wider. Clothing seems more colourful. More household utensils are available. Supermarkets have speeded matters for big-city shoppers – as often the husband as the wife. It is only an impression, but it seemed to me, judging by the crowded state of simple restaurants, that eating out has increased in the big cities.

These neighbourhood eating houses are full of interest. Here is one in Shanghai's Nanking Road. It is in the middle of a shopping district, and people come in with bags and bundles – food, textiles, and now and then a camera, radio, or watch. Noodles (boiled or fried) are the speciality of the house. They are, of course, the preferred staple in Shanghai, as boiled rice is in South China. A hearty restaurant, a *carrefour* of gossip, noisy with chatter and laughter.

The range of diners reflects the relative prosperity of Shanghai, with its sophisticated industry and higher wages. Here are four men, colleagues it seems, who take their noodles swimming in soup (*t'ang mien*) and already have four empty beer bottles in front of them. Beside us a quiet couple, intellectuals carrying books whose titles I can't catch, who eat fried noodles (*ch'ao mien*) and later hefty slices of the universally popular water-melon.

Décor is at the level of a public toilet. Chairs are the old wooden kitchen variety, and the wooden floorboards are hospitable to many a splash or piece of food (but no cats or dogs or flies). It is all a little different from the fancy banquets our Shanghai hosts serve at the Peace Hotel. (For a big fish dish at these feasts, a battery is put in the fish's head, so that two bright electric eyes stare out at you, as if in protest, as you hack at the fish.) But the food is excellent. It cost us under Y3 (the yuan is about 17p) for two. To remember what dishes to bring to what table, waiters fix a numbered clothespin on a bowl in the centre of the table: 7 is noodles with fish, 16 is chicken soup. No writing down is called for, and the evidence of what you've eaten and will pay for sits there as a row of pins; 7, 7, 16, 11, 4: total, Y2.90. Stacks of small red stickers hang on the walls. A notice says: 'If you have an illness, put a sticker in your bowl when finished, and special care will then be taken in washing the bowl.'

In 1964, there was in Peking more sense of foreboding about the international scene. And today, where there is anxiety it seems to centre on Russia, whereas in 1964 it centred on the United States. Some symbols sum up the change.

In 1964, I reached Peking the week after the clashes in the Gulf of Tonkin. One of the first sights, as the plane from Russia slid over the lovely hills into the heat haze of the capital, was a vast mass rally. It was one of many in those weeks, at which a total of twenty million Chinese raised their voices and fists against U.S. actions in and off North Vietnam. The cloud of Vietnam, and, even more important, foreboding that Washington might escalate the war into China's southern provinces hung over the entire visit.

In 1971, foreboding is replaced by buoyancy. The only American missile talked about in Peking last summer was Henry Kissinger. And when war pokes its nose in, it is not from South Asia but from North Asia. The mounds of earth in the streets of the northern cities tell the story. The air-raid shelters are insurance against 'our northern neighbour' – the Prime Minister's sardonic phrase, the night we met him, for the Soviet Union.

Today, China has attained, in reasonable degree, two goals it has long held most desirable. It is more *independent* than it has been since Liberation (and well before), and it is probably more *secure* than at any point since Liberation. To put a complex process briefly, until recently China has (since 1949) always felt itself beholden to the Soviet Union, or threatened by the United States (or the Soviet Union). Today, it is not at all beholden, and much less threatened.

It is perilous to generalize about conditions in China today; a striking impression is of variations up and down the nation.

At Tsinghua University, a briefing for the visitor sounded like a lecture on the evils of Liu Shao-ch'i (so much so that an Australian trade unionist inquired with interest, 'Does Mr Liu come from this district?'). At Sun Yat Sen University in Canton, on the other hand, no one in several hours mentioned Liu, or revisionism, until I raised the topic myself. And then the answers were formal and without passion.

In some towns (as Nanking), military men were much to the fore, in particular institutions, and in general. In others (as Shanghai), much less so: some institutions had no P.L.A. men at all on the Revolutionary Committee which governed them.

In Kwangtung province, the birth-rate was given as 3 per cent; in neighbouring Hunan province, it was only 1·5 per cent.

In Sian, the visitor was strongly discouraged from mingling with crowds. In Shanghai he was perfectly free to do so.

At the Clay and Plaster Figures Factory in Wusih, only 'revolutionary' figures were to be found. 'Scholars, beauties, generals, and emperors' are no longer produced, as they were before the Cultural Revolution. Yet at a handicrafts factory in Peking – where an ivory-carved memorial to the visit of the American ping-pong players was being prepared (see page 152) – I saw being fashioned just these decadent 'scholars, beauties, generals, and emperors'.

One week in Peking, Mr Y praised the straightforward simplicity of the captions and displays at the buildings in Shanghai where the C.C.P. held its first Congress. When I visited the buildings, however, I found the exhibit being dismantled, 'because it contains errors.'

In some places (as the Communications University in Sian), people looked blank when asked about the effects of the 'Socialist Education Campaign' (a drive, mainly in the countryside, during the early 1960s). Yet at the Arts and Crafts Factory in Peking, a lot of convincing mention was made of the effect on the factory of this campaign.

A visit can bring into relief the sharp diversities of China (which our study of documentary sources does not always do). It is not trivial to stress these variations. The Chinese do some tasks well and others less well. Temperament in this province is not the same as temperament in that province. Remote parts of China – however faithfully they may speak Peking's phrases – do not always live as Peking lives. Moreover, a certain regional differentiation – and a rapid pace of change – may itself be a major characteristic of China since the Cultural Revolution. It is only an impression, but China seemed to me less uniform in 1971 than in 1964.

5   Driving in Shensi

The name Yenan rings with eloquent echoes down the corridors of Chinese Communism's history. In this remote town the Long March ended in 1935. The infinitely longer march of building Communism began. I was happy when the Foreign Ministry agreed without hesitation to let me go there. 'It is good for you to get out to Shensi province,' Mr Ma Yu-chen adjudged. 'Before you talk with leading figures, you must see places where the roots of the Chinese revolution lie.' I followed the same route as the first visitors to Red Yenan in the 1930s. From Peking to the flat and dusty provincial capital of Sian. Then north by car to the loess hills and caves of Yenan.

We set out from the Sian Guest House after an ample lunch of steamed mutton (a speciality of Shensi). In one car was Hanoi's Consul in Peking, with an aide and a host from the Revolutionary Committee that runs the province. In another car I travelled with Mr Chou Nan of the Foreign Ministry, Mr Liu Ju-ts'ai of Luxingshe, and a second Shensi host.

The two Russian Volgas quickly trace an unimpeded way through Sian's symmetrical avenues. It is a regal old city, where some Chinese dynasties have had their capital. The city wall, some forty feet wide in charcoal-coloured brick (dating from the Ming dynasty), is still visible here and there. Beside it runs a stream in which boys fish peacefully. Along the tree-lined streets swarm hand-drawn carts, bicycles, and pedicabs bearing either a passenger or goods on a tray. The low commercial and residential buildings are grey or beige, and the dirt lanes and surrounding wheat fields lend a dusty colour tone. Against these subdued hues there leap out red-painted political slogans and notice boards. The people of Sian are tall, long and craggy of face, and forthright in manner. Some sense of their city's noble past seems to lend them a sturdy, unapologetic confidence. Since Liberation, Sian has been one of the inland cities that have benefited from Peking's policy of shifting enterprises from the east coast (thus reducing the lopsidedness that the Treaty Port decades introduced into China's economy). In 1949 Sian had 500,000 people (1·2 million in the environs); today it has 1·2 million (2·8 million in the environs).

Soon we pass through vegetable districts, and then find ourselves amidst gently undulating wheat fields. Poplars line the road. For beautification? More likely, it seems, to shade the asphalt road from sun which might melt it. No cars pass us, but many trucks. The big ones have leafy branches sticking up all around – maybe to keep the heat off the peasants who recline on top of the loads. One truck veers to left and right as it comes toward us. Our driver pulls quickly to one side and stops. As the truck sways by, its driver puts his head out the window and explains gaily, 'I'm a learner!' We plan to drive five hours, then stop overnight, halfway to Yenan, at the market town of Huang Ling.

The river Wei appears, broad and majestic in the crawling flow of its muddy waters. The valley of the Wei River is the heartland of Chinese civilization. Here, not on the east coast well known to foreigners, Chinese culture took on its modes. Chou Nan is a scholar of classical Chinese – especially its poetry – and an excellent travelling companion for these parts. He quotes for us poems about the region. Li Po, the great poet and great drinker of the T'ang dynasty, is among his favourites. And he gives us a couplet from another T'ang poet, Chia Tao, to express the interconnection of all things. ('When the autumn winds ruffle the Wei, leaves fall upon the whole of Ch'angan [Sian].') It is an extraordinary sight to watch farmers getting in the wheat beside a delicate aqua and orange pagoda of seven balconies, twelve hundred years old. Is it from living in the shadow of such traditions that they get their deep gaze and simple grace?

Winding north from Sian, the slogans become less grandiose and more prosaic. Around Sian, the themes were often 'imperialism' and the unity of all 'workers of the world'. But here it is 'Plant for the sake of revolution', or 'In agriculture learn from Ta Chai'. (Ta Chai is a successful unit of a commune in Shensi province, held up for emulation.) Others deal with the importance of fertilizers and conservation. Few are freshly painted. Many of the more informal ones, scrawled at will on any available spot during the Cultural Revolution, have now faded.

Some are on notice boards. Especially in the villages, where they are generally headed '*tsui-kao jih-shih*' ('supreme instruction'). But many are woven more naturally into the environment. The mud walls which surround houses are a good spot for a lively exhortation. Circular white stones are set into the wall at two- or three-foot intervals. On each is painted a big red character. So the mud walls are alive with high-minded suggestions.

We pass one slogan on a roadside wall: 'Long Live Chairman Mao Tse-tung.' But the last character of the slogan is missing. A hole has been made in the wall to make way for a path where its round white tablet previously was. It seems a symbol of the workaday spirit in China at present. A path is more useful than one more slogan, so why not give it priority? Chairman Mao can best be honoured not by 'formalism' but by plain hard work.

On the walls of a sprawling complex of mud buildings I notice an intriguing sign. It reads: 'This kind of training is good!' Then follows a number. I point it out and ask what it refers to. There is a pregnant silence as we drive past. Maybe it is a camp of correction for 'remoulding' errant urban elements? The Shensi comrade says with a frown that he has no idea what it could be.

In the Sian area, cotton is the number two crop after wheat. Further north where the land is less fertile there is more millet. 'Rifles and millet' were memorably coupled as the twin meagre resources of the Communist army in austere Yenan days. The main animal is a rather spindly sheep. Some are white, some are black; they are raised both for meat and wool. The scene is rich in yellow and various shades of green. The golden fields are dotted with red flags. These bear the emblem of the brigade (major unit of a commune) or the team (smaller unit) which is at work in that spot. The land in north Shensi is not un-fertile, but the hills make cultivation difficult and the rainfall is uncertain. Before Liberation, famine often stalked the area. In the two years to 1929, for instance, no less than 2·5 million people in Shensi (almost one third of the province population) died of starvation. Peasants wear blue and white, and in the Shensi manner some put towel-ling around their heads. The conical straw hat is much less common than in the south. Girls are so rosy-cheeked they look made up for a theatrical performance.

The countryside is electrified, but power machines (trac-tors, harvesters) are rare. You realize why Chinese become so enthusiastic about tractor-making plants when you watch the tedious hand labour in these wheat fields, and picture the enormous difference tractors would make to the work. Even in the towns of T'ung Ch'uan ('copper river') and Huang Ling ('yellow tomb') there is no indoor plumbing. Donkeys are the draught animals. But men and women can often be seen pulling hand carts, especi-ally near T'ung Ch'uan, where there are coal mines and brick kilns. (In the T'ang and Sung dynasties this district boasted famous pottery kilns, whose exquisite products exist today in museums across the world.) This is a new China in that socialism has replaced semi-feudalism. Men work for a wage and share weal and woe in communes. But it is not yet a new China in the mode and rhythm of its productive life. Slogans urging 'self-reliance' are every-where. You realize – when you see the lack of technology – that these slogans are no mere ideological affectation, but a recognition of simple necessity.

As we drive, the official from Shensi talks about overall agricultural performance in the province. Grain output was 63 billion catties at Liberation (one catty is half a kilogram). By 1965 it was 100 billion catties. In 1970 the figure was 120 billion catties. It is steady progress. But it is not spectacular, considering that the present province's population of 21 million is almost double that at Liberation. Three factors have improved agriculture in Shensi in recent years: better seeds, more waterways, levelling of land. There has also been much success with localized experimentation since the Cultural Revolution. 'One brigade,' my host related, 'found that by planting sweet potatoes by the whole potato rather than by the shoots, yield went up by a hundred per cent. This improvement now spreads all over the province.'

I dozed for a while, and stirred to hear the others in interesting conversation. I was in the front seat with the driver. Mr Chou, Mr Liu, and the Shensi host chatted in the back seat. The usual topics recurred. Provincial variations; inquiries about families; stories about the vagaries of travel by road, train, and plane. They dealt with each other in complete equality. But what struck me were the long, keen exchanges on the theme of economic development. How backward China still is. How important it is for China's national pride to modernize the economy. Each would relate problems that he knew of, success stories he had come upon. They were talking not for my benefit – I probably appeared to be asleep – but because the issues of development interested them and mattered to them. These three men, at least, are modernizers as well as patriots.

After a pause, Mr Chou asked the man from Sian, 'Where were you during the Cultural Revolution?' The mood changed abruptly. The bubbling momentum of talk about steel and cotton gave way to subdued and fragmentary remarks. The Shensi official answered: 'I was in Peking.' But he offered no elaboration. They made non-committal remarks about the period of the Cultural

Revolution. You sensed them brooding a little, thinking their three sets of private thoughts. The conversation was not open and shared and spontaneous as it had been on cows and computers. Were the memories of the Cultural Revolution troubling?

Further north its gets cooler and more hilly. Every inch of land must here be utilized. Boys weed and prune with hand-clippers right up to the edge of the road. The hills are terraced (often sown with millet) and the soil is a brighter colour. There is less wheat and more maize. The skin of the peasants is browner. North Shensi is one of the worst areas in China for erosion, and you see the two weapons used against it: terracing and tree-planting. Now and then, stopping to stretch our legs and drink a bottle of *ch'i-shui* (soft drink), we get into conversation with passers-by amazed to see a *wai-kuo jen* (foreigner).

While we pause in a beautiful orange valley called Chin-suo-kuan (Golden Key Pass), two peasant boys come up to say hello. I ask them where they are from. 'We came two years ago from Kiangsu.' In China today you find a lot of such movement of people across provincial lines. We also come across eleven Middle School students sent here from Peking to gain 'practical experience'. As with the two boys from Kiangsu, it was the Cultural Revolution which triggered their transfer to a new province and a new life. The motivation is economic only in the most indirect sense. It is for political reasons that the scrambling has occurred. To keep the youth of China realistic. To teach them about their own amazingly varied country and its many problems. Ultimately, to ensure that the whole nation is united around its fundamental tasks.

By sunset our Volga cars roll up the dusty main street of Huang Ling (named 'yellow tomb' because near by lies the Tomb of the Yellow Emperor). It seems like a cheery work camp, but it is a district headquarters of some tens of thousands of people. There is industry – mainly related to minerals, and construction of a railway north to Yenan – which operates by laborious methods. At the brick kiln there are no trucks for transport, let alone a branch railway track. But many donkeys. In the main street, too, donkeys shuffle by pulling squeaking carts.

Children, looking very healthy and dressed in gaudy colours, toddle by in groups. Lots of people carry cabbages they have bought from a central supply which is spread out on the roadside in the Chinese manner. There is a cinema and a Cultural Palace for Workers. Also public toilets, which smell outrageously. Many buildings are mud with thatched roofs, though there are also some modest new apartment blocks. Loudspeakers play the familiar revolutionary operas and ballets. Close your eyes and all regional difference, all gap between city and country, vanishes. These opera-ballets, by bonds of melody and lyric, make the whole nation one vast audience of 800,000,000.

We spend the night in a Guest House consisting of caves surrounding a courtyard. It is the pride of Huang Ling, and though simple (no running water, no toilets), it is extremely comfortable. Eager girls serve us the kind of feast you soon accept as routine in China. It centred on millet soup and various forms and combinations of noodles. Local hosts chuckled when Mr Liu, who is Cantonese, declined the noodles and asked for boiled rice.

The Vietnamese Consul was cordial, though our first exchange foundered on a linguistic *faux pas*. He asked about my politics. I replied using the Chinese phrase *Kung tang* which means 'Labour party'. But the Consul thought I put in a middle word, *ch'ang*, between *Kung* and *tang*, which makes the phrase not 'Labour party' but 'Communist party'. The Consul murmured nice things about the Australian Communist party and made to embrace me. His aide broke in to correct matters. The Consul transmuted an embrace into a handshake.

The caves have stone floors and are beautifully cool. To wash, you carry a basin of water from the courtyard into your cave. Trying to sleep, I hear loud chopping sounds. Why are they chopping wood in midsummer? But the sound is not of chopping. It is of chess pieces being slammed down on the board. The Vietnamese Consul and Mr Chou are playing China's favourite game, seated on tiny chairs just outside my cave. Beween the cicadas and the Chinese chess, a night in Huang Ling is not as quiet as expected.

The next thing I hear – at 6 a.m. – is a hearty rendering of 'Sailing the Seas Depends upon the Helmsman'. Loudspeakers carry it to every corner of the town. An ancient Chinese saying runs: 'Rise at dawn and sweep the courtyard.' This is just what the red-cheeked girls of the Guest House do. They work with discipline, yet also with a gaiety that is infectious – even at dawn. Before breakfast I wander out of the gate of the Guest House, and turn into a side street. People are already at work though it is not yet seven. Mr Chou soon appears, and we then turn around and wander straight back to the Guest House.

At breakfast the drivers join fully in the conversation. Each Chinese at the table is from a different province, and the talk is about regional quirks of food, accent, and custom. It is surprising how often conversation in China turns on these themes. I have stressed the 'mental unity' in China today, and the deeply felt national pride. Yet equal stress must go on the cultural variations in this nation which is the size of the continent of Europe (and far more populous than the whole of Europe including the Soviet Union).

Before continuing toward Yenan, we go in sacred silence to salute the Yellow Emperor (Huang Ti). His tomb is among gnarled old cypress trees on a hill above Huang Ling. One's sense of China's fantastic past is made acute by the mound opposite the tomb. It was built by Emperor Wu of the Han dynasty, to mark a visit he made to the revered spot. Wu's dates are 141 B.C. to 87 B.C. He visited the mound where we stood that morning 2,100 years ago. Yet at least as long a stretch of time separates

Han Wu Ti from Huang Ti as separates ourselves from
Han Wu Ti!

On the way up to the tomb is a temple dedicated to
this legendary emperor (who is said to have reigned during the third millenium B.C.). The Communist government has restored it in careful and tasteful fashion. Many
a stele (upright slab with inscription) has been put here
by later emperors to honour Huang Ti and his supposed
invention of pottery, the working of metal, and the wheel.
It is startling to find one stele among them dated 1959.
Here, in the handwriting of Kuo Mo-jo done in 1958, is
Communist China's own respectful glance back to antiquity. Its tone is nationalistic. Kuo's stele describes
Huang Ti as 'father of the Han people'. I ask the Shensi
official what effect the Cultural Revolution had on the way
this historical site is viewed. His answer is out of no Marxist catechism. 'The Cultural Revolution gave us a fresh
appreciation of what a very ancient civilization China has.'

As we stroll in the cobbled courtyard of the temple, the
mood of contemplation is broken by a messenger. Up he
dashes like a boy in ancient Sparta bearing news. He
holds aloft a washcloth that someone has left in his cave
at the Guest House. Nothing must be lost by the visitor to
socialist China! Everyone has turned from the steles and
stares at the cloth. It was mine, and there was no choice
but to step forward meekly and claim it. I had nowhere
to put a wet facecloth at that stage of the morning, but
consideration of principle outweighed logistical detail.
Thenceforth I guarded it like a precious gem. It is embarrassing to have one's carelessness shown up by the
fantastic carefulness of conduct in China today. The messenger brushed aside my thanks. He got on his bicycle and
pedalled back to the Guest House as suddenly as he had
come.

The road to Yenan led on through gorges of orange
clay. It is now unpaved, and deeply corrugated. There are
trickling rivers, almost lost in wide sandy beds. The
water is sometimes jade-coloured with the reflection of

grey-green trees that dot the banks. At one river, history constrained us to stop.

The Chiehtse River is no surging torrent but it is famous. During the war against Japan, it marked a boundary between Mao's part of China and Chiang's part of China. It was a line that separated China's recent past from China's emerging future. South of the river was Chiang's faltering county of Loch'uan. North of it was Mao's poor but vibrant Fuhsien County. Across it many a human (and journalistic) drama unfolded. Mao wrote of the Chiehtse at the time: 'North and south of the river are two different worlds.' But today the river witnesses no drama and forms no demarcation. A concrete tablet stands on the river-bank. It bears the text of Mao's telegram in October 1949, thanking Yenan comrades for their message of congratulation on the founding of the new régime in Peking. On one side of the tablet, Mao himself has scrawled a handwritten exhortation: 'Bring the glorification of the revolutionary tradition to new heights.'

We pass a slogan that heralds the proximity of Yenan: 'Hold the Spirit of Yenan Forever Bright.' But today 'Yenan' is not merely a town. Nor is it a special world of its own as in the heroic days when Mao, Chou, and others were moulded. For today Yenan is simply part of China, and all of China is a Yenan. We also pass the site of one of the C.C.P.'s notable meetings in the days of the anti-Japan war. It is a collection of long low mud huts on a barren hillside. Here the enlarged Political Bureau met in 1937, and Mao wrote his essay 'For the Mobilization of All the Nation's Forces for Victory in the War of Resistance.'

We reach the town of Fuhsien – a single main street, tiled roofs in the Chinese style, men nursing babies – and soon the light fades and the smell of rain grows stronger than the smell of dust. Eerie shadows stretch like a tangible grey mass across the valleys. A flock of black mountain sheep shelter from the rain against a rocky hill face, tended by a wizened shepherd with a face like a copper pot. Peasants run at a trot along the road with spades and picks on their shoulders. Some straggle, unconcerned, and the drenched blue cloth of their smocks sticks to them as a second skin. The dull light now has a bronze glow, refracted from the wet red soil of the hills.

I had read of erosion in north Shensi, but now it is a living process before our eyes. The hills are alive with rushing concourses of water, as if a mass of rusty-red serpents writhes downwards toward the embattled valleys. The river which was just now a trickle swirls angrily. Thunder drowns out our words of gingerly speculation. In a moment we face an amber torrent, like a rich caramel custard poured across the road. The driver of the Vietnamese Consul's car is ahead. He hesitates. Then his engine roars and he goes at the water. The Volga shakes like a toy – but both cars get through. We are all silent now. The driver is the only man in the car who counts. None of the intellectuals beside and behind him have any advice to offer. Only Mr Chou breaks the human silence. He recalls a line from the philosopher Lao Tzu to cheer us, and pronounces it with his usual confidence: 'The heavier the rain, the shorter it lasts.'

A few miles back a spill of rocks had protruded onto the road. On the rock nearest the passing traffic an old man was curled in peaceful sleep. But now all tranquillity has gone. Rocks tumble down upon the road regularly. The driver is fearful of landslides and rockslides. He asks himself aloud whether he ought to stop. Even the unflappable Mr Chou has a slightly furrowed brow. The driver's question proves academic. We turn a curve and find the way barred by a jagged red hillock of rocks. The cars draw up before it, helpless like two beggars at nature's gate.

Lao Tzu's maxim is not going to help us move those rocks. We get out to start the job. Except for the Vietnamese Consul, who remains sitting in his car. I enjoyed myself; but, even if I hadn't, I would not have risked looking like an unrectified intellectual inside the car. The drivers confer and decide not to try and remove the pile of rocks. They will rather level it off to a mound which the cars, by getting up speed, can drive up and over. It is an excellent idea. We remove the highest rocks and flatten the lower ones. The two drivers direct operations with resource and humour. We are soaked to the skin, and our legs are splashed red to the knee from the mud. After half an hour the heap of rocks has become an undulating curve. Two trucks which have approached from the other side will test it first, and try to flatten it a little more. It works. Like a buckjumper on a steer we negotiate our 'remoulded landslide'. What happened to later traffic I don't know; we drove on much relieved to Yenan.

Yenan was well worth the journey. Cradle of Mao's revolution, this town evokes the austere, comradely, non-urban ambience of Chinese Communism in its formative years. Its forty thousand people share a valley of intimacy and peace surrounded by steep golden mountains. The houses are simple, half-lit through windows made not of glass but of thin pale paper. The streets are rude, dusty tracks. Bicycles ply their way; a few donkey carts amble by; now and then there is a truck. The people are dark-skinned, dressed in blue costumes, extremely friendly. I stroll in the lively *hu t'ung* at dusk and catch the beautiful smell of corn being cooked. A small child suddenly looks up at me; she sees I am a foreigner and screams. After a moment of embarrassment I feel pleasure. The spontaneity is refreshing after the formalism of the atmosphere in Sian.

You see the places where the C.C.P. leaders worked and lived in the grim, heroic days of the war against Japan. Here is the meeting room of the Political Bureau. The floor is stone, the walls mud, the windows an airy void. There are wicker armchairs with blue cushions, little tables with teapots and cups. Near by is a ping-pong room, where the leaders tried their hand between sessions. The hall of the Military Affairs Commission, built by the cadres themselves, is a delightful building, with a ceiling of criss-crossed bamboo beams and rows of roughly hewn benches and tables in local wood. The ballot box inside is decorated with a hammer and sickle.

We stand on the spot where Mao gave his speech 'Combat Liberalism'. Stroll to the hillside where he read a draft of the famous essay 'Serve the People'. Inspect the table where he sat with Norman Bethune. Lounge on the stone blocks where he gave an interview to Anna Louise Strong. It is moving on this still, cool morning to tread the ground where today's China was seeded; the caves where Mao added the arts of government to the arts of the guerrilla; the valley in which hope pushed through against hopelessness.

The former houses of C.C.P. leaders are stone-floored caves set into the hills. I visit Mao's first cave, which he had to leave after the first phase of Japanese bombing. His writing desk, his washing bowl, his *k'ang*. The second cave, where he tended a vegetable patch as a break from meetings and writing. The third, in a date orchard, where peasants came in the evening to talk to him about their farming, and he broached for them the future of China. Sometimes they would bring him steamed bread, baked in the shape of a peach, which symbolizes longevity. Sometimes they would greet him with drums and gongs. We see also his fourth house, to which he moved in the grimmest days in order to be near the Military Affairs Commission.

In this fourth place Mao made one of his great and characteristic decisions. To abandon Yenan. Many did not want to do it. Was not Yenan the symbol of the revolution? But Mao, who had himself spoken with emotion of the 'caves of Yenan', showed masterly suppleness of mind. It is important to defend Yenan, he conceded. But the whole of China is more important than Yenan. Why not leave it to the enemy? It is after all only caves. When we come back we can build much better things. Mao's realism overruled sentiment. And just as well. For when the decision to abandon Yenan was taken, the Kuomin-

tang forces in the area were some ten times as strong as
C.C.P. forces.

In Yenan, you recall that 'self-reliance' is no ideal doctrine chosen from a gallery of alternatives. It was Mao's
way of using weakness as a springboard to strength. In
those days the C.C.P. had nothing. They made their own
soap. Cadres built meeting rooms with their own hands
before they sat in them to plan for China's future. Paper
was in chronically short supply. At the Anti-Japanese
University, students would sometimes have to write in the
sand; cork would now and then be available as a substitute for paper. About the only industry in the town was
a match factory. (I had often wondered why in Yenan, on
the occasion of important Party meetings, commemorative
matchboxes were produced; I suppose because it was the
only manufactured item that *could* be produced.) There
were so few clocks and watches that the usual method of
telling the time was a primitive sundial. Yet this is the
town where Mao wrote 92 of the 158 items in his *Selected
Works*.

Much that Mao counts as virtue, you realize when visiting Yenan, was evolved out of sheer necessity. The Anti-
Japanese University was simple and ardent. You read a
book with one hand and grew cabbages with the other.
Military spirit was to the fore. There was no 'nonsense'
about 'research for its own sake'. Since the Cultural Revolution, Mao seeks to make all China's universities follow
this pattern. Yenan was small enough for Mao to have
direct, affective contact with his people. It was a town
Rousseau would have liked. It had the 'natural' spirit
Rousseau extolled. In the Cultural Revolution, Mao tried
to bring back this ideal of direct participation. He is
restive with bureaucracies that arise (unsurprisingly) to
cope with organizing 800,000,000 people. He would like
the Party to be the spiritual power it was in the town of
Yenan. He cherishes leaders who are still tribunes of the
people, and have not become desiccated organization men.

A slight illness took my mind momentarily off history,

and brought great care and kindness from Yenan hosts. A doctor wearing a badge of Chairman Mao comes to see what is up. As the doctor examines me – in the usual Chinese way he puts the thermometer in the armpit – Mr Chou, Mr Liu, and Yenan friends gather around the bed discussing my condition in realistic detail. The doctor's pattern of training is typical of his generation (now in its forties). First he studied Western medicine (at Harbin); later he studied Chinese medicine (at Chengtu). He now blends the two styles, which is current practice. 'Which medicine do you want?' he asks me gravely. 'Western or Chinese?' Lying hot and weak, I have no views on this matter. 'Whichever promises the quickest recovery.' He gives me a final summarizing glance and announces: 'I'll give you some of each.' So I drink chrysanthemums soaked in a porcelain mug of hot water, and swallow Western drugs in tablet form.

A special song and dance performance was due that evening, and I decided I should not miss it. At the end of the show the doctor appeared from the crowd. He had attended especially to keep an eye on me. Back at the Guest House, he did a blood test and we talked. I had found one or two of the evening's songs tediously political. He defended them. But is *everything* political, I inquired: 'Is your reason for tending me political?' He vigorously affirmed that it was. 'I treat you as best I can because it is my internationalist duty to do so.' He spoke softly and with sincerity. 'Our whole system of medicine in China,' he added, 'derives from socialism. Only with socialism is there medical care at the best level available for whoever needs it.' I think the doctor was entirely right. Yet I also think his motive in treating me as kindly as he did was in part simple human compassion.

We did not return to Sian the way we came. There is no regular plane service to Yenan – nor any rail connection – but a special plane materialized to take some Japanese and myself back to the provincial capital. Throughout the morning there were consultations about the best time for departure. Chinese pilots are extremely cautious and do not fly if the weather is at all poor. Word comes that the morning rain has cleared, and as more is expected in the evening, the flight will depart after lunch. The tiny plane is an Ilyushin 14, built in China. You climb into it as into a hammock.

A young girl tells us the flight to Sian will take eighty minutes, and that photos should not be taken from the plane. No political quotations come with her remarks. As we roar up over the Shensi hills, she brings cigarettes (what smokers the Chinese are!), orangeade, peanuts, sweets, chewing gum, and notebooks with the calligraphy of Mao on the cover. We reach the plains north of Sian, and cross the yellow and pale blue waters of the river Wei. Clusters of green dot the land as Sian approaches. Soon chimneys swing into view, and the grey-green tiles of this stately town. It seems like cheating to swoop back to Sian as fast as this, after the laborious drive north to Yenan two days before.

6   The 'Cult' and 'Ultra-leftism'

One morning in Peking, I talked about trends in China
with an official (he once worked as a journalist in New
York) senior enough to speak his mind. For three hours
we sat on a vast white couch, then at a near-by table
where one reckless dish after the other was relayed by
wide-eyed boys. Mr Y – let me call him that – suddenly asked me: 'What do you think of the propaganda?'
Unsure of his line of thought, I murmured an incon-
sequential remark. 'I think it's awful,' he resumed, screw-
ing up his face. 'It's boastful. And too many adjectives
and adverbs. Take the exhibits at Shaoshan [Mao's birth-
place]. They are overdone. And why must it end with the
atom bomb – as if the point of the revolution was to
make the bomb!' My own tongue was loosened by his
remarks; I added criticisms. 'But you know,' Mr Y continued, 'it's not as bad as it was.'

That is true. Giant-sized white plaster statues of Mao
have come down in Peking and other cities. His photo no
longer adorns the daily Hsinhua news bulletin. During
the super-enthusiasm of the Cultural Revolution, it was
not uncommon for people to wear two, three, or even four
badges of Chairman Mao. Today it is common to find
people without even one badge. The *Red Book*, you might
say, has given way to books. (A statistic got in Sian shows
how far the glorifying of Mao went: during the Cultural
Revolution, in Shensi province – whose population is
about 21 million – 100 million copies of works of Mao
were published!) And not only books by Mao. A driver
in Canton has Engels' *Anti-Dühring*. No longer do sessions at factories and communes and flights on planes be-

gin and end with readings from Mao, as they did during the Cultural Revolution. Study has gained an edge on incantation. A workaday spirit has squeezed out rhetorical excess.

I stumbled across two startling examples of the trend. On Peking's Street of Eternal Revolution are the offices of the Municipal Revolutionary Committee. In the late-afternoon rays, as Peking sang with the bicycle bells of people riding home, I passed this building on my way to dine at Rewi Alley's house almost next door. Behold, four workmen were swiftly removing the huge Mao portrait from over the doorway! Random thoughts peppered my mind. A *coup* in the Revolutionary Committee? Making way for a *larger* portrait? Neither. Part of a general winding down of the personal display of Mao and his aphorisms.

Another afternoon, I returned to the Peking Hotel after a visit to the Peking Petroleum Refinery. On our sixth floor, the smell of fresh paint. Two quotations from Mao, in white upon red, had been painted out since lunch. I almost missed them, so cheery had they been beside the dark panels. But no replacement went up in ensuing days. Maybe the exhortation had won its incarnation in labour – the word become flesh.

Of course, slogans and quotations still abound in China, and I often puzzled over what relation the propaganda has to the worker's daily round. One Sunday afternoon I was sitting in my room at the Hsin Ch'iao Hotel, after a morning at the Ming Tombs. In the golden sunshine, the trees of the Legation Quarter made dappled pools of light and shade on the warm asphalt roads. It is 5.30 p.m. People meander home from diversions in the parks, from swimming in the splendid new pool near by. Others are back from shopping trips in Wang Fu Ching street, with bulging shopping bags and smiles of satisfaction. Most wear blue shorts, white shirts, and plastic sandals. Out of a taxi hops a Chinese official, and disappears into the hotel. Then President Ceausescu's car drives by.

He has also been at the Ming Tombs today, and now returns to the Romanian Embassy which is in the same street as the Hsin Ch'iao.

On the radio there suddenly bursts forth the 'Red Guard Programme'. For a moment it seems almost comically incongruous. The tone is shrill, and there are constant broadsides against enemies. Sitting there in my room, two quite different ways of summing up the mood presented themselves. Listen to the radio: here is China as 'Mao Tse-tung Thought'. Look out the window: here is China as a simple Sunday afternoon. Is it two worlds? No, it is one.

I listened further to the Red Guards. It was really a civics programme. News from Ta Chai, and descriptions of this model village's achievements; debates between one group of Red Guards and another; announcements about forthcoming community activities; uplifting messages to encourage better citizenship. It comes in the form of 'Mao Tse-tung Thought', I reflected, because it has to be given a dramatized form if it is to reach 800,000,000 people.

Given the size of the population (and the divisions of this far-flung nation), myth is a necessary tool for a strong government. Of course, it need not be this particular myth of 'Mao Tse-tung Thought'. But some myth is required, if the 'Sunday afternoons' of the 800,000,000 are to fit together in a workable, prosperous organism. Especially since the Chinese government aims not only at being a strong government, but at making an egalitarian China. Ultimately, the point of the propaganda is to make equal citizens of the entire 800,000,000.

Another related current trend in China is criticism of 'ultra-leftism'. That may seem puzzling; it not Mao an ...? The point is, ultra-leftism had its day, when the main job was putting down 'revisionists', but that day is past. Yesterday a weapon, today a target. The rebels have been called off, damped down. The order of the day is noses to the grindstone of productive work. Has the wind changed because the Cultural Revolution succeeded, and now it's back to routine? Or because the 'line' of the Cultural Revolution was utopian, did not work, and had to be replaced by a rebuilding of the Party along old lines, and by a dispersal of the hot rebels to turning lathes and feeding pigs? Here I can only describe the fresh mood.

At the Red Star commune near Peking, I saw a laundry. But it was not a laundry. Those were not clothes pegged to a line, but *ta tzu pao*, posters newly done in black on green paper. Members of the brigade had written them willy-nilly and awaited responses from the Party Committee. I had time to read only three before companions led me elsewhere. The theme was unmistakable: 'AND WHAT OF THE ULTRA-LEFTISTS? WHAT WERE THEY DOING DURING THE CULTURAL REVOLUTION? THEY WERE NOT AT WORK – WHAT WERE THEY DOING?' Little doubt but that they were demonstrating. Coursing up and down China lighting fires of revolution.

One of these *ta tzu pao* is worth pausing over as an instance of a widespread line of criticism of ultra-leftists. It was too long to read on the spot, but I photographed it – with the permission of commune members – and read it later at leisure. In the usual way it starts with a 'supreme directive' from Mao, then applies it to a concrete case. The directive urges citizens to 'defeat and smash the anti-revolutionary, conspiratorial organization, May 16'.* The text is then headed: 'A bad element has infiltrated the Red Star commune – Wang Hsu-tung.' The peasant who wrote this *ta tzu pao* announces that he is going to 'speak up'. It is wrong, he thinks, that amidst the struggle against May 16, 'our factory [one of the commune's small-scale plants] is still stagnating in silence.' He says 'it is an illusion to suppose that if nobody says anything, that means there is nothing to be exposed.'

The writer of the *ta tzu pao* chooses to expose a student

* The May 16 organization was an extreme-left network which – it is now claimed – mouthed Mao's line but actually opposed it and even planned (in 1967) a *coup*.

whom he suspects of extremism. Wang Hsu-tung is a 'self-proclaimed student' from a technical institute who 'wears glasses' and 'first came to our commune toward the end of 1966.' He is denigrated as a 'mysterious character'. He 'went out early in the morning' from the high school dormitory where he slept, and 'came back late at night ... Obviously he was engaging in some conspiratorial activities.' And now the pith of the case against Wang: 'He divided the people,' and he was 'the main cause of the violent struggle that occurred in various of our factories.' This rather angry literary assault, scrawled in lively prose with a black brush on green paper, was one of many against suspected May 16 elements at the Red Star commune.

I doubt that these posters would have been written if the Party did not welcome their message. In fact, the message is omnipresent in China. In schools, you are told that ultra-leftists wanted to do without teachers altogether. Some urged an end to universities, saying simply that life is the classroom. Some said you learn *only* by practice – theory is useless. These ideas are now all rejected.

At the Number 61 Middle School in Canton, it seemed that even some of Mao's own (more 'leftist') ideas about education are pruned in their application. The chairman of the School's Revolutionary Committee – one of the few white-haired men I met in China – referred to 'naughty' pupils. What do they do wrong? 'Well, they come late to class – and they leave very early.' I quoted Mao, who said if a student is bored let him leave the class; that is all right. There was laughter at the table, some of it a bit nervous. How would the jovial Hunanese chairman meet this? He spoke with a touch of intimacy, his tone an appeal to common sense. 'Look, if the teacher is really bad, pupils may leave. But they must come back.'

At Tsinghua University, a conversation reflected the trend of the times. Political workers who briefed our Australian group showed an ideological zeal that seemed to border on ultra-leftism. One of them, responding to a question, said China had no need of intellectual exchanges with other countries; all necessary knowledge existed within China. Surprised by this, the visitors queried the answer, and some argument ensued.

The zealous cadre with gleaming eyes appeared to be out of line with Mao's view, which is that good things can and ought to be selected from abroad (and from the past). As tension rose, a Chinese Foreign Ministry official, who was accompanying the visitors to the university, intervened to contradict the Tsinghua spokesman. He referred to my interview with Kuo Mo-jo some days before (at which he had been present). 'Kuo Mo-jo, President of the Academy of Sciences, said this week in an interview with Mr Terrill that there *should* be and *will* be international exchange of scholars between China and other countries.' He turned to me with a certain air of triumph: 'Is that correct, Mr Terrill?' The Tsinghua spokesman looked uncomfortable. The Ministry official had seemingly invoked Mr Kuo to damp down an ultra-leftist error.

In factories, students are often the target when ultra-leftism is criticized. I found this especially so in the smaller cities. 'They lacked experience.' 'Easily deceived.' 'Bad elements led them to extremes.' The 'bad elements' are usually identified as those in May 16. They are to be distinguished from ultra-leftists, in most explanations, but not all, by three points. They were an organized conspiracy, not merely, like the hotheads, a wind blowing where it listeth. The contradictions between them and the people are 'antagonistic'; between ultra-leftists and the people, the contradictions are 'non-antagonistic'. Third, the May 16 group took armed struggle to the point of committing criminal offences.

At a Nanking factory I came across an example. A P.L.A. officer, sent to meld the factions, had been kidnapped and held for three days by elements now suspected of being May 16. In this factory, I saw a freshly written *ta tzu pao* which aggressively inquired: 'Where do the May 16 elements think they can hide?' Many of the factory's workshops were plastered with the slogan *'i-ta san-fan'* ('one hit, three antis'). Counter-revolution is to be hit; corruption and graft, speculation, and waste are to be opposed. The interesting thing was that the slogan – which is susceptible of either anti-rightist or anti-leftist application – was being used overwhelmingly against ultra-leftists.

Nationally, the tone was set during my visit by the trial at two public meetings of the 'Red Diplomat', Yao Teng-shan. Yao had crossed the threshold into crime by burning the British Office in Peking in 1967. This was not his only crime – Yao even detained Chou En-lai during the former's giddy weeks of power as 'head' of the Foreign Ministry in the summer of 1967. But the British Office affair has been made a symbol of leftist excess. No opportunity was missed in my presence to condemn it.

The French Ambassador, Étienne Manac'h, told me how Mao himself raised the matter in conversation. Maurice Couve de Murville was in China, and Manac'h went with him to see the Chairman. 'Were you in Peking when the British Office was burned?' Mao asked Manac'h. No. 'Were any of your present staff?' No, a complete turnover of Embassy staff had occurred since then. Mao persisted. 'Well, you must have *read* about the incident?' He wanted to speak of it. He criticized it as 'indefensible'. It is ultra-leftism, he said; 'I myself am a centre-leftist.'

In Canton, I found signs of retreat from leftism, in the social style with which I was received. During the Cultural Revolution, T'ao Chu, the leading political figure of Canton, was attacked for the error of spending time and money on entertainments, catering, and beautification, in order to impress visitors to South China. T'ao Chu's civic zeal was brought to mind by an exchange at a banquet in Canton the evening before I left China.

The restaurant, one of China's finest, was the famous P'an Ch'i (now Yu I, 'Friendship'). Its elegant balconies, furnished in ebony and mother-of-pearl, overlook a lake bordered with willows. Some quite fantastic sweetmeats were being served. One especially took my fancy – a spiced coconut *purée* wrapped in a hot pancake – and I ate several. The host, himself a hearty eater, tried to broaden my approach. 'Do you know, Mr Terrill, this restaurant has more than *one hundred* varieties of sweet cakes. Recently some foreign businessmen could hardly believe this. So I ordered all one hundred kinds brought to the table!' Mr Yang was quite ready to do the same for me, but my stomach was not equal to the challenge. Yet what price T'ao Chu's 'errors'? Was not Cantonese chauvinism rearing its delightful head once more? I realized, again, that much backpedalling has taken place since the excessive leftism of the Cultural Revolution.

7   Kuo Mo-jo on Cultural Life

New shoots appear in intellectual life, after the winter blight of the Cultural Revolution. Some of them were spoken of in an interview – reported in *People's Daily* and other organs within China – given me by the leading intellectual of the Chinese government, Kuo Mo-jo, Vice-President of the Standing Committee of the Congress, and President of the Chinese Academy of Sciences. A rich, in some ways theatrical, personality, Kuo has trailed an astonishing array of writings and cultural activities (as well as having been Vice-Premier), and is now one of the most prominent members of the régime.

He has the square, rugged Szechwan face; bright, emotional eyes – more so when he takes off his glasses. Heavy lines arch between eyes and nose, and two more curve down from nose to mouth. His hair is receding, and he relies on a hearing aid. The strongest impression of his mind is of facility, suppleness. To use favourite Chinese images, he seems a willow, not a pine. Several aides were with him, as were several officials from the Foreign Ministry with me. Kuo fascinated the whole circle. Tossing out puns and rhymes, he seemed conscious of addressing not only his interviewer, but the circle of assistants who listened to him with awe. He has been called a 'cultivated leopard'; I saw mainly the cultivation, but glimpsed the leopard.

Photos were taken in the foyer, beside wrought iron wall pictures and calligraphy in the style of Anhwei province. Kuo signalled the taking off of jackets – leaving him in grey trousers and a white cotton shirt – and we sat down in the cavernous splendour of the Great Hall of the People and talked (through interpreters) for almost three hours. Nearly eighty, Kuo looked at me and said, 'You are like the rising sun at eight.' Since the Cultural Revolution, 'young' (up to thirty-five), 'medium-age' (thirty-six to fifty-five), and 'old' work together in China as a 'three-way combination' on many tasks. 'I suggested to Chou En-lai,' joked Kuo, 'that we need to add a fourth category for those over seventy-five – "super-old". But he thought it sounded too much like super-power!'

Kuo Mo-jo is considered a romantic, which seems indeed to be true. I asked him if he was still interested in any of the European writers he once devoured and translated, including Goethe and Nietzsche. 'The poems of Goethe are good,' he replied, 'but the man I really like is Shelley.' He confessed regard for another romantic work. 'The *Rubaiyat of Omar Khayyám* is also wonderful. You know it is rather similar to the poetry of Li Po [a famous poet of the T'ang Dynasty]. Not in subject matter – Li Po didn't just write of wine and women – but in style.' Mr Kuo was starting to talk with some verve. But then he stopped. 'We do not read any of these people nowadays ...'

The President of the Academy of Sciences acknowledged that research had been affected by the Cultural Revolution. The scientific sections never stopped work. But the humanistic and social-science sections have been suspended for a period of 'struggle, criticism, and transformation' – with the interesting exception of archaeology. Digging for national treasures went on through the turmoil. It even benefited at times, as Red Guards, coursing through the country, hit upon the edge or sign of an unearthed piece. Mr Kuo talked with an antiquarian's enthusiasm of the finds in the Cultural Revolution period, an exhibition of which I previewed that morning in the Forbidden City. Of many of them – one superb jade 'death-suit' from the Han dynasty, its tiny green pieces stitched together from wire of pure gold – he had read and written, but now could examine for the first time.

Research in all fields is poised for fresh advances. Kuo announced a new phase in the remarkable story of Chinese research on insulin. In 1966 insulin was synthesized, in work done jointly at the Academy and Peking University. Now the second stage, structural analysis of insulin, has been completed. It began in 1967, and was done in the Institutes of Organic Chemistry and Biochemistry of the Academy. Amino acids have been synthesized, surpassing even the work done by Hawkins in Britain. Important implications follow for our understanding of the origin of life. The results of the second stage, Mr Kuo told me, were assessed at a meeting on 15 July 1971.

The Chinese cultural statesman also unveiled a reorganization of the Academy. Dire rumours have circulated about the fate of the Academy. The facts are these. In accordance with a general principle of the period since the Cultural Revolution, the Academy is being drastically decentralized. Mao's idea, Kuo reminded me, is that initiative should always be a double thing: from above and from below at the same time. 'China is so vast. We have found that you cannot do everything from the centre.' Sixty of the Academy's one hundred research institutes are being thrown down to 'root levels' (under the authority of the provincial Revolutionary Committee), or shifted to 'other organizations' (the Army; productive agencies). Sections outside Peking which were formerly 'branches' will now be under local authority, though 'overall policy' will be set by the Academy. A further twenty research institutes will henceforth be under 'dual leadership', central and local together. The remaining twenty will remain with the Academy in Peking as in the past. The effect, it is hoped, will be a better integration than before of research with its application in the practical tasks facing the Chinese nation. Later in Canton, a biologist at Sun Yat Sen University confirmed that three

Institutes – Microbiology, Entomology, Botany – are now under Kwangtung provincial authority, no longer under the Academy at Peking.

From Mr Kuo (and other high sources) came news of further activity in research and publication. The *Modern History* by Fan Wen-lan, distinguished historian who died two years ago, is being revised and augmented by new chapters. The work is proceeding in the Institute of Modern History of the Academy and will appear before long. The archaeological journals, *Kao-ku* and *Wen-wu*, will shortly resume publication. A large new batch of the writings of Lu Hsun is on the way.

'Normal' intellectual contacts between China and other nations, Mr Kuo explained – 'students, lecturers, materials' – will be resumed as 'struggle, criticism, and transformation' are wound up. I was not entirely reassured by the way he phrased the Government's future intention: 'We will give new assignments to those who have remoulded themselves well.' But it was interesting, and a fresh piece of information, that religious organizations have not been done away with, but only 'suspended' for the duration of struggle, criticism, and transformation. Chinese delegates will soon be selected to go to international conferences of intellectuals. 'We have already begun to exchange scholars again,' observed Mr Kuo. 'You have come; the Japanese philosopher, Matsamura, came; Japanese economists and historians also; Professors Galston and Signer from the United States came here. And many, many American scholars have *asked* to come.'

Kuo Mo-jo made warm references to his contacts with Americans. He recalled Professor John Fairbank, 'my old friend from days in Chungking, and later from Shanghai'. I wondered if he expected to meet Fairbank again. 'I would like to see him in Peking.' Then Kuo added as a kind of afterthought, 'It is probably beyond me now to go to Harvard.'

One of the problems in reactivating exchanges, the Chinese leader remarked, is the shortage of interpreters.

You have to train them when they are young. 'My Japanese is not perfect because, although I have lived a lot in Japan, I was no longer a young man when I went there.' He recalled how well certain sons of Western missionaries who were born in China or Japan learned to speak the languages of these countries. He spoke of Edwin Reischauer, and of James Endicott, a missionary whom he used to know in Szechwan province. 'Endicott was very active in the peace movement.' Kuo, who has himself been one of the leaders of the World Council of Peace and similar groups, suddenly paused. Then he added quietly, in a reference to the influence of the Soviet Union in these movements, 'Of course, that was before the peace movement degenerated . . .'

Kuo Mo-jo said that an upsurge of language teaching is due. Stress will now be upon English, French, German, Arabic, and Spanish – in that order. 'We are also going to give attention to the tongues of Africa, such as Swahili, and the tongues of small nations, such as Nepalese.' The Peking Foreign Languages Institute will again – after a break for the Cultural Revolution – enrol regular students 'this winter'. Chairman Mao himself, Kuo Mo-jo informed me, is setting an example of language learning. At seventy-seven, he pursues English, and he likes to toss around newly learned phrases such as 'law and order' and 'anti-Mao'.

Forays into bookshops confirmed the upward cultural trend, though actual stocks are still meagre except on the technical side. Recently published fiction, mostly short stories written by young 'workers, peasants, and soldiers', is available. Its quality is not arresting. Mr Kuo confessed as much himself, comparing them sadly with Lu Hsun's 'unshakeable' work, and with the famous Chinese historical novels *Dream of the Red Chamber*, *All Men Are Brothers*, and *Western Pilgrimage*. These last are not in the shops, yet people of all ages manage to read them. Chairman Mao, Mr Kuo said, not long ago read *Dream of the Red Chamber* for the fourth time.

Why, I asked Mr Kuo, are there no writings from Chinese authors today which compare in quality with these giant works of the past? 'There is a lack of life about recent writings, and a lack of vivid and direct language.' Mr Kuo argued that the Cultural Revolution has done something to rectify this situation. 'Most authors come from the ranks of the intellectuals, and the intellectuals have been divorced from the masses. Their range of life was small; they did not know the language of ordinary people.' The point puzzled me. How could it be that Chinese writers between Liberation and the Cultural Revolution were more divorced from the masses than were Lu Hsun and his friends before Liberation?

But Kuo Mo-jo swept on to state his high hope for the literary results of the May 7 schools. Here the writers are being 'remoulded'. Most members of the Writers' Union, the Chinese leader observed, are in these schools, and meanwhile the activities of the Union are 'suspended'. 'In the countryside, the intellectual learns the living language of the people. There will come new and good plays, poetry, and novels.' Mr Kuo explained to me that writers at the May 7 schools do farm work only half the day. 'For half of the day they write, and many works have been produced that now await publication.' I looked at this Renaissance figure of China's cultural life, and wondered just when these works will appear; he has a major say in what will or will not be published.

In one of several paradoxes, Mr Kuo exclaimed, 'So I am optimistic; yet also pessimistic.' The pessimism was about himself. 'I am not able now to really go among the masses, that is why I am pessimistic about myself.' Looking back over the decades, he contrasted himself with Lu Hsun. While Lu Hsun was 'using his pen to further the revolution', he, Kuo, went to Japan in 1928 and stayed there ten years. 'I went there in the first place because of bad health.' Kuo's eyes were large with nostalgia. 'But to have been out of China then! All that was happening! Ching Kang Shan; the Long March; Yenan.' His explanation of why his years in Japan were so rich in literary output was characteristic of the restless, ardent revolutionary that he is. 'I had nothing to do, so I did research. I sat down and let my pen run.'

Letting his pen run for me, Kuo wrote in flourishing Chinese characters two lines from Lu Hsun: 'Fierce-browed, I coolly defy a thousand pointing fingers: Head bowed, like a willing ox I serve the children.' They are from a poem, 'In Mockery of Myself', of the early 1930s. The 'thousand pointing fingers' are the Kuomintang enemy. Lu Hsun's message – which Mao has praised – is that the intellectual should be an 'ox' for the sake of the masses. Kuo Mo-jo turned on me a sad gaze. This is the ideal. Lu Hsun is the 'banner holder of culture for the new China'. But he observed softly that when this poem was written, 'I was in Japan and not serving as an ox for the people.'

I questioned Mr Kuo about language reform, in which he has been involved since the mid 1950s, when the government began to give the matter high priority. At one stage, it seemed that Peking intended to phoneticize the Chinese language, and (however gradually) do away with the picture-language of Chinese characters. Kuo Mo-jo's remarks to me summarized the government's present thinking. 'Romanization is the ideal solution, that is true; but it is very difficult.' Experience has modified earlier intentions. 'We used to train children to write a romanized version, then to learn the characters later. But what did we find? When they started the characters, they forgot the romanized form.'

If China were to romanize its language, Mr Kuo summed up, standard Chinese (*p'u-t'ung hua*) must first be completely popularized. Otherwise, the loss of the characters would threaten the nation's unity. 'China could even break into a number of separate states,' Mr Kuo brooded, 'each with its language, crystallized by romanization.' So it seems best, he continued, to concentrate on simplifying the characters, rather than planning to abolish them. 'You can see for yourself that this has been a great help to ordinary people. Everyone is reading; it is a surging tide.'

The literature stores do indeed seem busy. Handbooks on technical subjects pour from the press and sell briskly. I bought a new one on Chinese medicine. It is in two parts, to cope with the widely differing climate and vegetation of the country; one for North China, one for South China. There are many simpler handbooks in every branch of applied science. Books long unavailable have reappeared. In the Hsinhua bookshop in Peking, I bought Hao Ran's 1966 novel *Bright Sunny Day* (in Chinese). A week earlier I could have got the great classic, *Book of History* (ten volumes, in *pai hua*, or modernized Chinese). It had sold out almost as soon as it arrived.

I bought one of the two works by Mr Kuo on the history shelf, essays entitled *Chung-kuo ku-tai she-hui yen-chiu* (*Research on Ancient Chinese Society*). He is supposed to have said during the Cultural Revolution that it should be burned. I asked him, nevertheless, to sign my copy. He was surprised that it was on sale, and had not before seen this edition. He made no effort to burn the book. Yes, he 'rather regretted' having written it, he said without earnestness. That did not stop him from autographing it with a flourish.

Secondhand bookshops, where still open, are disappointing. At the Eastern Market in Peking, in 1964 a great place to rummage for old books, there is little now but engineering texts and dictionaries. In Canton I chanced upon a more promising one. From the door I could see sections on history and social studies. Young people browsed in silence. But I got no further than the door. A man sitting in the entrance barred my way with his leg. Quietly and quickly he said: 'Foreigners are not allowed in here.'

(From the bookshop I went to see what had happened to the old Catholic cathedral. Massive Gothic, with towers 160 feet high, visible all over Canton, it was done by a

French architect in 1863. I did not expect it to be open for services. No churches in China have been since the Cultural Revolution. I found it being used as a distribution centre for building materials. Stacks of bricks and timber were on the grounds. Up the aisle steered a girl with a wheelbarrow. The altar bore red-and-white quotations from Mao. As Mr Liu – my Luxingshe aide – and I beheld the hum of activity from the gate, a man came out of a near-by doorway and said, 'He can't go in there.' Mr Liu replied, 'I know.' We watched for another moment, and I took a photo. Back we drove, in unaccustomed silence, to the Tung Fang Hotel. It is possible that I might have felt less uneasy about these closed-up places of worship if I could have talked to Chinese believers about their experiences; but I was not able to do this.)

The interview with Kuo Mo-jo lingered on the question of 'tradition' and its tension with 'modernity'. Mr Kuo himself had been active in the May 4 Movement of half a century ago, when a (Chinese) struggle for national dignity was blended with a (universal) quest for scientific ways. He insisted that Chinese policy today is still to take the 'positive elements' from outside China. 'We reject the position of Hu Shih, which favours indiscriminate Westernization. We also reject the position of Ch'en Li-fu, which stands totally against anything from the West.'

Mr Kuo spoke of the new revolutionary opera-ballets, to illustrate how China meets the issue of tradition and modernity. 'These works are not purely Chinese. They are not Western. They are a new thing; revolutionary works which blend both.' He stressed the role of the piano, as if he thought this would especially move me. 'Have you not seen our pianos? Were you impressed with that? Here we are using something from the West.'

As we chatted about the opera-ballets, I remarked that the themes were rather relentlessly political. He beamed at my *faiblesse*. 'You see, we live in China under the dictatorship of the proletariat.' He now grew earnest. 'If we do not consolidate it in the minds of all the people,

China will become social imperialist [the designation for Soviet society].'

Here was the major theme of this extraordinary octogenarian. The revolution in culture is necessary in order to consolidate what was begun at Liberation. This concern for the continuance of the revolution, said Mr Kuo, is Mao's great contribution to Communism. 'Lenin died too soon to carry it through. Stalin lacked time for the research necessary to spell it out. Mao has now summed up the experience of the international Communist movement.' A twinkle came into the eyes of Kuo Mo-jo. 'Of course, we should be grateful to Khrushchev for his errors.' He quoted Chairman Mao: 'We should award Khrushchev a medal weighing one ton for the valuable lessons his mistakes have taught us.'

8 Nights at the Theatre

The ceremony of going into theatres was sometimes embarrassing. As a 'foreign friend', I could not wander in with other patrons and find a seat. Our car drives up at the last moment. The audience is already seated. We enter from the lobby amidst tumults of applause. It is the custom to respond by clapping, as you walk the length of the theatre and take a reserved place near the front. Outside Peking, audiences gape in wonder at the foreign friend. Sometimes you hear speculation in adjacent rows as to the nationality of the foreigner. 'Is he French?', 'Probably Romanian.'

Though China's finest acrobats are at Wuhan, the Shensi Acrobatic Company which I saw at Sian was good enough to impress a foreigner. The keynotes were ingenuity, humour, suppleness, and striking use of colours. There are mass scenes to begin the evening. Leaning, bending, and circling in combinations, the actors turn themselves into a wobbling sea of daffodils. The girls trill at a whisper to suggest daffodils waving in the breeze. Then comes a fantastic variation on the traditional dance of the red scarf. Each dancer readies a length of flaming silk. Nimble limbs race and twirl. The scarves blend into a melting furnace of colour. Suddenly the molten mass becomes set in a pattern; all movement stops. The red scarves are stretched to depict the red star of the Communist party of China.

Having saluted political reality with such a spectacle, it was as if the performers now felt free to get down to solid artistic business. The next hour was the only hour I spent in the Chinese theatre that had not a trace of politics in

it. Gymnasts dash out in long white trousers with enormously wide cuffs. Their cheeks are like red carnations
(nowhere but on the stage do you see cosmetics in China).
In pairs, one stands on his head on the head of the other.
To make things difficult, they pair big with small, and
the big one is on top of the small one! Then the upturned legs of various acrobats link up. A new batch trots
onto the stage and leaps up like grasshoppers to make new
levels of precarious balance twenty feet in the air. I get
nervous at the risks, but looking around I find that no
one else appears to be. The audience is keen, and earthy
in its humour, but not excitable. They applaud in a
rhythmic 'clap-out' manner. No performer comes forward
for an individual 'hand'; only collectively do these panting youths absorb with faint smiles the loud applause.

The gymnast of one moment is a musician the next.
Ten minutes later he is back as a clown. Before the night
is done he is a hectoring propagandist. No wonder you
see fatigue around the eyes as they stand still for a bow.
This jack-of-all-trades style, it was later explained, was
stimulated by the Cultural Revolution. Specialization,
on the stage as everywhere else, is frowned upon. Communes have to strive for 'overall development', growing
a variety of crops they had never thought to grow before.
Stage performers likewise are required to strive for new
skills. Efficiency seems at times subordinated to the impulse to dare the impossible and the bid to become 'all-
round' socialist citizens.

The crowd loves the magicians. The feats themselves
are not beyond the ordinary. But superlative is the corporate rhythm of teams of magicians working together,
the gracefulness, the clever use of suspense. It is ballet,
and satire, as much as magicianship. A favourite theme
is the gap between appearance and reality. A man who
looks dumb turns out to be smart. Imminent disaster is
undercut by triumph. Another recurring theme is resourcefulness. The crowd warms up when a character
seems hopelessly disadvantaged, but manages by a cun-

ning stratagem or by 'self-reliance' to overcome the obstacle before him.

The serried rows of perspiring patrons also hugely enjoy the throwing of boomerangs. I wondered when and how the art of boomerang throwing had been transmitted from Australia to China. But I found out that the performers did not even know the boomerang was an Australian weapon! It was not a proper boomerang, anyway, I pointed out to them. The boomerang is bent like a dog's leg; this Chinese boomerang was in the shape of a cross. No wonder it seldom came back to the feet of the thrower!

Despite poor acoustics – the theatre is a mock opera house built in Soviet style during 1953 – the music was as good as the acting and gymnastics. A flautist, and, for dramatic moments, a trumpeter accompany the sketches and acrobatics with virtuoso skill. Maybe they came from the Shanghai Conservatoire, which turns out first-rate solo musicians. Two boys make marvellous sounds on an instrument that is a hymn to resourceful self-reliance. It is a xylophone *à la maison*. They evoke a melody by striking not the usual row of wooden bars graduated in length, but a row of kitchen bowls of odd shapes and sizes. What a symphony of tone they get out of these humble bowls! They grimace hilariously as they play. Now in mock anguish as they strive for a perfect tone. Now in feigned surprise as a startling or amusing sound echoes from the bowls. It is characteristic of the evening: musicianship, mime, and humour mixed together.

One of the best acts was the mimicry. Three boys (who moments before were doing handsprings) gather around a microphone and make quiet sounds. Their lips and mouths twist, their eyes bulge. Amplified, the hisses and puffing and whistles turn into a civilization of noises. The audience loves these concrete evocations of sounds they hear in daily life. A train seems to pass right through the middle of the theatre. Birds squawk and twitter. The loudspeakers are deployed to make the sounds seem all around. You could swear the building was full of cicadas. Trucks rumble by; babies cry. The patrons shake with laughter. Then the mimics do an air raid. Planes zoom down and drop bombs. In the stalls, humour ebbs rapidly into tense concentration. The older ones in the audience are all too familiar with these awful sounds. The young ones seem unengaged. They are taught to expect these sounds to explode again one day over China, but there is no concrete memory to produce in them a deeply felt response.

During the intermission, I am led to the comfort and seclusion of a side room. It would have been better to mingle in the lobbies, rather than sit glazed like this with my official companions. Only for a moment do I leave the V.I.P. room – on the unanswerable pretext of going to the toilet. Outside the theatre doors is a campfire atmosphere. Groups squat on their haunches chatting and smoking. Bony knees stick upwards like cranes at a construction site. In the gloom, cigarette ends light up the faces with a copper glow. The talk is not fussy, or merely polite, but quiet and earnest. You feel you are not in a theatre audience but with a community. Here, for once, is not China at work or China on parade, but China at ease. When the intermission was over, I had to enter again to an ovation. It seemed ironic to be shepherded aside from the masses, then 'joyously welcomed' by the masses.

The ambience of the auditorium is convivial as people chat and wait for the second half. In shirt-sleeves you feel on the formal side; singlets are the norm. The women have plaits; belts keep in place the floppy trousers of the men; all wear plastic sandals. A sprinkling are half-dressed in the uniform of army, navy, or air force. Smile at someone and unfailingly he or she will smile back.

Onstage, politics reasserts itself, yet not at art's expense. A girl who looks and talks like a pillar of political orthodoxy strides on and hurls at us a quotation from Chairman Mao. (Ninety per cent of the super-enthusiastic ideologues I came across in China were women.) I almost laugh at her pent-up stridency and piercing whine. She emits her message: China will not fight unless attacked, but if attacked the nation will fight like mad.

Two brilliant sketches with a war theme then unroll. The first is a skirmish between a girls' militia and American soldiers. Rousing music begins. Sophisticated lighting effects add to the mood of drama. The story is flashed on two oblong screens – long and narrow, for the Chinese characters on this occasion are written in the traditional top-to-bottom manner – hoisted on either side of the stage. The Americans are attacking China. The girls spearhead people's war against them. Amidst the scenes of struggle and social upheaval, one thing above all strikes me. The girls are portrayed not as outfighting but as *outwitting* the U.S. invaders. They trip Americans up. They isolate or humiliate Americans. But we are seldom shown them shooting or bayoneting an American. In the audience there is a matching sense of watching a game rather than a war. There is much laughing, little tension. Making the Americans look stupid is the artistic nerve-centre of the sketch.

The second sketch caught a similar mood, but this time the invaders were Japanese. The theme was how a clever underdog can overcome a cruel but blundering invader, and make him look ridiculous. Peasants nabbed Japanese soldiers from behind bushes, set booby traps for them, even engulfed them with large vats dropped with exquisite timing from the branches of trees. The audience was delighted. But beside me were six Japanese; a delegation of the Japan–China Friendship Society. Would friendship take such barbs in its stride? The delegation was divided! Four of the Japanese still gripped the Red Book of Mao quotations (which all six – I noticed in Sian and Yenan where we were sometimes together – carried practically all day in all places). These four applauded sedately and, though they did not laugh as the rest of the audience did, a smile never left their faces. The other two – whose Red Books had somehow slipped from sight – did not laugh, applaud, or smile.

Many of the dozen shows I saw at theatres in China were opera-ballets. These standard eight works reflect the norm and the sum total of theatre in the period since the Cultural Revolution swept 'bourgeois relics' from the stage. The most popular of them is *White-haired Girl,* a tale of awful suffering and breathtaking heroism during the anti-Japanese war. I saw it in Sian. Like the other opera-ballets, it is heavily political. In its construction, however, the old is blended with the new, and the foreign with the Chinese. Much of its ballet is in modern Western form, which the Chinese got from Russia. Interspersed with this come sequences from classical Peking opera – like the dance of despair by the father of the imperilled white-haired girl. The orchestra is basically Western, yet the *hseng* is also used. This instrument is made of pipes tangled together like intestines, and dates from the period of the Warring States (before Christ). I noticed, too, the *p'i pa,* a stringed instrument as old as the T'ang dynasty.

Sitting in the front row, it was fascinating to watch the orchestra of Chinese musicians playing Western strings and woodwinds. All were in white shirt-sleeves with badges of Chairman Mao. It was a hot evening, and the men had rolled their trousers to the knee. Cups with tea or water sat beside the sheets of music. This is Sian's leading theatre orchestra and the standards are high. Unforgettable were the faces. Shining black hair streaked across the sweating brows. Weary, patient eyes. Some of the mouths are fastidious; others have a philosophic setness about them. The faces are clear-boned, almost gaunt and above all they look tired.

During the intermission I snatch a moment – returning from the toilet to the V.I.P. room – to talk with two violinists. They are fanning themselves in the open air near the stage door. With a foreigner they are cheerful and friendly. Their tiredness is understandable. Each day they give at least one performance, and since the Cultural

Revolution they spend part of each day on political work, including study of the writings of Marx, Lenin, and Mao. It must be taxing for professional violinists to start broadening their pattern of work in middle age.

Theatre reigns supreme in the world of Chinese entertainment. The cinema is important – yearly cinema attendance in China is at least 4 billion – but it relies heavily on the theatre. There are films of the eight opera-ballets which are based squarely on the theatre productions. Some 500 million patrons are said to have seen the film of *Red Detachment of Women*. I made it one more by attending a screening on a stifling evening in Canton.

It is my favourite among the dance-dramas, and this version is well danced and brilliantly coloured. The setting is the lush island of Hainan during the ten-year civil war; the theme is struggle against landlords and Chiang Kai-shek's forces. I wondered if a 1971 audience still feels deeply about this bitter past. In front of me sit an elderly couple. When the heroine is beaten black and blue by the despotic landlord's gang, there are tears in the old lady's eyes. Later, the landlord is worsted, and his grain distributed among the poor peasants. Young people around me roar with delight. The old couple are silent but evidently moved.

A paradox attends the impact made by the performance. The theme is grim and earnest. Yet as a spectacle the drama is lavish and exciting. The costumes are gorgeous, and so is Ching-hua, the heroine. The music is stirring. Watching the faces around me, I wonder if young and old are not reacting differently. For the old, the theme outweighs the spectacle. For the young, perhaps, the spectacle holds them at least as much as the theme. The action, passion, and elegance must be quite something for the Canton worker, not to speak of the peasant in a remote pocket of China. The roars of delight – when justice caught up with Nan, the landlord – smacked of straightforward excitement rather than of intense emotion.

Some scenes of *Red Detachment of Women* – such as
the sword battle in the second act – draw on classical
Chinese theatre. But the soaring music is Western. Old-
style Chinese music does not lend itself to the new revolutionary opera-ballets. Both the piping thinness of its
instruments and its sedate rhythms make it too square
and intellectual. So Shanghai composers, working collectively, came up with new scores. Chinese folk songs are
blended in. Old Chinese instruments are used. But the
overall effect is of Tchaikovsky *à la chinoise*. Sweeping
string passages match the story well. It is ardent; it sounds
a tone of tragedy. It is as much like traditional Chinese
music as lyric poetry is like mathematics.

I was reminded of *La Bohème*, then quickly saw dis-
similarity. The deep feelings expressed in this Chinese
music are tuned to collective, not individual, endeavour.
Red Detachment, like Puccini's opera, makes an emotional tug on its audience. Yet *La Bohème* treats the heart
and an artist's impulses. The Chinese work treats society
and organized struggle for its improvement.

There are personal dramas, to be sure, within the collective drama of *Red Detachment*, but it is difficult for
the foreigner to gauge audience involvement with these
individual loves and follies. Individuals in the *audience*,
however, have their loves and follies. As the film begins,
I notice a girl sitting alone three rows in front of me.
Minutes later a young man saunters in and sits beside
her. His sauntering does not hide the prearranged nature
of the rendezvous. They sidle closer; they whisper; they
hold hands. For one brief moment the girl returns her
gaze to the screen – while the boy takes off his shirt, folds
it neatly, and resumes position in the cooler comfort of a
singlet. By Act Two these determined lovers are wrapped
around each other like mating crabs. When the film is
over, the boy leaves first, the girl a few moments later.
Red Detachment of Women was for this pair no more
than an excuse for a tryst that was perhaps not possible
elsewhere.

The final act of *Red Detachment* brings a martyr's death reminiscent of the death of Jesus Christ. A heroic Red Army cadre named Hung is captured in the very last lap of struggle. Before help can come, he is burnt on a pyre in a harrowing scene. Not a rustle could be heard in the theatre as Hung was made to mount the readied logs. Was evil to prevail? The flames licked up and destroyed him. It seemed unbearable. Then began a startling transfiguration. The light from the fire turned into a noble and generalized glow. The music stirred from a double bass of death's despair to swelling arpeggios of hope. Hung's embers were now the seat of a glorious new light. It was a resurrection! The Red Army arrives and liberates the area and Nan the landlord is shot. Hung is dead, but undying is the revolution. The masses join with the Red Army, and fantastic songs of battle and hope ensue. As a finale there erupts a rendering of the *Internationale*, an orgy of sound and colour and movement in the name of unshakable historical optimism.

How do young people enter theatrical work in China today? In Sian, I visited the Red Guard Art Troupe, in which some two hundred actors, dancers, and musicians learn their art. I wish I could convey the lively spirit and joy in their work of these performers. In the Troupe's theatre I talk with actors. They are preparing *White-haired Girl.* They train very hard. They have great opportunities before them, in a nation which values the theatre as China does. A banner over the stage reads: 'Art to serve workers, peasants, soldiers.' In the ballet rooms I meet dancers. Vivid in pink and blue, they leap and pirouette as lilting folk songs are played on a piano. Many are strikingly good-looking. As one pair dance an heroic *pas de deux*, I notice among those at the side awaiting their turn several half-clad couples in intimate conversation. Supervising them with a critical eye is an instructor, a bohemian to his elegant fingertips, who was trained at the Peking Dancing School, 1957–9. As the dancing pumps rustle and thump on the floorboards, I look up and there is a slogan: 'Rehearse for the Revolution!'

The thirteen artists of the Red Guard Art Troupe whom I interviewed had fathers with the following jobs and backgrounds: miner, peasant, poor peasant, worker in Sian, retired cadre, servant to a landlord (before Liberation), peasant, rich peasant who was himself a singer, apprentice in a fruit marketing company, worker in Sian, peasant, worker at the Red Flag shoemaking factory in Sian, peasant. In the whole Troupe, some ten per cent had fathers who were intellectuals. The vast majority of these young enthusiasts, therefore, would have had, in China before Liberation, not a ghost of a chance of a career in the theatre. To enter this well-regarded Troupe there are three requirements: sound ideology; good body; fine primary-school record.

The Cultural Revolution had a marked effect on the Red Guard Art Troupe, yet not in a heavy-handed or disruptive way. A P.L.A. Propaganda Team came to educate the Troupe in 1967, but it left in 1969. Already in February, 1968, matters were sufficiently stabilized for a Revolutionary Committee to be formed. Though these Committees in theory comprise one third army people, the Troupe's seven-member Revolutionary Committee has no P.L.A. personnel at all. Nor does any other military note surface amidst the trills and cries of these buoyant studios. I asked one group of three budding ballerinas in what ways they had learned from the 'P.L.A. work style' (which everyone in China these past years has been called upon to emulate). They looked utterly blank.

But the Cultural Revolution has altered the content and style of the Troupe's work. Before 1966, it specialized in national songs and dances, prepared many programmes for children, and never ventured out of the city of Sian. During 1967 the artists spent eight months in the countryside 'getting re-educated'. In Sian itself they also joined in the war of the wall posters, in which Mao's line was pitted against Liu Shao-ch'i's line, and a profusion of 'left' lines were later pitted merrily against each other.

Now there is more 'revolutionary content' in their songs and dances. Programmes for children are greatly cut back. With simplified costumes and properties, the artists go often to the rural areas, both to entertain the peasants and to learn the realities of Chinese life which the Chinese stage must now portray. I talked with two boys who danced for peasants in the tawny loess hills of north Shensi.

'It was not easy,' said one of them shyly. 'We had no stage, not even a smooth floor. We had to flatten and sweep a piece of ground to dance on.' The second boy chimed in: 'Peasants love revolutionary dances and songs.' How can you tell? He laughs at my dullness. 'By the applause!' The first boy amplifies. 'We got a letter from some peasants. It said that a drama we did – which dealt with agricultural struggles – gave them new inspiration for terracing the hills, and even some practical tips on how to do it.'

Since the Cultural Revolution, every artist spends one hour each day studying the writings of Chairman Mao. When performances are given, it is now two a day, rather than one a day as before 1966. Learning and rehearsal time for *White-haired Girl* now runs three months, where previously it ran five months. A small and earnest violinist tells me there is an important current slogan: 'Learn as you perform.' Most interestingly, the *Chineseness* of their work, in form and content alike, has intensified as a result of the Cultural Revolution. More Chinese instruments are used in the orchestra. More classical Chinese swordplay is put into the ballet. Costumes of peasants (not generals, courtiers, beauties) from Chinese history have been carefully traced and reproduced in the plays.

The Troupe has applied 'self-reliance' in making its own properties. Yet I found rather mixed results in the case of ballet shoes. The chairman of the Revolutionary Committee – not an artist himself, Mr Cheng is a Party cultural worker from Szechwan – tells me proudly the Troupe no longer purchases 'expensive ballet shoes from Shanghai'. They are made here at the school by the dancers themselves. It is an achievement of the Cultural Revolution. I asked to see the workroom where the shoes are made.

It turns out that theory leaves practice lagging. The Shanghai shoes used to cost £1·50 a pair to buy, Mr Cheng explained, and now the Troupe itself can make them for 50p a pair. But I find that 50p is the cost of materials alone. Who paid for the sewing machines? 'The state supplied the machines.' The shoemakers pore over their scissors, threads, and brightly coloured leather. They are not dancers. These two gentle old craftsmen are 'veteran workers' who came in from outside to set up the shoe-making room. Where are the dancers? 'Oh, the dancers help with repairs,' replied one of the veteran workers cheerfully. Add together the cost of machines, the wages of the veteran workers, and the cost of setting up small-scale workshops to replace purchasing from Shanghai. It is doubtful, I conclude, that anything has been saved out of the £1·50 per pair of shoes. Nor are the dancers getting a very thoroughgoing experience in self-reliant manual toil. Fulfilling the principles of the Cultural Revolution can prove an unwieldly process.

In addition to opera-ballets, the Chinese people are offered frequent concerts. In the metropolis of Shanghai and the town of Yenan I enjoyed two quite different types. Shanghai has some Big City atmosphere; you reach automatically for a jacket and tie to go out in the evening. In the concert hall it was so warm that most patrons were in shirt-sleeves, but there was a 'concert-goers' air in the foyers. Beside us in the balcony were TV cameras providing a live broadcast for greater Shanghai's 10 million people. The programme was a varied bill of orchestral fare. Western composers are virtually never heard in

China today, even in Shanghai. If you hear Westernized music, it will be music composed by Chinese – probably a team – in a more or less Western manner. You may listen to something that reminds you of Tchaikovsky. You will not actually listen to Tchaikovsky, for he has now been set aside as 'sentimental'.

But tonight the instruments are mainly Western. An ensemble of two violins, viola, double-bass, and piano play short works by local composers. Every instrument, including the first-rate piano, is made in China. There is no prejudice against the piano, or against any foreign instrument in itself. 'Make foreign things serve China' is a common slogan today. It may be the most internationalist cultural slogan China has ever had. Western music may be 'decadent'. But why not use Western instruments to make better Chinese music? The orchestra has so much brass and woodwind that it is really half-orchestra and half-band. The *p'i pa* and other ancient Chinese instruments are represented. They give piping and throbbing 'Chinese' overtones to the naïve, rousing music.

Items are announced by a girl with a voice somewhere between a wail and a scream. She utters a quotation ('Chairman Mao teaches us ...'), and the name of the piece to be played, then she strides off the stage like a robot. A vast picture of Chairman Mao adorns the proscenium arch. When the solid soprano and the austere baritone sing, the words of the song flash on screens to left and right of the stage. The chamber musicians wear blue overalls (does this make them 'workers'?). Members of the orchestra and chorus wear a straight and heavy grey uniform lit up by a Mao badge.

An astonishing scene ends the concert. The entire chorus and orchestra, together with other musicians and including the conductor of the orchestra, take out of their pockets the Red Book, and, waving it, sing with gusto the political song 'Sailing the Seas Depends upon the Helmsman'. The audience join in, first gingerly but soon with full vigour. The song is rhythmic and compelling. The concert hall becomes a temple of patriotic political incantation.

The handling of 'foreign friends' during the intermission had none of the formalism which I experienced in Sian. A room had been prepared for our comfort (I was with Mr Whitlam and his group). Its tables were well stocked with beer. The Australian group had made its liking for this beverage unmistakably clear on numerous occasions (after a while, the Chinese even began putting beer on the Australians' breakfast table!). I went to the guest room briefly with Mr Whitlam, but soon wandered out to stroll in the lobby. Shanghai hosts raised no problems about this. I explained that I wished to get some air, and have a look around. Without hesitation they left me to my own devices.

In the elegant lobbies people chat with little shyness. Two boys in tight pants come up and say 'hello' in English with an American accent. A sprinkling carry books (not the Red Book) in their hand. More than half are smoking, and several times a cigarette is offered. At the box office a lively scene unfolds. People line up for tickets for later performances. But the lines have turned into a surging mass. Evidently there is sharp competition, or perhaps some grievance at the procedures. Jostling occurs, a few voices are raised. A portly man shrugs his shoulders in irritation, a lady addresses firm opinions on the situation to her neighbour, a child cries at the confusion. All eloquent tribute, no doubt, to the popularity of the show.

Back in the hall I chat with a northern Chinese official about the Shanghai character. 'People from Shanghai are sharp-minded and quick to learn,' the dry diplomat observed as a tactful beginning. I did not treat that as his final word and waited for more. Soon he added, with a gesture of the hand to make the words seem non-committal, 'Of course, it is said that Shanghai people talk too much, and that they are not deep.' I ask him how Peking people differ from those of Shanghai. The northerner in

him overrides an impulse to be discreet: 'Peking people
are quieter and they think more.'

The concert at Yenan was quite a different kettle of
fish. It was a folksy offering of a ragbag collection of songs
and dances. The Shanghai concert was extravagantly political in its packaging. The Yenan concert was vividly
political in its every breath and note. I walk down the
aisle in the usual way, with a Japanese group and the
Consul of North Vietnam in Peking. The hall is small
and intimate, and decorated in the favourite Chinese
shades of red and green. There is nothing urban or practised about the audience. Elbows leaning on knees, youths
stare with open mouths at the foreigners. Military men sit
in groups; many of the audience – judging by their rough
hands – are peasants.

Bouncy songs are accompanied by whining, piping
Chinese instruments, as well as violins and assorted
drums. Singers strain their lungs to project the heroic and
Promethean lyrics. One song – which accurately reflects
Peking's policy on the issue – says China hopes for foreign
aid but, if it is not forthcoming, can perfectly well rely on
Chinese efforts alone. Another is a haunting hymn about
the conquest of nature for human purposes. 'Overcome
the wasteland; transform it; make it serve man.'

A third song, which is combined with a ballet sequence
and tickled along by a flute accompaniment, spells out a
crucial theme of life in China today. Though China is
backward, the Chinese people are pulling together and
they will make progress. The chorus runs: 'We are only
ordinary workers, but we are very happy.' I look into the
eyes of the youths singing those lines. How many are
students from Peking and Shanghai, sent to Shensi to
start a new life on China's frontier, being taught to
look on manual labour not as a grind but as a privi-
lege?

A charming girl in plaits and a long pink gown trips
on to sing a solo entitled 'Why Do I Have So Many
Uncles?' She sways and chuckles her way through this

interesting song. The 'uncles' are her 'revolutionary comrades'. Before the revolution, she had many uncles because the extended family pattern was still in existence. Now it is different. *China* is today's extended family! That is why she has so many uncles. The lyric cleverly makes past Chinese tradition serve present Communist purpose.

A Foreign Ministry official pointed out to me that the concert was strong on Shensi provincial colour. It was an impressive feature of the evening. Many of the songs you could hear in no other province of China. Some of these were ancient folk songs, by no means dating only from Liberation, let alone from the Cultural Revolution. Shensi costume was worn (such as towelling around the head). The most lively applause of the show greeted these local songs, and also a flute solo of great ingenuity (the only item without words).

Naturally, some of the Shensi songs are set in the 'Yenan years' of the 1930s and 1940s, when the province gained glory from the presence of the C.C.P. leadership. One song was about the receipt in Yenan of Mao's famous telegram after Liberation. It contained a marvellous line expressing the deep 'sense of place' of the Chinese. 'Even the mountains, even the rivers rejoiced to get the telegram from Chairman Mao!' These political odes were sung in no perfunctory, dutiful way, but with enormous zest and feeling.

One item the concert had in common with that in Shanghai. At the end came a rendering, which ebbed into a demonstration, of 'Sailing the Seas Depends upon the Helmsman'. Arms beat up and down with the song's martial rhythm. Voices shouted its lines of adulation to Mao. The atmosphere was not feverish, or even emotional, but it was loud and enthusiastic. Verses of the song came and went like courses at a Chinese banquet. A signal was given that the 'foreign friends' should mount the stage and shake hands with the performers. The song rolled ever onwards. Up we went to greet the panting, sweating, painted singers and strike a blow for international friendship.

The six Japanese each had a Red Book which they waved as the performers waved theirs. I felt a little empty-handed but did not regret it. There was one other man without a Red Book. I looked beside me and saw the Consul of North Vietnam. His fine long fingers held no book. A weak smile broke his bland expression. The foreign friends were now in centre stage, amiable targets for the popping flash bulbs. The Vietnamese and I clapped gently as the song staggered to its final verses. The Japanese waved their Red Books; the bright covers matched the red of the Mao badges pinned to their business suits.

9   Work

Here is an apartment block at a 'New Workers' Village',
in a textile-mill district of Shanghai. We knock on doors
and talk with those we find at home. It is 4 p.m., and
those on day shift are still at work. Children play noisily
under the spreading plane trees which shade the space
between blocks. A group of neighbours sit fanning themselves, talking about prices, drinking tea. Mrs Tan is at
home with her son, who is back from Anhwei province
for a month to see the family. He was sent there for practical work after finishing Middle School. The family of
five have two rooms, plus a kitchen shared with two other
families. Father earns Y72 per month, mother Y58 (a pen-
sion, three quarters of her wage before retirement). Rent
is Y5 per month. Another son, graduate of Communications University at Sian, works in a mining-machine factory in remote Tsinghai province. A third is on a state
farm not far away, earning only Y24 a month. Furnishings
are of the simplest. But the beds, mosquito-netted and
covered with *tatami*, are comfortable. There is a radio
and a bicycle. Mrs Tan is saving to buy a sewing machine,
which will cost her Y150. Food for each person costs about
Y 15 per month. Meat is not cheap; Y 0.65 for a kilo of
salted pork. Only grain products are at present rationed.

The Tans' conditions of life are fairly typical. Com-
munal provision in the Workers' Village is cheap and
above the standard of private provision. Medical care
costs Y1 per person per year. Many go twice a week to
the cinema – at tiny cost. TV is available, with two and
a half hours of programmes each day, only at the factory;
no worker has his own set. 'Pure entertainment' put on

by advertisers does not exist. Drama, political commentary, documentary – these are the staple, and technically they are quite well done. TV has little hold over people, and I often found myself – perhaps in a hotel lounge – the only person watching a programme. People in China *talk* – endlessly, over tea, through long meals – at times when Westerners might sit at the TV or dress up and go out to organized entertainment. Nevertheless, the Government is pushing ahead with experimental development of colour TV.

At the New Workers' Village, the Revolutionary Committee has a special section devoted to birth control. Its chief gives me three reasons for the vigorous promotion of birth control: it makes possible better care for children, better care for mothers, and greater concentration on production. Women prefer the pill, but physical devices are still the commonest method. The least preferred method is sterilization (of either the man or the woman). Experiments proceed with acupuncture, but the official said it is 'not a very popular' method. I could not find out just where they put the needles, or when.

Political meetings take a certain amount of the workers' time. Few seem either gripped or repelled by them. In hotels or factories I once or twice peered into a study meeting that reminded me, in its tight-lipped zeal, of an Evangelical Bible class. More often the ambience seemed languid; books drooping from the wrist, eyes far away – even, once at Canton's Tung Fang Hotel, a card game going on simultaneously. The issues of the Cultural Revolution did not seem to affect greatly these placid folk in the New Workers' Village. But its aftermath has – especially the sending of youth to far-flung spots for experience in factory, farm, and mine.

In Canton, I talked with an interpreter (Mr Hsieh) about his daily life. A graduate of the Canton Institute of Foreign Languages, he now works for Luxingshe, the China Travel Service. He lives in a room at the Luxingshe hostel. His wife works far away in a Hunan factory. With the two children, she lives with Mr Hsieh's parents in Changsha. Twice a year man and wife see each other.

Each day, Mr Hsieh and his colleagues study from 6 a.m. until 7 a.m., when they breakfast. If there is a tourist to be accompanied, they go with him until lunch at 11.30, followed by rest until mid-afternoon, and further interpreting after that. When they have not been assigned to a tourist, they read English texts (or favourite Chinese novels; Mr Hsieh had just read *All Men Are Brothers*). By contrast with 1964, when I saw interpreters reading classics of English literature (Charles Dickens, Oscar Wilde, Jack London), their English texts all seemed to be translations from Chinese (*Peking Review*, works by Mao). For reference, Mr Hsieh had *A Handbook of English Usage*, written by John Tennant and published by Longmans. In the evenings, the interpreters often have meetings to discuss questions arising from their work. When there is no meeting, many go to films or plays. Two half-days a week are consecrated to 'political study'. Would Mr Hsieh (a Hunanese) prefer to live in Changsha? He answers with a broad smile, 'Chairman Mao says we must serve the people. I will work where I am needed.'

Mr Hsieh was a quiet, courteous man, his Hunanese temperament milder than that of a Cantonese. Only once in a couple of days did he become ardent, and that was when I asked him about the Cultural Revolution. He was almost lyrical, and repeatedly I had to ask him to slow down to a talking speed which I could follow. He had been a Red Guard. He spoke of the evils of T'ao Chu (former Canton leader); of travelling here and there; of writing *ta tzu pao* (posters). What made his memories warm, it seemed to me, was that in the Cultural Revolution he had been a *participant* in activity that was freewheeling and daring.

Here are six silk-spinners in Wusih. Four women are Party members; the two men are members of the Communist Youth League. I spoke with them just after the announcement of Mr Nixon's visit to China. On that they had little to say, and only, it seemed to me, what they had been told to (except one youth – did he miss the briefing? – who amidst the polite nothings about 'traditional friendship between the Chinese and American people' burst out, his fist to the bench: 'Nixon is a bad, bad man'). But of their own lives they talked freely.

Mr Wang earns Y41 a month, his wife (who works at another factory) Y48, of which they save about Y200 each year. In the bank, gaining 4 per cent interest, is Y1,200. They have two children, and Mr Wang's mother lives with them in their three rooms. The other four who are married earn an average husband-and-wife wage of Y109 per month. Average annual savings for each couple are Y275; bank balance, Y830. Affably, the women giggling now and then, they told me things which show the persistence of the 'old' in new China. Of the six (whose ages average thirty-five), five visit the graves of ancestors not less than once a year. Of the five married ones, four used 'go-betweens' to get their spouses. The go-between either introduced them (with marriage in mind), conveyed the proposal, or served as intermediary to satisfy the queries of the spouse's parents. From Y50 to Y100 was spent on the wedding dress. (For marriage, three days off work are given, for maternity, fifty-six days, all on full pay.)

These silk-spinners I found not untypical of city workers. Here are four women at a chemical-fibre factory near Nanking. The wages are a little higher (average Y124 per couple each month), houses roomier. All have two or three children and use birth-control pills, available free at the factory, as a matter of course. Most have one or more grandparents living with them – taking care of the infants. The two children of one woman are living with her parents in Shanghai. She sends Y30 each month for their food and sees them three times a year. None of these mothers have ever, they said, struck one of their children. None would talk to me about sex education.

None use any cosmetics; three of the four have bicycles in the household; all have radios; three of the four have

sewing machines. Between them they can name and discuss the careers of six Chinese women prominent in
national affairs. The militia, to which they all belong,
keeps them fit with running, shooting, swimming in the
Yangtze. It also involves them in study groups on Vietnam
and World Revolution.

What do these makers of chemical fibres feel about
their work, and what do they like to do after work? I
asked each of the four: 'What has been the most exciting
day in your life?' Two said the day they joined the Party;
two said the day they started work. Later as we strolled
to the car, I tried to get one of them, a pretty mother of
three, to spin out her answer. 'Was having babies exciting?'
I asked casually. 'Was that as exciting as first coming to
work?' She lit up like a torch. '*Of course* it was – but, oh,
that's different, isn't it?' We reached the car, but she
could hardly be stopped ... about what grandma said ...
why the girl was rowdier than the boy. She spoke of
Spring Festival, for which there is three days' holiday. 'It
comes next to Sunday, so we have four days for a big
family reunion.' Yes, they go to the cinema – 'Have you
seen *Red Detachment of Women*?' she asks. Of course
they drink a lot of wine.... 'Yes, babies are very exciting,'
she mused as I left her, 'except when they're naughty.'

The girls heartily praise the social amenities of the
factory. Working conditions, I could see for myself, are
also good. The cut in bureaucratic personnel brought by
the Cultural Revolution is popular among workers. In
this Nanking factory it was a cut of nearly 50 per cent –
elsewhere I found an average of about 40 per cent. 'They
were not necessary,' said one of the girls simply, referring
to the excess administrators. On the other hand, there are
no trade unions – I was told – in this factory or elsewhere.
Industrial theory, if it existed, would be based on an
assumed harmony – stemming from the Thought of Mao
– not on conflict. And the worker cannot decide that he'd
like to work in another factory, or another trade, and
simply seek and get a different job. I inquired of the

spokesman of the factory Revolutionary Committee, 'Can a worker transfer work by his own individual decision?' I might have asked if the leopard can change his spots. '*I-ting pu-shih!*' ('Certainly not!') You must find your freedom in the collective; you cannot bid for it as an individual.

Some statistics by province, supplied to me by Revolutionary Committees, show why the worker is better off than in the recent past. Take Shensi. The value of fifteen days' industrial production in the province equals that for the whole year of 1949. The value of industrial production in 1970 was double that of 1965. (Shensi, it should be added, is one of the inland provinces particularly built up by the effort to reduce industrial concentration on the eastern seaboard. Textiles, a leading Shensi export, used to have to go to Shanghai for dyeing and other processing. Today all is done in Shensi, and finished products go direct from Sian to the foreign market.) At Liberation, there were 20,000 pupils in the Middle Schools of Shensi. Today there are 710,000 pupils (population of the province has about doubled).

In rural areas, standards are lower, and in remote counties you seem to step back in time. Many old folk are illiterate. Planting and harvesting are often done by hand. Few young people (ten a year from this commune, five from that) have gone to a university in recent years. The shadow of the past is long. I found ex-landlords and ex-rich peasants still referred to as such, even after twenty-two years. Up to 30 per cent of them are still not considered sound enough to be given the rights of ordinary commune members, and some 'reactionary' ones are 'under supervision'.

Household income averaged Y70 at the Ma Lu commune in the Yangtze Delta (one of China's four 'rice bowls' – others are the Pearl Delta, Szechwan Basin, and Hunan); Y65 at the Red Star commune near Peking. Under the work-point system, wages depend upon work done (and since the Cultural Revolution, on 'attitude').

At Red Star, highest household income was 80 per cent more than lowest. Education and health care are fairly good and extremely cheap. At the Ma Lu commune, each person pays Y2 per year as a medical fee, and gets free service in return. At the commune schools, Y4 each year for each child covers all fees and books.

From 'private plots' (which took up 5 to 7 per cent of the total land in the communes I examined) comes additional income. Frequently, commune officials accuse Liu Shao-ch'i and his associates of having 'exalted' private plots. Yet I never found evidence that the percentage of commune land devoted to private plots has dropped since Liu and his revisionists were put down. Trying to explain why the figure was still 5 per cent – as it had been before the Cultural Revolution – the Vice-President of the Revolutionary Committee at Red Star commune said a little lamely, 'Before the Cultural Revolution, commune members paid more *attention* to their private plots.'

A Ma Lu commune official estimated the products from plots to be worth only Y18 per person per year. Yet I knocked on a door and was told by the lady who answered that her family's plot brings in Y200 by raising three pigs a year, and keeps the family in vegetables as well. Again at Red Star, a family who were expecting my visit – a seven-year-old boy had rehearsed an aria for the occasion – said they earned only Y100 a year from their plot, but informal questions in the fields brought forth higher figures.

Enormous variation marks rural conditions. In ten hours' driving through the wheatlands of north Shensi, I saw only two tractors. In Hunan, by contrast, the nippy two-wheeled tractor, now made in many Chinese cities, was everywhere, and here and there four-wheelers also.

Along the unpaved roads of north Shensi you do not see much sign of 'modernity'. Carts inch by with rocks for the building of the Sian-Yenan railway – they are pulled by a man or woman. At a brick kiln near T'ung Ch'uan ('copper river'), there seem to be no power vehicles to

Work

carry the finished bricks, let alone a branch rail track;
donkeys or people pull the loads. By the roadside, scores
of people of both sexes and all ages squat, breaking up big
rocks into smaller rocks by hand for the railway construction. Mostly the wheat is harvested with a rude scythe –
often a piece of metal tied to a handle with string.

As for threshing, I learned a new method on the rolling
plains of Shensi – and promised the laughing peasants
I'd transmit it back to Australia. These brown, wily types
– who look quite dramatic in their headdress of towelling,
a provincial feature – take the wheat, after they have cut
it, and spread it out on the road. On the paved part of
the journey north from Sian we drove over frequent
stretches of it. The vehicle is the thresher. When enough
trucks or wagons have passed over the wheat, boys take
away the husks, and the grain is swept up by grateful
farmers and put in bags. Of course north Shensi is not
among China's richest parts. Yet the vast majority of its
villages are electrified, which cannot be said of the really
backward pockets of China.

Birth-control campaigns do not meet with equal success in all places. In Kwangtung, the birthrate figure given
me was 3 per cent. In Hunan, 1·5 per cent (in Changsha
it was down to 0·97 per cent last year). Seldom did I find
such earnestness as when provincial officials talked of
their birth-control efforts. A cloud came over a lively
banquet in Canton when the 3 per cent rate was announced. 'It's the old problem,' explained a senior editor
of the *Nanfang Jih-pao* (*Southern Daily*). 'Peasants have
a daughter. They think, that's no good. So they keep
going till they get sons.'

Industry is being made to 'serve agriculture'. In Shensi
I found a new price system in operation since the Cultural
Revolution. Transport cost, to any part of the province,
is included in the set price of the item at the city of Sian.
Previously transport, so backward in China, was a heavy
additional item of cost. Hence the purchasing power of
the commune, and of the individual peasant, is enhanced.

113

Industry grumbles, of course, but at present it grumbles in the air.

Travelling through the hills of Kwangtung, I had been impressed by the amount of terracing done since I saw the province in 1964. Of course it enlarges the cultivable area. Yet I wondered. Won't eventual mechanization be extremely difficult? Next day, a Canton official jumped at the question. He put down his chopsticks and turned to me for emphasis. 'Our factories will have to adjust. This is China; this is the situation. They will have to produce machines, design new ones, which will work on terraced hillsides.'

Certain basic achievements in rural life are undeniable. Simple education improves by leaps and bounds. Kuo Mo-jo disclosed a new figure on literacy in China. Just under 10 per cent, he said, are now considered illiterate. This is the lowest figure ever given for illiteracy in China. It compares with perhaps 70 to 80 per cent at Liberation. The terrible exploitation and inequality of pre-Liberation days has gone. (In 1949, landlords and rich peasants between them made up 7·2 per cent of the population of what is now the Ma Lu commune, yet occupied *79 per cent of the land*, according to commune officials.)

The power pump, as a boon to water control, is a thing of emotion in the Chinese countryside today. The pumps are on the banks of waterways. On the plains, wells are dug. In the hills you find reservoirs. In these ways, the ancient evil of flood and drought has been considerably throttled. In Shensi a vivid statistic is offered. Last year, 3·5 million mou of land (the mou is one sixth of an acre) were newly irrigated in the province. From 1949 to 1965, 7·5 million mou had been irrigated. In the 2,000 years before Liberation (yet how do they know?), 3·5 million mou – the same figure as for the one year of 1970! In Hunan, waterworks done in 1970 made 900,000 mou of land newly available for cultivation.

There is still the saying in Kwangtung, 'whether you get a harvest depends on water; whether you get a good harvest depends on fertilizer.' But here progress is mixed. Organic fertilizer is generally relied upon. Not enough chemical fertilizer is yet made in China, nor is it always of good quality. Much has to be got from Japan. (Mr Whitlam tried to interest the Chinese in Australian chemical fertilizers – but the price was too high.) Agricultural production figures suggest steady but not rapid advance. Grain output in Kwangtung, for instance, is now just double what it was in 1949 (population is up by more than one third). In general, it is social advance – in health, education, security – rather than immediate economic advance which strikes the visitor to rural China today.

10   Southward by Train

After a sun-baked stay in the placid city of Changsha, I was due next in Canton. My two companions, Mr Chou of the Foreign Ministry and Mr Liu of Luxingshe, did not want to go by train. 'We will roast,' reasoned Chou, who is a prudent and measured man. 'The train travels all day from Peking. At Changsha you board it at 10 p.m., and by then it's an oven.' But I insisted, so Mr Chou took back to China Airlines the tickets already bought for to-night's flight. We would go by train. I would see the southern countryside as I wished. Mr Liu, who loves the technical frills of flying and hates heat – though he is Cantonese – would have to bear it. Which he did with good humour. 'But you'll be sorry,' he warned.

I thought the precaution of drinking a few glasses might guarantee sleep for the night hours of the trip. Opportunity came at a dinner, given as a farewell by the Foreign Affairs section of the Hunan Province Revolutionary Committee. The sickly *huang chiu* and the devastating *mao-t'ai* (rice wine) flowed freely as usual. As we left the hotel – a cavernous place, built in Russian style during the 1950s – a group of Laotians appeared in the foyer. They are delegates of the Pathet Lao. We had exchanged notes when our paths crossed – as they often did, for there are few foreigners in China. They are going also to Canton, they tell us, but by air... Mr Liu turned upon me a meaningful glance.

At Changsha railway station a small P.L.A. man comes forward to carry my suitcase. It is fearfully heavy with books and Hsinhua news bulletins. But I let him take it up the long crowded platform. It's not often nor everywhere, I reflect, that I get served by an army man; savour the pleasure! As the Changsha hosts say good-bye they ask, as is current custom, for criticism of their work on my behalf.

For once I offer them. The Guest House was comfortable, but was it not also isolated? I never got the chance to wander around the town. To which Mr Lin (a local man) made the usual point about safety. Also, I continued, I had wanted to see a law court in action. Mr Lin says visitors are *never* taken to courts. Perhaps it's worth making these points anyhow, for they are discussed at post-mortem sessions after the visitor has gone. Good-byes were prolonged and amicable.

The train, labelled 'Peking-Canton Express', is less hot than feared, as the day further north in Hupeh province has not been hot. But it shakes and we don't sleep much. The compartment is comfortable in an old-fashioned way. Straw mats cover the berths and each pillow is wrapped in a towel. There is a table with a lace cloth; on it a fairy-tale light with a pink silk lampshade, and an optimistic potted plant. Red carpet welcomes the feet. My berth has written on it: 'Supreme Instruction: Serve the People. Number Nine – Lower.'

Each passenger has a covered porcelain tea mug. The mugs are endlessly refilled by an attendant who makes cheery remarks in a broad Hunanese accent. The radio is on, with a forceful political commentary, but Mr Chou, reading the thoughts of all, turns it off by a switch under the table. There is a Western-style toilet at the end of the corridor (as well as several of the 'crouching' kind). Hot and cold water is abundant. Several travellers in the carriage – who look like officials – use streamlined cordless electric razors for their morning shave.

Fitful sleep ended and the sights of South China's rural life absorbed us. There was a tranquil and unhurried air. By 6 a.m. peasants are in gentle circulation, washing themselves, standing around in singlets with mugs of tea. Smoke issues from kitchens, and children in gaudy clothes run around and point at the train. By contrast with the north, the houses are generally not mud but brick, and the donkey has given way to the water buffalo. The train enters the Nanling mountains and snakes through valleys and rounded hills which are almost feminine in their curves and undulations. Every cultivable niche is under rice or vegetable. Now and then – to satisfy the perverse principle of 'overall development' – there is inferior wheat, just as in the area near Peking peasants are required to raise dry-grown rice.

You can see the point of the Kwangtung saying, *'ko-shan ko-su'* ('Each mountain has its own customs'), for the land is broken constantly by mountains. And from this topography you get a clue to the independent-minded Kwangtung mentality. Communization is more difficult here than on the northern plains. Not only because of the hills – cultivation is sporadic: where can the bounds of each commune be? – but because of the hill-people and the localism of their ways.

The terrain accounts for other features of South China life. Fragmented settlement has made it easier for the aboriginal peoples to continue their separate ways of life. The Yao minority are numerous in the valleys we traverse. Unlike North China, where the coastline is generally flat, the coast of South China is rocky, hilly, and indented. Life oriented to the sea is therefore more common. Cantonese cuisine is notable for its fish specialities, and the seafaring motif is recurrent in the history of South China.

The early morning sun glitters on the water of the rice paddies. With shoots protruding here and there from the silver expanse, the fields look like flawed mirrors. We cross the Pei Chiang (North River), in which logs float obediently downstream to a paper mill. On a riverside path, an old woman makes her way with baskets on a pole. Brown as a nut, she wears the old-style black garments of oiled silk, and the brilliant sun lights her up like a shining ebony spider.

Long hours in the train loosen Mr Chou's usually measured conversation. He takes swipes at Russians as we chat about travel. A diplomat, he has moved a lot through Russia, Europe, Africa, and Asia. 'Russian air-hostesses,' he remarked as we lolled on our berths with a mug of tea, 'powder themselves instead of attending to the passengers. Every little thing you want – even a glass of water – you have to ask them for it. Otherwise they never come near you.' Mr Chou was in an interesting mood. He was not faulting the Russians this morning for being 'revisionists'. He was picking holes in their way of life.

He cast a cold eye on Soviet aviation standards. 'My wife always gets anxious when I travel on a Russian plane. Never when I travel on Chinese planes – as with you these past weeks. She knows Chinese planes are safer.' I asked him if planes ever crash in China. 'Very few.' But he would not let go of the Russians. 'Once, our Minister of Culture was killed in an air crash in Siberia. And I could tell you of many Chinese diplomatic couriers who have lost their lives (and documents) in Russian air accidents.' Chinese officials, I recalled, seldom travel to Europe via the U.S.S.R. these days. They prefer the southern route using P.I.A. (Pakistan) or Air France – both of which fly from Shanghai.

Chou Nan is convinced life is better in China than in Russia. So are other Chinese I met who know both countries. When it comes to comfort, convenience, and cooking – to things which count in daily life – Chinese officials do not envy their muttering neighbour to the north.

The train wound on through the Nanling passes. Sheer slopes faced us on the one side, lush valleys lay green and gold on the other. A breakfast was prepared for us in the dining-car. For the foreigner, fried eggs and bacon with huge chunks of bread. For Mr Chou and Mr Liu, a kind of porridge made of rice and beans, and with it pickled turnip, tomato, and slices of pork. They drink nothing, but I have one of the few cups of coffee of my weeks in

China. Our entry into Kwangtung evokes some acerbic comments on the province from Mr Chou. He comes from the province of Liaoning, and is a northerner to his fingertips. The morning advance southward seemed to give him apprehensions. As if one must gird one's loins for such nether regions.

The radio is now on again. A girl with a voice like an old violin gives a health talk. She is Cantonese but is speaking the national tongue. I remark on how clear – for a southerner – her Mandarin is. 'Better than usual,' is Chou's grudging judgement. (Mr Liu, who is Cantonese, is safely asleep on a top berth.) He goes on to wonder what weird dishes we may find ourselves eating in the days ahead. I recall in silence that in imperial China northerners would sometimes take their own food with them on trips south, rather than risk their digestion to the fertile gastronomic imagination of the Cantonese. (In fact Mr Chou ate dog with gusto a few days later in Canton; I stuck to less domestic beasts.) We touched on the history of South China, and his main comment was unflattering. 'Emperors used to send people to Kwangtung to get rid of them,' he observed as an end to the topic, 'much as Russian Tsars sent people to Siberia.'

This trace of disdain for Kwangtung on the part of northerners may not be unconnected with Peking's detached attitude toward Hong Kong (which is part of Kwangtung province). People wonder why such an intensely patriotic country allows Britain to keep Hong Kong as a residual jewel in its imperial crown. No doubt it is in part a practical question: Hong Kong pays China in useful foreign currency for food, water, and other products sold there. Yet there may also be a touch of northern *hauteur* in Peking's casual tolerance of 'barbarians' in Hong Kong.

Once we reached Canton, Mr Chou found much to praise. He had not been there for a decade. 'In those days,' he recalled, 'I would go into the shops and find no one could speak the national tongue. Very tiresome. But now it is quite different. I can talk with anyone.' But one day we had a contrary experience. It was an afternoon with the 'boat people'. These are the Canton fishermen who have long lived on boats. In recent years the government has settled almost all of them (some sixty thousand) in new housing on the banks of the Pearl River.

I went to interview them because I was interested to see how they had adjusted to life on the land. (Some throw rubbish out of the doors and windows the way they used to throw rubbish from the boat into the river.) Most of those we met were old. Brown and leathery, shrewd from a lifetime on the water, they were attractive people, blunt in comment and fertile in stories. But they spoke Cantonese only. Mr Chou was not able to hide his disapproval. As one fisherman spun the story of his life, Chou turned to me and said in a loud and dignified voice, 'His words are as meaningless to me as to you.'

The train stations are marvellous human theatres. Young and old scurry in and out of carriages with boxes, melons, water bottles, and nameless bundles on sticks. Some carry babies; some carry chickens. Peasants are amusing when they are met by an intrusion from the technological world. The train seems to them a capricious monster, not to be relied on or trusted. They frown and rush and shout instructions to each other. Safely on with their paraphernalia, they look surprised to have made it.

You see that they are not ordinary peasants as Asia knows peasants. They pull newspapers and magazines from bags and read. Mao badges spot their garments like red tail-lights. Loudspeakers bring world news into the carriage and they comment on it. Some whistle arias from familiar opera-ballets. This is not the kind of countryside life Marx recoiled from as 'rural idiocy'. These patient faces are not lost in a backwater of history.

True, machines have hardly entered their lives. But a sense of corporate national purpose is evident. These farmers can tell you what Mao is trying to get at in his Cultural Revolution, and what China stands for in the world of nations. And the hand of organization touches them. They go to meetings, sign papers, belong to groups with economic, community, or political aims. We pass two columns of marching boys. A little cup hangs on each knapsack. Instructors lead the boys in political songs as the file wends along the ridge of a silver-coloured rice paddy. In a sense these people are 'moderns'.

Like moderns, they enjoy a wide range of simple manufactured items. From the train you see the straw hats, hand carts, and rude scythes of time immemorial. But look closer. The people wear bright printed cottons and plastic sandals. The plaits of the girls are tied with gay ribbon. Many have transistor radios and most have bicycles. All have the usual simple personal toilet articles. These are peasants with a difference.

At a small station not far from Canton, two boys catch the eye. One is swimming with two water buffaloes in a pond. Peasant houses are scattered around the yellow water. Chickens scratch idly at the foot of near-by trees. It is the searing midday hour. The buffaloes splash around, their black skin shining like a wet umbrella. The boy, jumping on and off their backs, is naked except for a straw hat in the southern, conical style. Now and then he stands still, just his head and the hat showing above the muddy sheet of water, savouring the coolness.

As he tiptoed beside the buffaloes, a phrase from a writer on Chinese agriculture in the 1930s sprang to mind. The Chinese peasant, observed R. H. Tawney of the precarious position landlordism put the peasant in, is like 'a man standing permanently up to the neck in water, so that even a ripple is sufficient to drown him.' When Tawney wrote, desperate reality lay behind the image. As I watched the boy and his buffaloes, the carefree ambience seemed to signal the fantastic improvements in China since Tawney went out to make a study for the Institute of Pacific Relations. Mao's government has not brought the Chinese peasant great prosperity, but it has given him unprecedented security. No ripple can finish him now.

Another boy is on the platform of the railway station. I lean out the window, watching travellers buy tea and unleavened pastries. The train radio blares, but few listen. The business at hand is to get a drink and a snack. The small boy catches my attention because he carries a rifle which glints in the sun. He is not in uniform; what is he doing? I notice he is looking not around him but up at the trees. A mild sense of relief. He is shooting birds. Sparrows, by the look of the tiny corpses. His weapon is an air gun, and the basket strapped to his waist is for his feathered victims.

Such punctilious public service must amaze those who knew the fearful chaos and lethargy of China before Liberation. It springs from traits that can remind the visitor of a vast Boy Scout camp: a sense of belonging; a spirit of service; hearty use of simple methods where streamlined ones are not available; the presence of willing hands on all sides; an irrepressible buoyancy.

As we reach the Kwangtung province capital a typhoon is not far distant. It makes the city cool and grey, refreshing after the heat and glare of Changsha. Canton is a garden city, lush with tropical vegetation. Buildings are shabby, in faded memory of the war of slogans and quotations during the Cultural Revolution. Portraits of Mao and quotations from Mao adorn almost every building. I realize Changsha (though it is Mao's home city) has far fewer of these than Canton. In Changsha, institutions have Mao trappings on display, but the whole city is not draped and placarded the way Canton, despite recent modifications, still generally is.

Mr Yang of the provincial Revolutionary Committee's foreign affairs section is at the station to meet me. We drive together to the Tung Fang (Eastern Hotel; in 1964 it was called *Yang Ch'eng*, Goat City Hotel). I am tired from the overnight journey and unable to make much conversation. Carelessly I inquire, 'Are you Cantonese?' Mr Yang is taken aback. I look at him and realize how silly the question is. He is tall, with square, angular

features. (Cantonese are smaller and rounder.) He says
to me with wounded astonishment, 'Do I look like a
Cantonese?' He is from Shantung and proud to be so. In
Canton he is doing his duty.

By now the typhoon has swept in from the coast and
the city girds its loins for nature's tantrum. As we alight at
the Tung Fang, trees wave and veer in a crazy fashion.
Rain is whipping up and the light is eerie. Around the
hotel grounds staff members scurry under sheets of pale
green plastic. A few enterprising girls and men are already
chopping up fallen tree-parts.

From my balcony I look out over the Pearl River delta.
Silver clouds swoop down to invade the trees and taller
buildings. Dull rays cast an ochre-coloured light here and
there. The whole scene seems to sway before the torrent
of wind and rain. After the baking temperatures of
Hunan province, the cool air is seductive. And the gloom
broken by lightning and muffled sun rays lends an amusing psychedelic flavour. I had always wanted to see a
typhoon. Yet watching the winds' occasional acts of de-
vastation, I was glad this typhoon hit Canton only at a
tangent.

Canton has none of Peking's grandeur, but all of south
China's earthy, inventive fascinations. Stroll among a late
afternoon crowd in the city streets. The hot air clutches
at you as in a steam bath (the Tropic of Cancer runs just
north of Canton). For protection against the heavy rainfall, the pavements of the commercial districts have wide
stone verandas. In these semi-enclosed corridors, every
variety of ingenious Cantonese dish can be seen and
smelled. Herbs and roots of Chinese medicine can also be
sniffed. Their hard, piercing odour mingles with the
smell of glue and paste from Chinese offices, and that of
fresh rain on the luxuriant vegetation of the city's environs. Among sounds, cicadas compete with bicycle bells;
underlying both there is the singsong drawl of the Cantonese dialect (which people use – rather than *p'u-t'ung
hua* – for informal talk).

Off the main boulevards, commercial life gives way to a ceaseless round of community life. In a small alley, a girl in a floral blouse does homework at the door of her home. Sitting on a chair, she leans forward, legs apart, and writes against a second chair drawn up to face the first. Her plaits fall down over a notebook in which she laboriously traces Chinese characters. I was transfixed for a moment watching this girl write the ideographs with which I have wrestled so pathetically as a foreigner. What is to me a challenge from over a far horizon is to her a casual chore before supper. These are *her* characters, as surely as her coal-black hair and nimble limbs and silky skin are hers, and they can never be the foreigner's.

The girl's little brother dashes by with a bowl of boiled rice, grinning broadly. A youth in striped singlet turns into the alley with a chicken carcass in each hand. An old man comes by from the other direction with bits of pork and a bunch of bamboo shoots. Inside a niche in the wall, a lady works at a sewing machine. Her children surround her, reporting their day at school, pestering her with questions. I ask if I may take her picture, and she shyly says no. Here and there people squat on a stool or a stone slab; knees high, head bent down, chopsticks fussing, bent in concentration over a succulent dinner.

As in other parts of Asia, many people (especially women) hold a fan or newspaper over their faces when exposed to direct sun. An old lady stumps by, heavily bent by a stick across her back, from which are suspended two enormous bundles of small scrap iron and nuts and bolts. Clothes hang drying on strings and poles across the alley, flags of humanity hoisted above this stoic, resilient, resourceful south China community. Later, I look down upon the same scene from a tall building, and now there is something extra. On the roofs of the lower structures, a whole realm of life comes into view: neighbourhood restaurants, people asleep, gardens in boxes, little boys playing football.

These pulsating alleys are crowded and far from afflu-

ent. Yet no one is in rags; no one sits around in that state
of hopeless-looking poverty all too familiar in Asia. Clothing is simple, clean, neat; food is wholesome. No one is
ingratiating toward the visitor. No one badgers you to
buy something, much less to beg something from you.
You are a visitor and you are respected, but no special
attention is paid to you, and you do not feel uncomfortable. What struck me, above all, was the equality of the
life of these alleys, and because of this there is dignity
even when there is poverty.

Canton can boast some fine tables. One evening I took
my hosts to the Pei Yuan (Northern Garden) Restaurant,
a lively place with glossy black furniture and airy windows
looking out on ponds and bridges. I had left the choice
of dishes in the hands of a Cantonese. When the handwritten order of dishes was presented to me (as the host),
my eye lit on the characters *kou-jou* (dog flesh). There
was no doubting its arrival, for the smell was strong. All
except me – northerners included – ate it heartily. I half
closed my nostrils, and concentrated fiercely on the champagne until the next dish came steaming in. The others
did not like the champagne, which is made in north-east
China, and chose instead the *huang chiu* (yellow wine),
too sweet for many Western palates. Mr Chou was soon in
fine form, with culinary tales from his diplomatic experience. The cook at the Chinese Embassy in London, he
recalled, once went to Covent Garden to buy a hen. His
English being less developed than his kitchen skills, he
approached a market attendant with the words: 'Please,
I would like a madame cock.'

Another meal unfolded the night before I left China,
at the Friendship Restaurant. Like the Pei Yuan, it is set
in a garden bordering a large pond. The host, Mr Yang
of the Foreign Affairs Section of the Revolutionary Committee of Kwangtung, leads me to a group of ebony chairs,
inlaid with pearl, on a second floor balcony. There is talk
with journalists from the *Nanfang Jih-pao* (*Southern
Daily*) before dinner, and we look directly down on diners

in the garden. They lean noisily across large circular tables speckled with dishes and fallen pieces of food. Lit by the glow of sunset, the round tables look like an array of golden sunflowers.

In preparing a farewell banquet, they have decided to satisfy my every known whim. Having remarked the previous day that I liked shrimps, I now found shrimps on all sides, done in many cunning ways (some with honey). Since I had ordered champagne the night before – when host at the Pei Yuan – there was now a constant flow of champagne, though I knew most of the Chinese didn't like it. Here were pineapples (some fresh, some hot), bananas, and other favourite fruits. Halfway through the meal there appeared a delicate clear soup, served in an oblong hollowed-out melon! The sweetmeats I have already described (page 78).

As the relay of dishes bore us down, talk slid off Kwangtung politics to matters both smaller and larger. Mr Chou grew philosophic about parting, and ventured some summary judgements on the state of the world (in his indirect, poetic way). Mr Yang railed against hijacking. 'We oppose that kind of thing. It's not revolutionary.' I remarked – at a low temperature – that some of China's friends in the Middle East seem rather keen on it. Mr Yang shrugged his chopsticks. 'We can't be responsible for everything they do.'

The food was served by the two finest waitresses I have watched. If they are relics of the past, they are relics worth preserving. In their forties, they had a concentrated earnestness but were not fussy. I watched the faces coming out of the kitchen door: there was a professional pride that seemed lodged deep within these women. The long, slim hands would make a tiny twist or flourish as they set down a new dish, or proffered a wet towel from behind. Each diner had four glasses, and no glass was permitted to get more than one quarter empty before the relevant bottle materialized at its rim. During the endless toasts, the waitresses melted into the background and stood prim as cypresses beside an ebony pillar. How such specialized waiting skill fits in with Chinese society today I do not know. To come upon these women was like walking off a London street and finding inside a hotel two characters from the world of Charles Dickens.

Soon after reaching Canton, I went up to take the waters at the hot springs of Ts'ung Hua. Once more, like an itinerant musician, I packed my bag, and we drove by the edge of the Pearl River delta and up into tranquil hills. The typhoon has subsided, but we pass and dodge many broken tree-portions. The fields here give two crops of rice each year, as well as one crop of winter wheat. Further out from Canton, there is much jute and cassava. Trucks pass us laden with a sharp-edged mountain reed. In Canton it will be turned into a rayon-like fibre, which the Chinese are still experimenting with but so far find promising (and dirt cheap).

At the *Pin-kuan* (Guest House) we sink into simple comfort. Each visitor has his sunken bath, into which the therapeutic waters gush. The Guest House is not for tourist use, and there are no slogans on its walls. Meals are taken overlooking rustling bamboos, and the blue-yellow waters of a river rimmed by sandbanks and backed with towering hills. Waiters announce each dish as they present it. I wonder which previous guests they are using as a working model for me, since they bring beer for my breakfast!

Early in the morning, I am drawn to the window of my room by the dull silver light. Rain-sheets hurl themselves at a forty-five-degree angle across the scene. They pelt into the river like a million cruel darts. The lovely hills are only intermittently visible through billowing cloud. A cluster of bamboos near the window creak and groan as they bend from side to side. Cocks crow pathetically in the distance. Opposite, a cottage nestles on the far bank of the stream, smoke curling from its chimney to meet the rain.

I go walking and find the environs well cared for.

Every thirty yards on the driveways, there are handsome green-tiled lamp-posts, each one capped with two vast spherical lamps. Trash bins are made of the same green tiles. There are boating stations and basketball courts. Also military men, some with fixed bayonets, some with Bren guns, for an army base is near by. A splendid gateway, half-hidden by waving trees, lies high above the Guest House, and here two soldiers turn me back. In the other direction, a stone bridge spanning the river is also guarded by P.L.A. men.

Before returning to Canton, we climb skyward through the mountains to see three waterfalls, named 'Galloping', 'Silver Bed', and 'Flying'. Mr Chou regales us with literary titbits. As we pass bamboos, two lines from a Sung poet come to him: 'Without meat to eat, a man becomes lean; without the quality of bamboo, a man becomes mean.' He recalls that bamboos and pines, together with the chrysanthemum, were three species to which virtue was attached in classical Chinese literature. He gives us phrases from the poets to describe the waterfalls as we approach their rushing freshness: 'long white cloud dropped from heaven'; 'heavenly girl washing her long hair'. The rain has gone, and sun lights up the falls like phosphorous. But underfoot it is slippery. Perching for a photo, I fall off the path. Mr Liu cries with dismay. Happily, I hit a ledge not far below and am barely scratched. Liu's face is a study in anxiety as he peers down at me and begs, 'Don't move, don't move. We will think of a way to get you up.' Bright yellow butterflies hover around his head as I see it framed against the sky. Coordinating a plan with voices loud to rise above the rush of the waterfall, Mr Liu and a Canton assistant pull me up to safety. There Mr Chou stands grinning, hands on hips. A few moments before my fall, he and I had been discussing ideological questions. Now as I brush myself down he declares grandly, 'I told you your standpoint was not firm!'

11 Education for Revolution

Education is a mirror to key values and problems in China today. I looked at six universities: Peking University, then not open to many foreigners; Tsinghua University, a polytechnic praised by the Government for its high level of political consciousness; the Communications University, formerly in Shanghai but moved in 1956 to Sian to help spread development more evenly over the whole nation; Fu Tan, a fine general university in Shanghai; Hunan Normal College for teacher training in Changsha; Sun Yat Sen University, a leading southern school at Canton. I also made visits to Middle Schools in Peking, Sian, and Canton, to a Physical Education College near Peking – where the basketball players, men and women, dwarfed my six feet one – and to a lively school of performing arts at Sian.

Schools, and especially universities (which I will stick to mainly), are in the grip of drastic experiments. Maoists – here I mean those who came out on top after the Cultural Revolution – said 'revisionists' led by Liu Shao-ch'i sabotaged the 1958 reforms. These would have made education more egalitarian, and linked it more with the world outside the classroom. 'Liuists' allegedly favoured professionalism, competition, over-specialization, and individual ambition. They liked to have 'professors rule the universities'. Exams for them meant 'ambush of the students'. They exalted *san chung hsin* – 'three core points' – namely, 'Teachers, Classrooms, Textbooks'. Ultra-leftists embraced the opposite error of *san fou ting* – 'three negations' – namely, total denial of the value of teachers, textbooks, and the classroom. The Cultural

Revolution, claim the Maoists, fulfilled the hope of the 1958 reforms and set China on the path to a truly socialist education system. It had two principles: unity of theory and practice; education to 'serve the working people'. I went to see how this works.

You wonder at first if you are on a campus at all. Here at Communications University (C.U.) in Sian are people, dressed in conical hats and blue peasant jackets, threshing wheat (eighty thousand catties were produced on campus this year). In the Middle School attached to Peking Normal University, girls are making chairs. Next door are boys, helped by 'veteran workers' from a near-by factory, making semiconductors. In Canton at Sun Yat Sen University (S.Y.S.U.) I found professors tending a vegetable garden, and many classrooms turned to strange uses. One is stacked high with peanuts, the next with rice – grown by the university (the campus has seventy mou under rice). When you sit inside these schools and talk, you find a sizeable part of the management to be neither students nor teachers but People's Liberation Army men, manual workers, and Party cadres.

After two or three years without classes, many universities began again in autumn 1970 with a small, handpicked enrolment. At Peking University (P.K.U.), where there used to be 9,000 students, the new class of September 1970 numbered 2,667. At Fu Tan in Shanghai, formerly with 9,000, there were 1,196; at S.Y.S.U., 547 where there were previously 4,700; at Hunan Normal College (H.N.C.), 440, against 6,000 before the Cultural Revolution. Teachers outnumber students at present. Here are a few current figures for teachers, those for students in parentheses: Fu Tan, 1,263 (1,196); S.Y.S.U., 869 (547); Tsinghua, 3,000 (2,800)

These hothouse students are a new breed. None come direct from Middle School, but only after two to three years at farm or factory. They must be 'politically sound' as well as bright and physically fit – much stress on health. If a would-be student is a 'sturdy pine' politically, and has been strongly recommended by local units, it is not even necessary that he be a Middle School graduate. I found, however, that Peking University can and does reject applicants who have been highly recommended politically, if they are 'simply not qualified' to do academic work.

An astonishing number of the new students are members of the Party or the Communist Youth League. At S.Y.S.U., for instance, 229 of the 547 students are Chinese Communist party and another 240 are C.Y.L. members. At Fu Tan, 359 of the 1,196 belong to the Chinese Communist party and another 458 to the C.Y.L. Almost all of the new classes are offspring of 'workers, peasants, or soldiers'. At Fu Tan, whereas in 1956 only 25 per cent were in this category, the figure is now 98 per cent; at S.Y.S.U., 97 per cent.

At Shanghai's Fu Tan, I drew aside one of the new students (call him Wu), a political science student. Dressed like everyone else in voluminous blue trousers, white cotton shirt, and plastic sandals, he is a peasant's son, thirty years old – the average age of the new students at Fu Tan is twenty-four. Between Middle School and coming to the university, he worked in the Bureau of Sea Transportation, and joined the Party. In the Bureau he earned Y49 each month, and following the rule for students who worked for ten years or more after Middle School, he keeps that wage while at university. (Other students get a state bursary of Y19.5.)

Wu is a canny man who knows and believes in Marxism. But he's sober as a judge – nothing at all of the panting Red Guard about him. He knows just why he's at university, and is grateful for this chance to study politics. He will probably go back to the Bureau when his course is done. Neither from Wu nor others of the 1970 batch of students I met was there any sign of student organizations of the kind that mushroomed during the Cultural Revolution. These students are handpicked, mostly from the countryside, outnumbered by teachers and cadres, and simply have their noses to the grindstone.

Life at university has changed. Courses are shorter: two or three years at Tsinghua, where it used to be six; three years at C.U., instead of five – the reduction is similar in all six universities I looked at. What has been left out, I asked repeatedly. At H.N.C. – a teacher-training college – they have dropped the courses on 'methods of teaching'. Not a great wrench, I gathered, partly because they'd been based on the ideas of the Russian educationist, Ivan Andreevich Kairov. At S.Y.S.U., maths courses have been integrated into dynamics, physics, and electronics. The student gets his maths along with one or more of these three subjects, and the maths department has been dissolved and poured into these three departments. At P.K.U., ancient history is cut back and attention placed mainly on the nineteenth and twentieth centuries.

These cutbacks have brought problems – and temporary confusion. One distinguished scientist, whom I talked with on four occasions, discussed this matter of shortened courses around and around. Yet I still felt puzzled about how, as at his university, five years' scientific training could be put into two and a half. Our last meeting was at Peking Airport, and we touched the question again. He concluded on a note he had not struck before: 'I was not myself opposed to keeping the five-year course. Now, well now, we just have to work out what we can realistically omit.'

In the classroom, lectures are less frequent. Teachers must distribute in advance what they used to give as lectures; the class then becomes a forum. Though proportions vary a lot, often half the students' time is spent outside the classroom, on labour and 'sharing experience' with people in other walks of life. Exams have lost their terror – at least for students. Mostly, they are now open-book exams. Often there is no exam at all; the student is assessed by exercises done throughout the term. Exam questions are worked out with student participation. Not memory but analytic ability is weighed. The exam is considered a test of the teacher no less than of the student – and an educative experience for both. At the end of the course, no diploma awaits the student. Certificates may be given – practice varies widely – with written comments on the student by his teachers and some of his fellow students.

In Mao Tse-tung's home city of Changsha, I visited a place which may be considered the seedbed of these 'new' educational ideas. It is the 'Self-Cultivation University' which Mao founded in 1921 and ran for two years. He had just returned from the first conference of the C.C.P. in Shanghai. With his usual practical skill, he obtained a fine building for the university. Today you can still admire its spacious halls and charming courtyards. Within them, the young Mao mounted an experiment in radical education.

Since the Cultural Revolution, the visitor may peruse the university's records and documents, and copies of its bold and fiery journal *Hsin shih-tai* (*New Epoch*). In the Self-Cultivation University, the purpose of study was frankly stated to be the transformation of society. Theory and practice were married; students made investigations among the peasants during vacations. There were few lectures; students read by themselves, thought for themselves, then held forums. No diplomas or exams existed. Students were not required to meet a host of regulations, and they could come or not come to 'classes' as they chose. For China in 1921, it was revolutionary pedagogy (no wonder Mao found Peking University stuffy and pretentious, when he went there from Changsha in 1918). The reigning warlord, denouncing the university as a school of subversion, sent in troops to close it in 1923.

Brief as its life was, the Self-Cultivation University was an early test of the ideas which have swung to the fore in Chinese education since the Cultural Revolution. 'Education for revolution' was Mao's theme at Changsha in the 1920s; he would like it still to be the theme for China in the 1970s.

Mao likes to be thought of as first and foremost a teacher. It is not surprising, when you note the persistence of his early zeal for education, and his brilliant sense of pedagogy. In Shaoshan, Mao's birthplace, where exhibits of his life and work are displayed, I saw a document which is worth quoting at length for its flavour of Mao the teacher. Written in 1917, it is a notice for a new Workers' Night School which Mao founded, together with other students at the Hunan First Normal School (where Mao was training to be a teacher). Signed 'Friends of School Society', its text reads:

Gentlemen, please hear a couple of words from me.

Gentlemen, what is the most unrewarding attribute you have? Do you know? The old saying is right: 'Can speak but cannot write, can write a few [characters] but cannot read, can count but cannot really calculate.' To be such a man is not too different from being a piece of wood or stone. So we must seek a little knowledge, learn to read and write, and do calculations, if we are to be an effective member of society. However, you gentlemen have to work in the daytime, and there is nobody to teach you. How can you learn? Well, we have come out with the best solution. We are establishing a night school at the First Normal School. It will meet two hours each night, from Monday to Friday. You can learn letter-writing, accounting and other such practical knowledge essential for everyday use. We provide the syllabus and all the course material; it is all free. For those who wish to attend these evening classes, please apply as soon as possible at the school office. Let us consider why we do this. The simple answer is that we wish all the workers well. Some might be aware of the difficulty which will be encountered when they try to go to school at night in view of the present curfew order. Well, we can guarantee safety. Each student will have an identification card issued by the night school. And if the soldiers or the policemen should ask, all you need to do is to present this identification and say that you are going to night school. If you do get into trouble with respect to the curfew, the school will act to protect you. So there is nothing to worry about. Do not hesitate; come and apply.

Some of Mao's characteristics shine from this leaflet: his drive, his practical sense, his burning desire to use knowledge for the making of a new world.

At P.K.U. I met the English class which was reading and discussing Aesop's fable 'The Peasant and the Snake'. They received me with clapping – though few, I found, knew where Australia is. On the walls of the airy old class-room was a picture of Mao, some quotes from him in English, and a world map. The teacher, a graduate of the University of Nanking, addressed the simply clad students by their full names. 'Comrade Wu Tse-tung, would you like to answer the Australian visitor's question?'

Since the teacher spoke with a B.B.C.-British accent, so in their halting way did her enthusiastic students. This group of thirty-five had begun English only ten months before, yet could talk in simple phrases – remarkable compared with Western students after ten months of Chinese. Mostly, the students quizzed each other, in staccato English, about the fable. The courtly politeness amused me. 'Who – will – answer – my – question?' Someone rises, is acknowledged, and with infinite pains stabs a reply. The questioner then says with a coast-to-coast smile: 'Thankyou – very – much. Please – sit – down – now.'

In a mixture of Chinese and English I questioned them (my Aesop was too rusty to go far into the fable, but I could see the moral being drawn from it: never trust appearances – that's what the peasant did, and he got bitten). Had they been out of the classroom on practical work, as the new order requires? 'Well, it's not so suitable with English,' explains the pink-cheeked daughter of a navy man. 'The class learning Mongolian did – they went to Mongolia for several weeks. What we do is spend one day a week on a [near-by] commune.' Were they sons of toil? Three of the thirty-five had military fathers; one an intellectual father; the others were sons or daughters (sexes about equal) of workers or peasants. All had, of course, spent the two or three years prior to September

1970 in manual work – and they looked fit, even tough. I could not help concluding, after thirty minutes with this bright-eyed bunch, that P.K.U. had recruited new students who are both working-class and able.

Curriculum changes are big and complex. Let me draw their flavour by illustration. Here is Chou I-liang, Harvard-trained professor of history at P.K.U. After meeting him at the university, I invited him some days later to a quiet dinner *à deux* in the city. Middle-aged, of scholarly mien, Chou has close-cropped grey hair and large serious eyes. His speciality was once Buddhism – 'but we don't do that sort of thing any more.' Now he works on Asian history.

But there has been little time for research in recent years, and his main writing work now is a modern history textbook, which will take account of 'new interpretations' since the Cultural Revolution. Thus Li Hsiu-cheng and Shih Ta-k'ai, figures in the Taiping Rebellion, were previously thought admirable, but are now seen to have been 'traitors'. The team working on the textbook is a three-in-one combination of youth (Red Guards in this case), middle-aged (historians thirty-six to fifty-five), and older scholars. Until the textbook is published, many lesser colleges – who take their lead from P.K.U. – will not resume teaching modern history.

Professor Chou's own students have centred their studies this term on a near-by coal mine. One day a week for a ten-week period, they worked as labourers in the mine (Chou too). Concurrently, they studied its history. It had been an American mine in the 1890s, then Belgian, and, later again, British. Three work groups each chose a special topic to delve into at research level. One traced the story of strikes in the mine. Another did the story of child labour; once, they found, forty per cent of the workers had been children. The third wrote a biography, based on oral data, of a veteran worker and his family. Drafts of it they read out to miners involved – a fiery baptism for the budding historians. Meeting history in the

flesh this way, Chou thinks, has proved an excellent
pedagogical method.

At Fu Tan, I talked with Liu Ta-chieh, professor of
Chinese literature. He was perhaps the only man I saw
in China who looked like an old-style intellectual. The
deliberate manner; the careful, almost ponderous way he
would split straws; the style with which he gripped his
umbrella and wielded his fan. What was the main change
since the Cultural Revolution in the teaching of his
department? 'Well, my textbook has been dropped,' replied
Professor Liu, gravely yet with no emotion, referring to
his influential three-volume work *History of the Development of Chinese Literature*. It had insufficiently stressed
'class aspects' of literature. Among other changes of emphasis, *Dream of the Red Chamber* is now treated 'less as
a love affair – as if there's a kind of love beyond class,
which comes from so-called human nature.' Professor Liu
had, it seemed, taken a buffeting in the Cultural Revolution. On the other hand, his salary was unchanged at
Y348 a month – just under six times the lowest teacher's
salary at Fu Tan (Y60).

He had assigned his new students an interesting project
to blend theory with practice. He selected a 1936 work by
Hsia Yen, a leading writer of the 1930s but no longer admired. Called *Pao shen kung* ('Contract Work'), its setting was a mill in Shanghai, now Number 15 Cotton Mill.
Hsia Yen, it is said, portrayed the workers in his story as
disunited and subservient in mentality, silently accepting
capitalism. 'We told our students to study this work of
Hsia Yen, then test the accuracy of the picture it presents. They live in Shanghai. They can go to Number 15
Cotton Mill, talk to old workers there, trace matters
through. *Was* it as the author suggested?'

While Professor Liu recounted this, my Luxingshe
aide whispered that when at Middle School, he himself
had read this story, and it was then presented as a fine,
sound piece of work. But today Hsia Yen is known as an
adversary of the great Lu Hsun. Needless to say, the stu-

dents who went to the Number 15 Cotton Mill found 'grievous distortions' in *Pao shen kung*. I am not saying the 'given' nature of the conclusion means the exercise had no value for the students; since I did not talk with them, I cannot tell.

These are tiny glimpses of a vast and varied educational experiment. The blend of theory and practice looks promising. There will be fewer electrical engineers, to recall the Canton driver's remark, who cannot replace a fuse. The learning process may benefit permanently. More to the point for the government, graduates will be more immediately useful to the economy, and the social gulf that always threatens China, between peasant and professional, will be minimized.

Yet problems are not lacking. In Changsha a student reasoned: 'I come from the countryside. Yet no sooner had I come [to H.N.C.] than I had to go back for "practical experience". I don't need that again.' He felt that, as one of the new breed, he was 'born red' and could now get straight down to study. In Canton there were grumblings from workers. This endless stream of students coming to the factory to get experience ... It takes time to supervise them ... Time is just not always available. Less serious, a new student at S.Y.S.U., who had been years on a commune, told me he found classroom discipline a bore. 'I'm used to moving around all day, but now I have to sit like a stone at a desk.'

The new order is egalitarian to a striking degree. This is true of the atmosphere of the colleges; respect based on mere status has apparently gone. And what education exists is open as never before to sons and daughters of the ordinary man. This is especially so of Middle Schools where the new order is fully operational. By cutting the years of schooling to ten, and taking pupils on a basis nearer to simple geographic proximity than to merit as tested by exam, China is making Middle School education almost universal. In Kwangtung province, these figures were given: in the past six years Middle School enrolment has leaped from 500,000 to 2·6 million (population of the province is 45 million); 95 per cent of those who finish Junior Middle School now go on to Senior Middle School. Middle Schools where the children of an élite are concentrated, like the former August 1 school for sons and daughters of military officers, seem to exist no more.

It remains to be seen whether this Middle School explosion can be matched by expansion at university level. At present, the road ends for nearly everyone after Middle School. I could get no national percentages, but clearly only a trickle of graduates from (expanded) Middle Schools can go on to (shrunken) universities. Understandably, there is a shortage of Middle School teachers. This will be made worse by the reduced college enrolment of the present period; it is hard to produce teachers when you are not sure what to teach them.

And if universities expand, what will happen to the present experiments? Can they be sustained if numbers in the universities climb back to pre-Cultural Revolution levels – some five to ten times the enrolment now? Enrolment, I was told at all six universities, is soon to be stepped up. But can special coaching for those not graduates of Middle School still be given, when there are ten times as many to coach? Can the pitch of 'political soundness' be kept up – surely there cannot continue to be 80 to 90 per cent of students belonging to the Party or the Communist Youth League? What about the increased burden on factories and communes which must receive students and guide their practical work? Will not troublesome student organizations reappear? Can decisions still be made by 'discussion' – rather than by rule, or entrance exam, or a grading system – when there are ten times as many decisions to make?

I talked about the future with Professor P'u Chi-lung at S.Y.S.U., a biologist whose Ph.D. is from the University of Minnesota. P'u's own research has been re-directed by the Cultural Revolution. No more esoteric topics that tickle his fancy, or publishing the results in learned journals. Now he heads a research project dictated by the needs of Kwangtung province. How to get rid of insect pests without using pesticides – which harm crops. He is developing new species which he calls 'insects to kill insects'. (As we inspected some of these monstrosities, Chou Nan dryly observed: 'It's like the Nixon Doctrine – "Asians to fight Asians".') This way biology at S.Y.S.U. serves the peasants of Kwangtung.

We strolled back from the laboratory to Professor P'u's two-storeyed home (the rent takes Y8 each month from his salary of Y360). He spread out his hands on the living room table and wrinkled his brow. 'It's all experimental. We're trying to make universities more in touch with our country, its needs. We're trying to make it socialist – the door open to anyone, and doing work that will serve workers, peasants, and soldiers. But what the future holds is unclear. When you're on a new road you just don't know what is around the corner.'

The prelude to a meeting with a Chinese leader is always the same. There is no fixed appointment time, but word is one day given 'not to leave the hotel'. Suddenly a phone call comes to say that the man you are to see has just left the compound where the Chinese leadership works. You leave immediately for the Great Hall of the People. The idea is to have the two parties arrive at the same time.

With Chou En-lai, Premier of the People's Republic of China since its inception the call is likely to come late at night. This war-horse of revolution works until 4 a.m. or 5 a.m. then sleeps until mid-morning. Our group (I was with my countryman E. Gough Whitlam, leader of the Australian Labour party) was advised late on 5 July 1971 to stay about the Peking Hotel. There would be an 'interesting film' that evening. The Foreign Ministry official did not explain why we were advised to put on suits and ties for the occasion. Just after 9 p.m. a call came: the film was off, Chou En-lai was on.

The Great Hall of the People is really the Great Hall of the Government. Only on highly formal occasions do the masses view its murals and tread its crimson carpets. A stone oblong in semi-Chinese style, it was built in a mere ten months around the time of the Great Leap Forward. Its fawn solidity stands guard over the biggest square in the world, Tien An Men; the Imperial City is to the left, the big museums opposite. The building's area of 560,000 square feet includes an auditorium for 10,000 people, a room decorated in the style of each of China's provinces, and sparsely furnished halls such as the East Room, where we found the Premier.

He enters from one door, we from another. A red badge with the Chinese characters 'Serve the People' lights up his tunic. He is all in grey except for black socks inside leather sandals and black hair showing strongly through silver fringes. Introduced to him by Ma Yu-chen of the Foreign Ministry (the man who attended James Reston at his hospital bed), I suddenly realized that he is a slim, short man. We talked for a moment of the background to the Whitlam visit; then he asked where I learned Chinese. Told 'in America', he smiled broadly and said, 'That is a fine thing, to learn Chinese in America!'

Recalling his amazing career over half a century, I marvelled at his freshness. This man has been a member of the Politburo of the Chinese Communist party since 1927 (well before Mao); was forty-five years ago a close colleague of Chiang Kai-shek's in Canton; played leftist politics in Europe at the time of Lenin; covered the last miles of the Long March through north Shensi in 1935 on a stretcher, gravely ill. Now he reaches across an epoch of China's modern history to face Richard Nixon in the ping-pong diplomacy of the 1970s.

Though he is like David to Mr Whitlam's Goliath (the Australian is six feet four), you quickly forget his height; it is his face and hands which rivet every eye in the room for the next two hours. The expression is tough, even forbidding, yet sometimes it melts into the disarming smile which used to flutter the hearts of foreign ladies in Chungking (Mr Chou was the Communist representative in Chiang Kai-shek's capital during the Second World War). The eyes are steely, but they laugh when he wants them to. The voice, too, has double possibilities. One moment he is nearly whispering, weary and modest. The next he is soaring to contradict his visitor, and the streaky, sensual voice projects across the hall. From a side angle, a rather flat nose takes away all his fierceness. The mouth is low in the face and set forward tautly, giving a grim grandeur to the whole appearance.

The small, fine hands, moving sinuously as if direct from the shoulder, serve his rapidly varying tone and mood. Now they lie meekly on the blue-grey trousers, as he graciously compliments Mr Whitlam on the Labour party's 'struggle' to get back to power in Australia. Now they fly like an actor's in the air, as he denounces Prime Minister Sato of Japan. Now the right hand is extended, its fingers spread-eagled in professorial authority, as he instructs me to study well a recent editorial in the *People's Daily*.

Sitting back in a wicker chair, wrists flapping over the chair's arms, he seems so relaxed as to be without bones, poured into the chair, almost part of it, as persons seem part of their surroundings in old Chinese paintings. Beside this loose-limbed willow of a man, Mr Whitlam, hunched together in concentration, seems stiff as a pine.

But the conversation is a freewheeling give-and-take. The Australian style, blunt and informal, fits in well with Mr Chou's. The evening has a lively, argumentative note rare in talks between politicians of different countries, rarer still when the countries represent different civilizations. When he disagreed – as on how widespread militarism is in Japan – the Premier would interrupt in English: 'No, no, no!' Talking of Australian affairs, he twice frankly said he hoped the Labour party would win the next election in 1972. Occasionally he struck a didactic note. 'As you come to China,' he said after suggesting a lesson Australia ought to draw (about the United States) from China's experience with Russia, 'we ask you to take this as a matter for your reference.' Both sides enjoyed themselves making barbs against John Foster Dulles's policies. The ambience was, in brief, keen and frank.

Mr Chou's aides from the Foreign Ministry and the State Council office had prepared him well. He knew, from reports of what his visitors had said to the Chinese Foreign Minister, that on Taiwan and China's United Nations seat no great problem existed between Peking and the Labour party. Mr Whitlam said a Labour government would switch Australia's diplomatic ties from Taipei to Peking, and vote for Peking's installation in the China seat at the U.N. (Mr McMahon's régime supported Washington's unsuccessful 'two Chinas' proposal in October 1971.) So the Premier hardly touched these bilateral issues, but instead pitched a complex argument about the overall problems of Asia. (The efficient briefing continued throughout the week. At the evening's end, Mr Whitlam happened to recall that his birthday was near. Five days later in Shanghai, the Australian found his birthday observed with a festive dinner and a large cake – tactfully adorned with a single candle.)

Mr Chou painted a picture of China threatened by three adversaries: the United States, Russia, and Japan. In one way or another, the Chinese press has given this picture ever since November 1969, when Japan – following the communiqué signed by Nixon and Sato – seemed to step up to the status of major enemy in Peking's eyes. Interesting in the Premier's remarks was the pattern of relationships he sketched between the three adversaries.

After preliminary talk, Mr Chou reached for his mug of tea, sipped, swilled with deliberation, then asked a question which turned the conversation where he wanted it to go. He was going to be very direct, he warned. What was meant by saying, as the Australians had said the previous day, that the A.N.Z.U.S. treaty (which binds the United States, Australia, and New Zealand in mutual defence) was designed to meet any restoration of Japanese militarism? 'That is a special approach to us, so I would like to ask you to inform us what articles or what points of that treaty are directed toward preventing the restoration of Japanese militarism?' Mr Chou was fingering the apex of Peking's triangular anxiety.

The Australian background was explained. After the Second World War, Australia was much less anxious to sign a peace treaty with Japan than was the United States (and to this day Australians are slower to forget Japanese aggression than are Americans). The United States signed A.N.Z.U.S. (in 1951) in large measure to reassure an Australia (and New Zealand) still fearful of Japan. This perspective on A.N.Z.U.S. 'down under' was shared by all shades of political opinion. The treaty was a purely defensive arrangement, concerned not with Communist revolutions in Asia, but with Japan – the only country that has ever attacked Australia.

The Chinese leaders leaned forward attentively. The Ministers for Foreign Affairs (Chi P'eng-fei) and Foreign Trade (Pai Hsiang-kuo) were present with senior aides, but the Premier did all the talking. 'You know, we too have a defensive treaty, concluded one year before the treaty you have.' He recalled with a grim, ironic smile: 'That treaty was called the Sino–Soviet Treaty of Friendship, Alliance, and Mutual Aid. And its first article was that the aim of the treaty is to prevent the resurgence of Japanese militarism!'

But what has happened, the Premier asked rhetorically, his eyes and hands now stirring to life. His answer, in a word, was that both Australia's ally (the United States) and China's ally (Russia) have gone back on their pledge to forestall any new danger from Japan. He alleged that the Pentagon 'is considering whether to give Japan tactical nuclear weapons or even something more powerful.' Does not the fourth Japanese defence plan total $16 billion, one third more than the amount spent on the three previous plans put together? The Nixon Doctrine, he noted, turns Japan into 'a vanguard in the Far East'. With a shrewd addition to the usual slogan ('using Asians to fight Asians'), designed to make his visitors feel their potential importance, he assailed the doctrine's motives. 'It is in the spirit of using ... "Austro-Asians to fight Austro-Asians."'

Then Mr Chou weighed the actions of the Soviet Union. He never referred to it by name but by sarcastic indirection. 'And what about our so-called ally? What about them? They have very warm relations with the Sato government.' Unveiling China's vision of the world, the Premier wove in two further themes. The Russians, he observed, are also 'engaged in warm discussions with the Nixon government on so-called nuclear disarmament'. Now his point came home: 'Meanwhile we, their *ally*, are being threatened by *both* [Japan, the United States] *together!*' He finished with an application to Australia's situation. 'So we feel our "ally" is not so very reliable. Is your "ally" so very reliable?'

The Premier had a formidable case. He had put it with passion and embroidered it with detail apt for Australian listeners. It was, Whitlam conceded, a 'powerful indictment', and the Australian took a few moments to marshal himself and probe its questionable parts:

the first theme had been Japanese militarism;

the second, the failure of Washington and Moscow to resist it;

the third, the charge that the United States and Russia are in collusion with each other;

the fourth, a deep scepticism that any country can really be the ally of any other, an assertion that each country is utterly alone in the world, with nothing but its own resources and its 'independence' to gird it.

Throughout forty days in China, these four themes met me at high levels and low. Later there is more to say of each. But stay now with Mr Chou, for he had a fifth theme in his analysis of the triangle of menace facing China. It was introduced by another of the curious historical analogies he is fond of deploying.

During the talk Mr Chou showed a kind of fascination with John Foster Dulles. I remembered with a certain shame what had reportedly happened between these two men at the Geneva Conference in 1954. After lunch one day Dulles walked into the chamber and found only one man there – Chou En-lai. An embarrassing turn of events! Chou held out his hand. Dulles declined it (one account says he murmured 'I cannot'), gripped his hands behind his back, and strode out. But this evening Mr Chou displayed no bitterness, just amusement, at Dulles; and a

hearty contempt for his policies. Recalling the circle of
defence pacts, multilateral and bilateral, which Dulles
made with nations on China's south-eastern borders – and
showing accurate knowledge of Dulles's role as an adviser
to the Truman Administration before he became Secretary of State – the Premier mused that it seemed to be an
imperative of the 'soul' of Dulles to throw a military
harness around China. He spoke, I felt, as a man gazing
down the corridor of history rather than as one faced with
burglars at the door.

Suddenly it became clear that this historical excursion
was for the purpose of analogy. He switched to the present. 'Now Dulles has a successor,' said Mr Chou with a
laugh that was not a laugh of amusement, 'in our northern neighbour.' The Premier was launched in earnest
on his fifth theme. *Today's military encirclement of
China is by Russia.*

This emphasis – that the Dulleses of the 1970s sit in
Moscow – was confirmed when discussion turned to present trends within the United States. Mr Whitlam said
that the 'soul of Dulles does not go marching on' in
America. American public opinion, he judged, would
not again permit its government to practice the interven-
tionism in Asia that resulted from the 'destructive zeal' of
Dulles. Mr Chou responded: 'I have similar sentiments
to you on such a positive appraisal of the American
people.' By implication he agreed that Dullesism was
now eclipsed in the United States.

Later he spoke admiringly of the strength of anti-war
feeling from coast to coast in the United States ('Even
military men on active service and veterans have gone
to Washington to demonstrate'). He frankly revealed the
source of his confidence about the future course of U.S.
policy: 'The American people will *force* the American
government to change its policies.' Casting around the
room, Mr Chou asked if his visitors had 'in the past two
years or so' been in the United States. They had. He then
summed up with heavy stress: 'So you realize from your

own experience that in these past years the American people have been in the process of change.'

Of course, the Chinese Premier disapproves of particular current U.S. actions in Asia; his words on Indo-China made that quite plain. But when he mapped *trends*, the United States did not seem to loom largest among his concerns. And when he analysed the dynamics within the triangle of threat, the United States was evidently not the ultimate focus of opposition. He lashed Washington less for its own activities than for its support of Japanese activities and for its collusion with Russian activities.

Caution would be wise in construing what Mr Chou said. Maybe the three threats to China are so diverse in character that comparing their magnitude is invalid. The Japanese threat is 'rising'. The Russian threat is 'immediate' in a crude military sense. The U.S. threat may yet be the 'biggest' if the three were to be measured objectively against each other at the present moment. A conversation cannot give systematic finality to this cauldron of slippery variables. Nevertheless, it was all very different from what Peking was saying in 1964 or even two years ago. Here was a picture of the world that featured power more than ideology, fluid forces more than rigid blocs, emerging problems more than well-worn problems.

Recall that the Premier was talking to Australians, and with an Australian political leader whose views on Taiwan were not opposed to his own. So the two chief bones of bilateral contention between Peking and Washington – the U.N. seat, the U.S. military presence in Taiwan – did not even come into the conversation. Maybe Mr Chou calculated that of the three threats to Chinese security, Japan was the one to stress to these visitors. The Russians are far from Australia. The American tie is intimate, and no Australian leader is about to break it. Japan, however, is both important to Australia *and* a country about which Australians have ambivalent feelings. Yet it was remarkable that Mr Chou did not raise – nor did his Foreign Minister the previous day – queries about the substantial and sensitive American bases (some related to nuclear weaponry) that dot Australia. Mr Whitlam told me he had expected – as I had – that the Chinese would harp upon these bases.

It was easy to see that Japan was in the forefront of the Premier's mind. Whichever country came up, he linked it somehow with Japan. He quoted the Japan Socialist party to buttress his point of view. Broaching the subject of nuclear weapons, he seemed more worried by potential Japanese weapons than by existing massive American and Russian stockpiles. Discussing the Australian Labour party's international connections, he wondered in particular if it was close to the Japanese socialists. Should not Mr Whitlam, when he left China for Japan – Mr Chou had somehow unearthed this unpublicized fact of Mr Whitlam's itinerary – make a point of having serious talks with the Japanese socialist leaders as well as with Mr Sato? The Komeito (Clean Government) party especially kept popping up. Mr Chou had met its leaders the previous week (I had travelled into China in their compartment and watched them photograph each other, the train, and the countryside all the way from Hong Kong to Canton). Was it not 'quite something for a Japanese, Buddhist, pacifist party' to make the shift it has this year (to a rather pro-Peking position)? Musing on the Labour party's prospects of winning power in Australia the following year, Mr Chou again brought in the Komeito party, and made a comparison with it. But seeing its inaptness, he diplomatically qualified himself: 'Of course it's different; your party is very near to power.' A few days later, Mr Whitlam was surprised that the Chinese put on his programme a Japanese film. Entitled *Our Navy*, it dealt with the Second World War and its background. The film was not out of the ordinary. But it seemed remarkable that the Chinese chose to show a foreign (military-political) film to a delegation visiting China; and no accident that it was Japanese.

13   Why Did Peking Receive Nixon?

Let us leave Chou En-lai there, broaden the canvas a little, and consider more of his remarks as they come into the story. As to diplomacy, I found Peking in a springtime mood of growth and hope. Some Western ambassadors, glazed by long years of boredom in Peking, flexed their muscles like invalids just out of bed. New ambassadors were arriving every few weeks, as the list of countries newly recognizing the People's Republic of China lengthened: Canada, Equatorial Guinea, Belgium, Italy, Nigeria, Chile, Kuwait, Ethiopia, Iran, Cameroon, Austria, Sierra Leone, Togo, Turkey, Rwanda, Iceland. The Chinese Foreign Ministry, severely short of personnel since the time of the Cultural Revolution, resembled a market-place bursting with products but short of salesmen.

A bevy of ambassadors accredited to Peking had just returned from a 'diplomatic tour' of South China. Nothing like this had occurred for years – for some it was their first sight of a Chinese city other than Peking – and they were accompanied in cordial fashion on the trip by a Vice-Foreign Minister. Contacts between foreign diplomats and Chinese officials have this year increased manyfold. The French Ambassador remarked over dinner that his last guest had been Ch'iao Kuan-hua, Vice-Foreign Minister and perhaps the leading craftsman of China's policy toward the West. (Ch'iao arrived in New York in November 1971, to head China's U.N. delegation.) The Indian and British chargés, so long in the doghouse, still glowed from getting a warm smile and pleasant words from Chairman Mao at the last May 1 festivity. It was all like rain after a long drought.

But the most poignant element was the contrasting stance of the Russians and the Americans. The whole situation had put the men from Moscow in a foul mood. In Peking, where men will measure time less in weeks than in decades, foreigners were reminded of China's phase of diplomatic openness in the early 1960s – but now Russia was the odd man out in China's diplomatic thaw, instead of America.

The pinnacle of the summer's excitement – it was salt in Russia's wounds – was the Sino-American meeting in Peking in the second week of July and the announcement that Nixon himself had arranged to visit the Middle Kingdom. During my first week in China, I spent a morning at the Peking Arts and Crafts Factory, where delicate work is done in jade and ivory carving, lacquer, and the incredible *nei-hua* (painting a picture on a tiny bottle from the *inside*). Here were superb things – one piece just done was going on the market at 100,000 yuan (£17,000) – and several craftsmen, exponents of *nei-hua* and designers of gaudy birds, were ripe with fifty years' experience. But the factory's star project, now in the design stage, was an intricate ivory-carved memorial – bats, balls, Glenn Cowan's long hair and all – of the visit to China by the American ping-pong players! No wonder the Russians gnash their teeth.

In the Chinese capital, during June, there were occasions to glimpse the unfolding of an apparently new American policy. It is a story of caution, uncertainty, yet basic consistency from the Chinese side. On Saturday morning, 19 June, two Chinese diplomats received me in a faded lounge of the International Club. Beer and cakes were served – ambitious fare for nine-thirty on a Peking summer morning. I expected a *tour d'horizon* of Chinese foreign policy, and some exchange on Chinese/Australian relations.

But these two officials had other fish to fry. America was their interest, and I was hard put to get questions in on other matters. We discussed the various positions on

China policy within the U.S. Administration and among Democratic senators and academics. We considered how McGovern differed from Kennedy on 'one China' and 'two Chinas'. Why the Pentagon seemed tougher over Taiwan than certain elements in the White House. What the nuances of Harvard Professor John Fairbank's 'culturalistic' approach to the Taiwan issue were, in contrast to his colleague Professor Jerome Cohen's 'legalistic' approach. The centre of gravity of their interest was entirely concrete and practical. Impossible to miss the difference from talking on equivalent topics to Americans. In America the thrust of the questioning of a foreigner is often 'What do you think of us?' But these Chinese officials, caring little what the foreigner thought of China, were concerned instead with the question 'How can China get what it wants?'

The second issue was the 1972 election. It was a thing of wonder to hear these officials of the most secretive foreign-policy establishment on earth discuss the foreign-policy angles of an American election. The cast of mind was like a blend of Jeane Dixon and the most ambitious kind of social science. They expected a statement, free of any ifs or buts, of who was going to win. It dawned on me that Peking might prefer to deal with a monolithic, dictatorial Washington rather than with the cacophonic pluralism of voices which democratic America is.

Like terriers to a favourite bone, they seemed to come back always to one issue. It boiled down to this. Which was the better prospect: the reasonable China policy of certain Democratic senators – with the uncertain chance of its becoming U.S. policy; or the less reasonable but evolving China policy of Nixon – with the certainty that here was a real live government you could do business with? I later learned that this was perhaps the crucial question on American policy facing Peking in the late spring and early summer.

The third issue was Henry Kissinger. How much power does he have over U.S. policy? Is it true that he is more

'open-minded' toward China than key officials in the
Pentagon and the State Department who also advise Mr
Nixon? Kissinger's alleged hostility to the Soviet Union
strikes the Chinese as one of his most positive attributes. I
remarked that Kissinger finds Moscow's methods baffling:
he sees decisions suddenly reversed, as if there were a
'government A' and a 'government B' tugging away in
different directions. One of the Chinese said that that was
exactly Peking's impression of Moscow. It reminded him
of a saying dating from the fluid Warring States period
(fourth century B.C.): *'ch'ao Ch'in mu Ch'u'* ('In the
morning for Ch'in, in the evening for Ch'u'). 'The Russians are just like that,' he said, 'you never know where
you stand with them.'

Struck by the interest in Kissinger's mind and writings,
I did not yet know how immediate these matters were for
Peking officials. But two features of the conversation at
the International Club stuck in my mind: the apparent
pragmatism of the analysis of American trends, and the
isolation of two policies – Taiwan and the U.N. seat – to
a degree that they seemed erected into absolute goals in
themselves, not to be qualified by other goals.

Many people asked themselves, during these days in
Peking, why the Chinese Ambassador to Canada, Huang
Hua, still had not left for Ottawa. He had been named
to the post months before, and his counterpart in Peking,
Ralph Collins, was already installed. Late in June, I met
a friend and colleague of Huang Hua, and asked him
why Huang had not left for Canada. This Chinese diplomat said to me: 'In April I talked to Huang Hua and
said, "When are you leaving for Canada?" He replied,
"Any day now." Two weeks ago I saw him again and
asked the same question, and he replied, "Any day now."'
In fact, Huang Hua was being held back in Peking to prepare for the visit by Kissinger in early July.

Over the next few days I went to talk with more
Chinese officials and with five European ambassadors (or

chargés, in the case of countries which do not have fully-fledged embassies in Peking) about Peking's American policy. Three points of note emerged concerning the genesis of the Sino-American flirtation.

A basis was laid in 1969, when Nixon saw de Gaulle and de Gaulle reported the talk to the Chinese, for an American move toward China which made it a little less difficult, two years later, for Peking to bring itself to believe that the U.S. President meant business. It is no secret that Nixon admired de Gaulle (this at least he has in common with Mao). He seemed moved to talk to the French President about some of his long-term goals. The man whom de Gaulle chose to relay Nixon's views to Peking told me of them, and of how they were received by the Chinese. Nixon declared to de Gaulle – in his third month in office – that he was going to withdraw from Vietnam come what may, and that he was going, step by step, to normalize relations with China. Peking was impressed with the first aim, and as events unrolled and U.S. troops came back from Saigon, began to realize that Nixon had meant what he told de Gaulle.

On the second aim – normalizing relations with China – Peking was more cautious. Could this travelling sales-man in the lurid merchandise of anti-Communism really bury the past on China policy? But at least an intriguing seed had been planted in the back of Peking's mind. Subsequent events – including Nixon's zigzag steps along the path of Vietnam withdrawal – suggested to the Chinese that the gap between words and deeds might be less in Nixon's case than it had been with Johnson. If he was doing what he said he would on Vietnam, perhaps he would on China also? This background – as European go-betweens testify – steadied Peking's hand during the Sino-American flirtation that swelled in the spring of 1971.

The second point is a double one about Laos. The 'in-cursion' into southern Laos in February deeply alarmed China. One of the highest officials in the State Department cynically styled the attack a 'widening down' of the war.

Peking was more struck by the 'widening' aspect than the 'down' aspect. I had known in January – through friends of China's whom Peking consulted on the matter – that China was concerned at the possible use of tactical nuclear weapons in conjunction with the build-up on the southern Laos border (and the evacuation of South Vietnam's northern provinces). When the 'incursion' began, Peking was anxious lest the government of Souvanna Phouma cave in under the pressure and fall to a rightist coup. Concerned also about northern Laos – Hanoi's chief concern, of course, was the Ho Chi Minh Trail in *southern* Laos – China had substantial forces put on alert in its bordering province of Yunnan.

But did Washington not assure Peking that the aims in Laos were 'limited'? A Northern European ambassador discussed this with Ch'iao Kuan-hua, Vice-Foreign Minister of China. 'We can never be sure,' observed Dr Ch'iao. He recalled the self-unleashing of General MacArthur on the Chinese–Korean border while Truman protested the 'limited' nature of the United States' Korean operation. 'We were fairly confident of Nixon's limited intentions in Laos, but not sure some General wouldn't take it into his head to provoke China, or cover failure with a drastic escalation.' This Chinese view of events, said Dr Ch'iao, can be discerned between the lines of the speech that Chou En-lai made during his March visit to Hanoi.

When the U.S.-backed incursion by Saigon into Laos failed, bringing none of the military and political complications that Peking earlier thought possible, Peking was buoyed. If anything, Chinese optimism about Indo-China was now higher than it had been before the Laos operation began. Saigon had (as a Chinese saying goes) 'picked up a stone to throw against the people's forces, only to drop it on its own feet'. It had merely given fresh evidence of its military and political weakness. Peking's conviction that effective U.S. force in Asia is in a large and long decline also deepened. For Washington did nothing drastic to salvage the Laos incursion. In fact, the flirtation with the United States would not have unfolded if the U.S.-Saigon thrust into Laos had gone well (or greatly widened the war). Yet its lack of success provided all the more reason – given the logic which underlies Peking's whole America policy – to put aside doubts and press on with the flirtation.

The third point concerned tactics, and hinged on Peking's reading of the American domestic political scene. In the early spring, Peking had reached the point of being ready to permit one or more leading Democratic senators to visit China. It was part of the ping-pong package: there would be opposition politicians, as well as sportsmen, journalists, and scholars. But before the decision could be implemented, the mutual coaxing between the Nixon government and Peking accelerated. Hesitations about the Democratic senators occurred. The option was the one that we had discussed at the International Club: to coax Nixon further, or to cultivate the Democratic opposition. The Chinese were not sure they could do both. For the time being, at least, they (evidently) resolved to keep the line open with Nixon and see where it would lead. Exchanges continued between Washington and Peking. Neither McGovern nor Kennedy came to China in June, though at one stage it had seemed certain that one of them would.

To understand China's actions, it should be pointed out that in important respects the Republicans are less unacceptable to Peking than the Democrats. This is because of their greater hostility to the Soviet Union. Democrats, one Chinese official pointed out, 'have been very keen on collusion with Moscow'. He cited Averell Harriman, and the East Coast foreign policy establishment generally, to support his point. During the meeting with Chou En-lai, I noticed that in his indictment of Dulles, he stressed that Dulles worked out and began implementing his evil schemes while advising Truman, *before* he became Secretary of State in the Republican Administration. One may go further back – to Dean Acheson, whom the Chinese did not like – and the point is reinforced: Peking has no love for Democrats. Especially today, because of the Democrats' alleged greater warmth toward the Soviet Union.

On 2 July, I spent four hours with an eloquent spokesman of the Chinese government in a suite at the Peking Hotel. Mr Y I called him in Chapter 6, in quoting his criticisms of Chinese propaganda; he, too, came to New York in November as a member of China's U.N. delegation. Though we planned to talk mainly of social developments and political thought, America was also much on Mr Y's mind.

One small measure of his interest in the U.S. press – it turned upon an interesting detail – was that in speaking of what Chou En-lai said to the American ping-pong team, he unwittingly quoted not from the Chinese text but from the U.S. press. The Premier had said, recalled Mr Y, that the event meant 'a new page' in friendly exchange between Chinese and American people. I pointed out that the Chinese text said merely that the event 'opened the door' to friendly exchange. Mr Y explained he had got 'new page' from the *New York Times*. His aide, who had been present at the meeting of the Premier with the U.S. ping-pong players, broke in to confirm that 'new page' had indeed *not been* Chou En-lai's original phrase. Mr Y (whose English is faultless) laughed when it was suggested that in recent months he seemed to be an even more assiduous reader of the American than of the Chinese papers.

This strategist and 'ideas man' has for many years dealt with international matters. He was like a ship in full sail when explaining the new phase in China's foreign outlook. It clearly pleased him. He had argued for it; he knew its rationale. He made several points which are crucial to understanding why Peking is going down the path of détente with the U.S.A.

'The opening up is going to go far,' he told me; 'it's a big thing.' He added sharply: 'And it's about time we did it, too.' But why has it now become possible? We spoke of the Taiwan problem, on which he gave the long-standing Chinese position and said that 'everything' in Sino-American relations depends upon the removal of this bone in the national throat of China. But why, I asked, had China started people-to-people diplomacy with the United States at a time when Washington's policy on Taiwan was just as it had always been? Nothing on the Taiwan question, it seemed, could account for the genesis of the ping-pong diplomacy. Mr Y had quite a different reason to give. 'Yes, you are right. The U.S. government made no change on Taiwan. We did it because of the new attitudes among the American people.'

This is not to say Peking was unimpressed by the gestures – in trade and other matters – which Nixon made toward China. Early in the summer of 1971, Chou En-lai inquired of a European ambassador in Peking: 'What was the impact of the ping-pong trip, within the United States?' Said the ambassador: 'It has helped the Democratic opposition to Nixon, yet it has also helped Nixon.' The Chinese Premier came back: 'I don't mind that. I am happy that China should take some steps in response to Nixon's.'

But if certain of Peking's specific gestures are a response to certain of Nixon's gestures, the reason for China's new readiness to deal with America lies deeper. Mr Y spelled it out in various ways. Essentially it amounted to this: China thinks *America no longer has the capacity to work its will in Asia*. Now Mr Y warmed up to broach broad themes of history and theory. The gist lay in a distinction between military power and political goals. Washington has the first, but is muddled about the second. Hardly new to those who have lived through the 'Vietnam years' in America.

But to hear it in Peking is to hear it in quite a fresh

tone. Mr Y is not bent on a theoretical discussion of options. This is not a 'dissenting' quibble from within the camp. The hour is long past when Washington missed its chance to grasp the fact that military power from outside Asia is unlikely to attain political goals within Asia. Now I was listening to a Chinese official coolly describe the consequences in Asia of Lyndon Johnson's failure to grasp the point. An abstract truth at home had become concrete truth here in Peking. At home one debates the point dialectically – still hoping that wisdom may prevail. From a Chinese in 1971, the point somehow strikes home with a more final logic, if only because it comes from outside you, and with the weight behind it of Asia's most influential government.

There was therefore a curious authority to Mr Y's analysis. A point I had made in the wilderness of theory and dissent since 1965 now stared me in the face as a cold, hard fact of international politics. The Far East is now the way it is because Asians like Mr Y saw, and Johnson did not, the political limits of alien military force. I realized, as Mr Y discoursed, to what effect the Chinese, with their long memories and their patience, had waited and watched through the 'Vietnam years' while America bloodied its head against a wall largely of its own making.

'The United States put a million men around China.' Mr Y did not say 'in Vietnam', 'off Japan', 'in Thailand', and so on, but 'around China'. And to what avail? 'It simply has not worked.' There was not a trace of moralism; he was like history's physician. 'You can't do that for long. First, you have to *pay* for them while they are out there, far from home. You have to feed them, supply them, and this takes taxes which the American people will not sustain.'

Some of his remarks came in Marxist dress, and the reasons he gave for the subsidence of U.S. power in Asia could be questioned. But he summed up well the nature of America's failure to prevail in Vietnam *and* the reasons why China is now ready to sit down and talk with the United States.

He came to a second problem that Washington has faced. 'You have the troops there; you start a war, fought with no clear aims; but how do you end it? It is so easy to start these kinds of wars, but not so easy to wind them up.' Finally he spoke of the various forms of power. 'The third problem was that spreading all those troops around China did not even increase the bargaining power of the United States.'

Do nuclear weapons increase a country's bargaining power? 'Only if the other country fears them,' he replied. 'If the other country does not fear them, then nuclear weapons are not a deterrent, much less a decisive force in international struggles.' Mr Y was making an assumption that seemed basic to his view of the United States – that the United States almost certainly would not *use* nuclear weapons. Here was one more sign of its flagging will. He is less confident that the Russians lack the will to use nuclear weapons.

But Mr Y did not merely mean that nuclear weapons are without power because they are unlikely to be used. He meant that they are literally without any power to change the world! For a country cannot be 'captured' – occupied and ruled – by the use of nuclear weapons; only physically laid waste. And the importance of nuclear weapons short of their actual use – their deterrent effect – exists only if the potential victim fears them.

Mr Y gave a picture of a China less pressured than in the past. More buoyant about its options. Possessing more room to manoeuvre. I sensed a link between enhanced international confidence and a readiness to be self-critical. Mr Y spoke of the overselling of national historical monuments. 'We have had so much escalating rhetoric here,' he confessed. 'Once I even went to two tombs in different places, each of which claimed to contain the same Han dynasty emperor!' The next moment he rather confidently dissects the troubles within the United States. It seemed that America's troubles were a kind of encouragement to this Chinese official (who does not hide from himself China's own troubles).

And America's troubles, Mr Y felt, meant that America would now give China less trouble. Having lived for so long in a world they never made, encircled by those one million Americans under arms, the Chinese are starting to think that they may take a share in shaping at least Asia's future patterns. Like the two diplomats at the International Club, Mr Y put greatest policy emphasis on Taiwan and the U.N. seat. He believed – and events so far have not shown him wrong – that there was a better chance now than in the past of China's getting an acceptable arrangement with the United States on these two long-standing goals.

He was candidly aware that some of America's 'troubles' arise from its democratic institutions. Mr Y is familiar with these institutions, and knows that 'the people' means something totally different in U.S. foreign policy than 'the people' means in Chinese foreign policy. In fact, it is not just or mainly that U.S. *power* to trouble China has declined. U.S. *will* to trouble China with energetic military activity far from America's own shores has sagged, because many Americans have lost confidence in the *morality* as well as the efficacy of that activity. Peking, of course, is not 'troubled' by the complication of an influential public opinion on foreign policy.

Mr Y was not blind to the sweetness, from China's point of view, of the displeasure caused in Moscow by the Sino–American flirtation. With his eagle-eyed watch on the U.S. scene, he had noticed things I had written. I recalled to him that in 1968 I had published (in *Motive* magazine) the prediction:

There will come eventually one small sign that Washington has accepted the Chinese present as a chapter in world history: the readiness of officials . . . to refer to 'Communist China' by its name, the 'People's Republic of China', the way they brought themselves to refer to 'Communist Russia' by its name, the 'Soviet Union'.

Mr Y had heard about the first occasion on which Mr Nixon had publicly used the phrase 'People's Republic of China' – when the Romanian President visited Washington. He had also heard that the Soviet Ambassador in Washington, Anatoly Dobrynin, phoned Henry Kissinger in agitation the same evening to find out the meaning of this outrageous verbal accuracy. The incident made him chuckle. Pleasant that China, which Mr Y was old enough to remember as the hopelessly 'sick man of Asia', could without lifting a finger cause a ruffle between the 'super-powers'. It seemed to me, however, that he saw the frustration of Moscow as a by-product of the Chinese-American détente, not as a major Chinese goal in the pursuit of that détente.

That week in Peking, Kissinger's name cropped up with a frequency that puzzled me at the time. On the morning that Mr Y mused on Kissinger's readiness to disregard Russian sensibilities if the science of power required it, Hsinhua, the Chinese news agency, reported Kissinger's arrival in Saigon. I did not know – no foreigner in Peking did, and precious few Chinese, since the Politburo kept the Chinese Foreign Ministry even more in the dark about the trip than Mr Nixon kept the American State Department – that a later stop on the same journey would be Peking. But three days later, on 6 July, the professor was again brought into the conversation, by Kuo Mo-jo, Vice-President of the Congress. During an interview about intellectual life in China, he interpolated musings about Kissinger's trip to Asia. Not again, I thought with a sinking feeling, for I wanted to draw the Chinese leader out more on cultural matters. But Mr Kuo would make statements about Kissinger that sat in the air inviting response. 'We don't know enough about the thinking of this man ...'

There were others in Peking who would have liked to know more about the 'thinking of this man'. On 10 July, Kissinger's main day of talks with Chinese leaders, I found myself at the North Vietnamese Embassy. The Hanoi official didn't know of Kissinger's presence – he would not have talked to me at length that day if he had – but he smelled a rat in Sino-American relations. His informality – putting a hand on my knee, drinking despite the morning hour – did not hide but rather underlined his anxiety at some of the developments that had unfolded in the spring and summer of 1971.

Of course, Hanoi was pleased that Peking stressed so much, and so unusually, the seven-point peace proposal that Madame Binh of the Viet Cong made in Paris on 1 July. But Nixon had launched 'sinister schemes', said the Vietnamese diplomat. He grew more explicit. 'We know that the ending of the U.S. trade embargo against China was designed to produce a response from China which might pose problems for our struggle.' Hanoi's nightmare, I gathered from other sources, was that a 'linking' might somehow be effected between Indo-China issues and the Taiwan issue. Knowing that some people in Washington have toyed with this idea, I now asked directly if North Vietnam had any fear that Peking might under some circumstances agree to such a linking. The answer was non-existent but eloquent. The man from Hanoi alternately smiled and furrowed his brow. He leaned forward and put his hand on my knee. 'What have the Chinese comrades indicated to you about this?'

Six days later I arrived by train from Nanking at the lakeside resort of Wusih. (The town's name means 'no tin'. In the Han dynasty, two thousand years ago, the district exhausted its tin mines.) Driving to a hotel in the midday heat, I heard the radio announcement of Kissinger's visit and Nixon's impending visit to China. Unadorned by commentary, it was identical with the seven-line story in the next day's *People's Daily*. There was no follow-up coverage, much less an orgy of speculation, as in the American press. The Chinese government closed up like a clam on informal talk with visitors about foreign affairs. Rich conversations of previous weeks were not repeated after 16 July. Nor was I able, despite earnest requests, to go back immediately to Peking.

My hosts in Wusih, like workers in the city's factories, showed interest in the announcement, but were reticent about commenting on it. The Foreign Ministry official travelling with me, however, did not hide his satisfaction. The U.S. President was coming *to* China; this he stressed. Nixon said he wanted to come; Peking graciously agreed; the meetings would take place on Chinese soil.

Into policy matters the official did not venture. This was not merely because the phone call he had just received from Peking briefed him only in outline. He seemed totally confident that China's policies (touching Sino-American relations) had not changed and would not need to change. He spoke as if China were a fixed point in a fluid world. The United States was rethinking matters. That is interesting, and can only be for the better.

China is always ready to talk should America drop its hostility toward China.

Such blandness lay also, it seems to me, behind the lack of public attention in China to the turn of events. Of course, foreign policy options are not debated out loud in China as in the United States. Still, you cannot overlook the almost offhand confidence of Peking's approach to the flirtation with Washington. The Chinese want certain things from the United States. But they have waited a long time for them. They can wait longer. Especially since they see American opinion stirring unilaterally in rejection of rigid and expansionist policies of the past.

It is Nixon who is committing himself most. It is he who is under pressure to deliver the goods. So the Chinese attitude is, in a certain measure, to sit back and see what Nixon brings to Peking. Peking has formulated an eight-point agenda of items to discuss with the U.S. President. On these items the Chinese position has not noticeably softened. But the Chinese think that Nixon will have to soften *his* positions on some items, if his requested trip to Peking and subsequent diplomatic dealings are to prove a boon to him and not a liability.

It is not surprising, then, that the Chinese were rather tough with Kissinger in the July sessions. The last of the three talks began (according to the distinguished French reporter, Jean Lacouture) with Chou En-lai dramatically declaring to Kissinger: 'I am charged by Chairman Mao Tse-tung to tell you that miracles should not be expected from Nixon's visit here. It is not an end in itself. Its success depends on real steps accomplished beforehand by the one who will visit.'

At the same time, the Chinese feel that they gain more than they risk from détente with the United States. They have been seated in the U.N. Equally important, the international status of the government of Taiwan slides quickly downward. A wedge, too, is inserted between Taipei and Washington. As a result of these developments, Peking's desired solution to the Taiwan issue becomes more likely. Russia gets stung. Not least, Peking obtains a dose of generalized prestige from the fact that President Nixon visits China, at his own request, before he visits Moscow or Tokyo. (Indeed, Peking will be ahead of Moscow and Tokyo in having *any* U.S. President visit it.) On the side of cost, there is a possible loss of credibility with various anti-imperialists. But Hanoi's anxiety – now less deep than last summer – is the only serious problem here.

A barometer of the atmosphere at the Kissinger–Chou talks is the U.N. issue (though it has never been the most important issue in Sino-American relations). I do not believe that Kissinger and Chou set the U.N. issue 'aside' when they met last July – as was often said in the press. Nor that Peking was ready to go ahead with détente regardless of what happened in the U.N. I believe the issue was set aside, after July, because the two sides knew what was going to happen in the U.N. Fragments of information available to me about the July parleys add up to a picture of delicate diplomacy-at-a-tangent. During the many hours of rather tough talks, the two sides gave each other a statement of intention on the U.N. issue. Since the talk dealt with votes and agendas in an international organization, each side could state what it would *seek*, but not guarantee what it would *attain*.

The distinction was crucial. It permitted two statements of intention to seem – to a beholder who wanted to see it that way – like an agreement on what would result. The Chinese were satisfied with what they concluded from this diplomacy by indirection. No sign exists that the United States was deeply dissatisfied.

First, it seems, the Americans indicated that they would support the seating of Peking in the China seat at the U.N. this year – which means a Security Council seat, as one of the permanent five members wielding a veto. Second, the visitors served notice that, should Taipei fight to keep some sort of U.N. place for itself, the United States must support this attempt. This place would be, at most, membership in the General Assembly. Third – here we enter the twilight land of signals – the U.S. side said it 'did not know' whether the attempt to keep Taipei in the U.N. would succeed or not.

The Chinese responded also in three parts. They took note with undemonstrative approval of Washington's decision to back the installation of the People's Republic of China in the China seat. Second, they warned that should the effort to retain the Kuomintang régime in some U.N. role be mounted, Peking would vigorously fight against it. Finally, the Chinese gave their own signal with all its overtones: the government of China was confident that the effort to salvage a role for Taipei would fail.

Given the context – that the mutual coaxing during the spring had gone well enough to bring Kissinger over the Himalayas to Peking, and that Nixon wanted to come to China within a year – the U.S. position in these talks could be interpreted as having an element of shadow-boxing about it. Secretary of State William Rogers' subsequent statement of 2 August did not mean quite what it said on the printed page. Yes, the United States will fight to keep a U.N. place for Chiang Kai-shek. But if the United States 'does not know' whether this will succeed, and China is sure it won't, the two sides are not as far apart as they seem. Peking was not as outraged by Rogers' statement as its press made out. Though enticed to do so by journalists, no Peking official said Rogers' statement meant Washington had gone back on anything Kissinger conveyed to Chou. Yes, the Chinese called the Rogers formulation 'absurd'. But they did not say that the United States had deceived China or broken a promise.

In Washington a certain backpedalling began. Mr Rogers confessed, with more sorrow than anger, that the United States had found through international consultations that 'there is a good deal of support' for assigning the China seat in the Security Council to Peking rather than Taipei. He added, 'We haven't made a decision about our own policy.' Two weeks later, Mr Nixon decided – in Peking's favour. Washington then came out with a double proposal for the U.N. debate: Peking to have the China seat; a separate, lower place to be salvaged for Taipei in the Assembly.

Meanwhile, U.S. spokesmen underlined that, though every effort was being made, success for this position could not be guaranteed. By the time Foreign Minister Fukuda of Japan came to Washington in early September, it smelled as if Mr Rogers were foreshadowing failure and looking around for others to share whatever blame failure might trigger. If Japan did not co-sponsor the U.S. resolution, he warned, this would have 'a detrimental effect' on the resolution's chance of success. Japan did co-sponsor, but the resolution failed.

The grief in Washington was not searing. Mr Nixon seemed more upset by the 'manners' of the voters than by the vote itself. Mr Rogers cried out 'we tried hard' more relentlessly than sincerity would seem to have required. George Bush, American Ambassador to the U.N., was not unhappy with his image as a mighty arm-twister. Given Nixon's fear of a right-wing rampage if U.S. fortunes in Asia should plummet, it is no surprise that Bush was told to make an elaborate effort to hold an Assembly seat for Taiwan. Yet the photographs of Kissinger conferring in Peking in the days before the U.N. voted were more eloquent than anything Bush did in New York.

Interestingly, Washington wished Kissinger's second visit to China to take place a little earlier than did Peking. According to the joint announcement of 5 October, the trip was to be in 'the latter part of October', but on the same day Kissinger spoke of going to China 'shortly after the middle of the month'. In fact, Kissinger reached Peking only on 20 October, by which time the U.N. drama was building to its climax. Moreover, the White House had said on 14 October that the visit would last 'about four days', but it actually lasted six days, even though business was not so pressing as to prevent Kissinger from going sight-seeing and to the theatre. So it turned out that Kissinger was still in Peking when the vital U.N. votes were taken, and signs are that Peking wanted it this way. Maybe the Chinese had in mind a slightly different course of events, should a slip-up have occurred at Turtle Bay on 24 and 25 October.

The gap between 'seek' and 'attain' had richly served Sino–American relations. Nixon lost a battle at the U.N. on 25 October, but salvaged a campaign (perhaps *two* campaigns). The Pakistani delegate at the U.N. aptly said just after the vote that one big reason for the outcome was Nixon's new China policy. (Chou En-lai himself said the same thing one month later.) Nixon's new China policy, in turn, ultimately benefited from the U.N. vote, as did Nixon's prospects for re-election. Meanwhile, Peking took it all so calmly that not a single Chinese newspaperman was sent to the U.N. to cover a drama climaxing twenty-two years of struggle in which China was the key party involved.

Within China, the U.N. issue seems a bagatelle compared with the Taiwan issue. At the Museum of the Peasant Institute in Canton, a vast wall map gives details of the Revolutionary Committee of each province. When you press a button, a light flashes on with the date on which the Committee was established. I pressed Taiwan (Taiwan is invariably included on any map of China within China). A red light flashed with the characters: 'We shall certainly liberate Taiwan!' The phrase is a theme song all over China.

In the beautiful hills near Sian lies the craggy cliff where Chiang Kai-shek was captured in 1936 by one of his own disgruntled generals – the famous Sian Incident. The place is now a lush and tranquil hot-spring resort. Emperors of the Han and Sui dynasties had summer palaces here, and the Communist government has built superb pavilions in traditional style to fit the history-laden ambience. My companions laughed and joked as we inspected the room from which Chiang fled – leaving his dentures behind – when shots pierced his windows.

We climbed the hill where Chiang had clambered in his nightdress. At the place of his capture stands a handsome portico. But it was built not by the Communists, to mark this spot of Chiang Kai-shek's personal tribulation, but by Chiang's own government, in 1946, apparently to try and blot out with glory an ugly memory! After 1949 the new government left the portico intact. Beside it, in red paint on the cliff face, they have simply added: 'We shall certainly liberate Taiwan!' As if to suggest that, just as Chiang was nabbed here, so in the fullness of time he will be nabbed in Taiwan.

No issue seems more important than Taiwan when you talk with Chinese, official or non-official, about international affairs. It is pointed out that in 1950 the U.S. government reversed itself on Taiwan. Until that time, Washington considered Taiwan part of China, and planned no support for Chiang Kai-shek's bid to set up an alternative China. Came the Korean War. As part of its military encirclement of China, the United States, it is recalled, then backtracked and began the long, increasingly ludicrous sponsorship of Chiang and his dreams. Ignoring that Chiang had lost out to a stronger and more popular force, the United States from then to this day has (officially) considered his group the government of China.

But now the movement at the U.N. has unfrozen the Taiwan issue. As Peking envisaged, the displacement of Taipei from a U.N. seat begins a 'softening up' of the Taipei régime's front of bravado. Practical talk on modalities will now become possible between Peking and Taipei. A Chinese official said to me in July that China would not go into the U.N. if the arrangements left Taiwan some kind of 'international label or status'. That statement implies that Peking expected resolution of the U.N. issue to go a long way toward resolving the 'international' aspect of the Taiwan issue.

So it is proving. A long-overdue downgrading of the Taiwan issue is taking place. In Washington, as in other capitals, Taiwan's importance in the whole landscape of China policy increasingly shrinks. U.S. officials seem now to think, for instance, that the effect of Nixon's new China policy on Japan is far more important than its effect on Taiwan.

Visiting China in the summer of 1971, I considered the key question over Taiwan to be *how* Peking's sovereignty over the island is to be reasserted. Of course there are people who argue fiercely against this. Some cry out – at this very late hour – for the lofty cause of self-determination. Others, forgetting that Chiang's brilliant future is entirely behind him, would back him to the hilt and even 'unleash' him against the 'mainland'. But the real question now is *how* an end will be put to the present false status of Taiwan, and its relationship to the rest of China modulated. Diplomacy must henceforth focus, it seemed to me, on encouraging Peking to reassert its sovereignty over Taiwan gradually, peacefully, and partially (granting the island a certain autonomy); rather than suddenly, violently, and without regard to the fact that the island is not just a province like any other province.

So I probed in Peking the possibility that China might give clarifications on three points. What method would it consider appropriate for taking over Taiwan? Would the province of Taiwan, after its liberation, have any military role, and if so, what? (Will there be major air bases such as the United States now maintains – the Ching Chuan Kang base and the Shulinko base – or nuclear weapons as the United States probably now has on the island?) What will Peking's economic policies in Taiwan be, and will there be reprisals against those who have opposed communism? Every side would gain, including Peking, if undertakings could be given on these questions which trouble anyone concerned that justice be done to the people in Taiwan.

On 18 June I learned, when dining with them, that Seymour Topping of the *New York Times* and William Attwood of *Newsday* would soon talk with the Premier on U.S.–China relations. The next morning was my session at the International Club with the two Chinese foreign-affairs officials. If the Premier, as rumoured, was going to say something notable on Chinese attitudes toward the United States, could he clarify one or more of these three questions about Taiwan? Appreciation for China's position within the U.S., it seemed to me, might increase if Peking would speak at least in general terms about the future of Taiwan. It would be harder for extreme anti-Peking elements, such as the 'China Lobby' remnants, to claim that a smile at Peking today will mean a bloodbath for the people in Taiwan tomorrow.

Two days later, the Chinese Premier talked about Taiwan with Topping, Attwood, and Robert Keatley of the *Wall Street Journal*. In the past, Chinese leaders have refused to discuss how they would deal with Taiwan if they re-took it (as well as how they would re-take it). It has always been claimed that this is purely an internal Chinese matter. But on 21 June Chou En-lai departed from this practice.

First, he stressed that the island would benefit economically by returning to mainland rule. Income tax would be abolished, existing wage scales would be kept, living standards would be 'gradually improved'. Second, far from there being reprisals, Peking will 'reward' Taiwan for the contribution it will begin to make to the motherland. In particular, the Premier said any unemployed residents of Taiwan who left the mainland in 1949 'could go back to their home provinces and they will not be discriminated against.' Hinting at Peking's probable attitude toward Kuomintang leaders, Mr Chou recalled that those leaders who have already gone over to the mainland – many did in 1949, a few did later – are being well looked after'.

Third, the Premier acknowledged that such clarifications do have a link with the prospects for Sino–U.S. relations (a marked departure from the old insistence that Taiwan's affairs are absolutely no one else's business).

Observing that Taiwan will 'benefit and not be harmed' by its return to mainland rule, he added, 'If this is done, then relations between China and the United States will be all the better.' In other words, Chou recognized the reality, if not the right, of American concern with the fate of Taiwan.

On 23 June I met at the Foreign Ministry one of the two officials who had talked with me at the International Club on 19 June. Accounts of the Premier's talk with the three American newspapermen had been published. He smiled as he held one report in his hand. 'Well, here is the clarification about Taiwan. The Premier has now spoken of what will happen to Taiwan after its liberation.' I remarked that Mr Chou had indeed clarified one of the three questions – what will happen to the island economically, and will there be reprisals. But not the other two.

In fact Chou En-lai had specifically confronted one of the other questions – by what method would Taiwan be liberated – and flatly refused to clarify it. 'How Taiwan will be liberated is our internal affair,' he had said to Topping, Attwood, and Keatley. The official in front of me on the steps of the Foreign Ministry said, 'Look, you will never get "clarifications" on these two military points.'

Nevertheless, when Mr Whitlam arrived, the Chinese were again asked for clarifications on the remaining two points. (On China policy in Australia, Mr Whitlam's position rather matches Senator Kennedy's in the United States. He accepts none of Chiang Kai-shek's claims. But he cannot shrug off all concern for what happens on Taiwan if and after Peking takes it.)

On 4 July, Whitlam broached the topic with Foreign Minister Chi P'eng-fei. By what means does Peking envisage 'liberating' the island? And will the island have any significant military role after its liberation? (This latter point is a matter of concern to countries close by to Taiwan, and directly affects the desirable possibility of

creating a zone free of nuclear weapons in north-east
Asia – whereby South Korea, Japan, and neighbouring
waters would be kept free of such weapons if China kept
her eastern provinces free of them.)

Mr Chi did not much like the question, yet it is note-
worthy that he did give an answer. In the past it has been
explained that China has no obligation to answer such
'domestic' questions. Mr Chi said two things with some
deliberation. 'China believes in political, not military,
solutions for such problems,' and then: 'The process will
not be too difficult.'

All this is far from a full picture of Peking's intentions
toward Taiwan. Yet it does offer clarifications and it does
convey a mood of flexibility. Mr Chou's and Mr Chi's
remarks indicate that China is unlikely to disregard
world opinion as the moment of opportunity comes for
it to reach out for Taiwan. Peking is unlikely to deal as
harshly with Taiwan as it dealt with Tibet. All signs are
that they expect a political bargaining process to eventually take place, in which Peking will make – at least for a
transitional period – certain concessions to whatever
elements in Taiwan are able to demonstrate political
strength.

But this political bargaining cannot begin in earnest
until Taiwan is fully defused as an international issue.
The U.N. developments have done this to a degree; the
big next step will be military withdrawal by the United
States from Taiwan. I understand that in July 1971
Kissinger talked to the Chinese about this matter. Before
the Chinese agreed to invite Nixon, the United States
side intimated that by the time Nixon reached Peking,
further reductions in the United States military presence
on Taiwan would have taken place.

In the Chinese view, there are two parts to the Taiwan
problem. One is the United States military presence on
the island. The other is the political gulf between Peking
and Taipei, and the methods of bridging it. Only the
first part, say the Chinese, concerns the United States (or

any other nation). Washington is not being asked to 'hand over' Taiwan to Peking – only to stop regarding its government as the government of China, and to take its bases away. This leaves the door open to give-and-take between the two sets of Chinese, and to a process of re-absorption that could stretch out over decades.

In his talk with me, the nimble-minded Mr Y observed, 'There's an easy way out for the United States on Taiwan. Simply announce a return to the position Truman stated in 1949–50 – that the U.S. is not going to interfere in the destiny of Taiwan.' We do not know, because it has not been put to the test, how reasonable Peking would be about the second part of the problem (Taiwan's political reintegration into the mainland) if the U.S. were, as Mr Y suggests, to solve the first part (U.S. disengagement from the problem) by returning to the Truman formula. It may well be in American interests to do this. To gradu-ally phase out Taiwan as a base, and concentrate Ameri-can bargaining power with Peking on trying to ensure that China will reassert its sovereignty over Taiwan gradually, peacefully, and with provisions for the island to enjoy a certain 'autonomy' in the Chinese tradition.

What overall impressions does the visitor to China get about Peking's view of America? Toward the United States, China has a mainly negative aim: to be free of the military harness that the U.S. has thrown around East Asia since the Korean War. China wants to consolidate its revolution. The only way America can help, in China's view, is by not interfering. The Chinese know they are still weak by the standards of the super-powers, yet they know also that they are rising. They consider that time is on their side.

There are strong lines of continuity with the past in these attitudes. Not so much with the Confucian past of the dynasties, but rather with the anti-colonial experience of the last century. Americans may be shocked by the sug-gestion, but the Chinese see *post-1945* America as a direct successor to the colonial powers which bullied Asia. The

period from the Opium War until the present is a seam-
less stretch of history to Peking. First, because throughout
it, China has faced superior material force on its doorstep. Second, because the Chinese mind has felt frustration, and often humiliation, when looking during this
period at the West. The West has threatened China; yet
the West is more advanced than China. It is a painful
mixture for the patriotic Chinese mind. To *keep the West
at bay* and to *catch up with the West* have both been
among China's concerns.

One reason that Communism wins wide allegiance in
China is that it helps China achieve both these aims. It
gives China the unity and the ideology to be anti-Western.
And it is a vehicle of modernization. But Mr Nixon
also made a contribution to easing the first concern. He
called a halt to American expansion in East Asia, and
actually reversed the process. This is what Peking has
always wanted. The Democratic administrations saw the
Chinese question too much as a mere problem of com-
munication. They offered Peking exchanges of doctors,
seeds, journalists, and other good things of life. But at the
same time they kept on building up the military harness
around China's throat. Peking scoffed at Johnson's
honeyed offers, and deeply feared his imperialistic actions.
But Nixon is delivering the goods. Month by month, he
draws back more and more ground troops from China's
doorstep.

With their long view of history, the Chinese sit back
and talk about this historic shift with a philosopher's
detachment. It was inevitable, they say, that the U.S.
should have found its East Asian adventures counter-
productive. China did not have to wait all that long to see
it happen. America's burst of global imperialism was, by
Chinese standards, an affair of a single evening. It only
ran from the quivering sense of power of 1945, until the
lesson of the powerlessness of power in Vietnam.

When the Australians met Chou En-lai, Mr Whitlam
started to rake over the embers of Vietnam, saying how

misguided the United States had been, what a tragedy the war was. But the seventy-three-year-old Premier cut him off. With a large gesture, he said grandly, 'What is past is past,' and went on to chew at the bone of Japanese militarism. Mr Chou feels able now to look beyond the twenty-five-year spasm of American expansionism in Asia. Dozens of talks that I had in China ran along the same lines.

Some Chinese dwell much on internal upheavals in the United States. 'We notice the obsession with sex,' one official remarked. 'It is the sign of a crumbling order. The late Ming period was the same. Sex was everywhere. Soon the dynasty collapsed.' But what occurs within the U.S. is minor to the Chinese. It is what the U.S. does in Asia that concerns them.

Of course, as China grows in power, its ambitions will increase. It will go, when it is able to, from 'strategic defensive' to 'counter-offensive'. China may not always be in a condition of relative weakness. It will not forever be in the mental situation of coping with a painful past. Positive goals will be asserted. Having 'stood up' (Mao's phrase), China is likely to 'stretch out'.

The Nixon visit to Peking began a dialogue that results from a shift in the balance of forces in East Asia. The United States is adjusting its role; Peking welcomes the adjustment. The tough bilateral issue is Taiwan (it is interesting – and not unpleasant in Peking's ears – that Henry Kissinger considers Vietnam essentially a problem of the past, and Taiwan the next East Asian problem). If Taiwan gets settled, the way is wide open for Washington and Peking to cooperate in whatever ways the flux of world power may at any point intimate. The conflict of interest between the United States and China is not extensive. (That between Japan and China is greater, and so is that between Russia and China.) The American and Chinese leaders are not rigid men, and they look out today on a strikingly fluid world.

One day in Peking I met a jade carver at a handicrafts

factory. He was a shrewd, humorous old man who has practised his art for forty years. I watched his nimble fingers and darting eyes. He was carving fruit and vegetables. Struck by the range of colours, I asked if they were natural. 'Yes, the jade has many different colours,' the craftsman replied. Then he explained to me an uncertainty about carving vegetables in jade. 'I cannot tell, when I start, what colour the jade is inside.' He showed me a jade piece, cut at an angle; the edge was green and the middle red. 'So I am not sure, at the start, what vegetable I will end up carving from the piece of jade. Take the piece I am working on now. If the inside is red, I will make tomatoes. If it is green, I will make cucumbers.'

So it may be with the relationship Nixon and Mao carved out. The lump of jade is the international context of the Sino–American dialogue. Who knows whether it will turn out 'red' or 'green'; whether what Nixon and Mao started will eventually make 'tomatoes' or 'cucumbers'? The Chinese leaders may be as uncertain as the jade carver about what product (beyond a Taiwan settlement) will appear. They are so worried about Russia and Japan that they may want to go far down the road of détente with the United States. But how far does the United States want to go?

One of Peking's finest residences is the former French Embassy in the old Legation Quarter. Its oak panels, stone balconies, and central location are no longer enjoyed by the French – who occupy a bare and functional villa in the new diplomatic section – but by the Royal Government of the National Union of Cambodia. The leafy compound bounded by a big red gate and two lions contains Prince Norodom Sihanouk and ten of his ministers who operate from China. It also contains the Chinese Ambassador to Cambodia, K'ang Mao-chao. Mr K'ang was too busy to see me (What does he do?), but the Prince himself passed a morning talking about the Cambodian tragedy, and offering impressions of the senior Chinese leadership.

Beyond the top of a spiral staircase the furnishings are mostly Chinese. Near my chair hangs a glinting mother-of-pearl montage of the Nanking Bridge. But when the Prince bounces in it is easy to forget you are in China. He is Latin-like and passionate. He tries to convince you of his opinions with frank and very personal argument. In all respects he presents a total contrast to Chinese style. The hands are small like the whole body, but the eyes are tremendous as he warms up. He has a most expressive way of turning his mouth down, now in candour, now in disgust. At times he edges almost off his chair, as when he describes the Vietnamese, with an expansive gesture of face and limbs together, as '*Très forts! Très*, très *forts!*'

At the conversation's end a photographer came in to take a picture. But was he really a photographer? He pointed the camera almost at our feet. When the picture was developed, the Prince let out a cry of dismay to find just our two pairs of legs – and those at a thirty-degree angle. The second effort was little better. Only under Sihanouk's detailed supervision – it was like the old days in Phnom Penh, when Sihanouk directed films and dramatic performances – did the beaming Cambodian assistant manage to get both the Prince and myself into a photo. Glossing the picture, Sihanouk jerked his head toward the photographer and asked me, 'Do you know who he is?' I knew only that he wasn't a professional photographer. 'It's Sisowath Sirik Matak's brother [Sisowath Metheavei],' Sihanouk casually remarked. 'He used to be my Ambassador in East Germany before the *coup*.'

The Prince referred back to an early part of our talk. 'You remember I told you Lon Nol, Sirik Matak, and the others listen to my broadcasts from Peking? How do I know? Well he [pointing to the former Ambassador] gets letters from Sirik Matak and others in the family. They describe the scene. On the evenings when my broadcast in Khmer comes – about 7 p.m. in Phnom Penh – they gather round the radio. They listen in silence.' Sihanouk's establishment in Peking is that sort of place – an ambassador takes the pictures. The Cambodian situation is that sort of situation – one brother runs one government, another works for the rival government, and the two of them exchange letters. Sihanouk is that sort of man – even his successors and would-be murderers are not immune to the emotional appeal of his patriotic commentaries.

The Prince had kept me waiting a moment at the start. He was sending a cable of thanks to President Kaunda. Zambia had just become the latest country to recognize his government. Sihanouk thinks the National United Front (N.U.F., the movement on which his government is based) will take Cambodia back by the end of 1972. 'By then Nixon will be forced to withdraw just about all his troops. And we can cope with Lon Nol and Thieu.' He felt good about the military situation. Two thirds of

Cambodia and 4 million of its 7 to 8 million people, he claimed, are controlled by the N.U.F. 'Lon Nol has to import rice but we have enough rice in our liberated areas. We also supply food – rice and fish – to the Vietnamese and Laotian forces operating in Cambodia.' He has no doubts about his own continued popularity within Cambodia. And it is hard not to be convinced of his argument that the people of Cambodia are far worse off now than when he ruled them.

Toward the United States, Sihanouk showed little emotion, but insisted that Washington stop 'interfering' in Indo-Chinese affairs. On the one hand, he demanded American withdrawal; not only of ground forces, but of air and naval forces. 'The U.S. may give weapons to Lon Nol, if it likes, but must not participate in the war itself. China gives weapons to one side; America has the right to do that also.' On the other hand, the Prince found something to praise in Mr Nixon. 'I am happy to see his statement that after the United States withdraws, if the fighting still continues, that is a purely Indo-Chinese affair. This is a reasonable position.'

The Prince has grave problems within his own camp. They stem from the fact that he, a Buddhist socialist whose career has been the very definition of non-alignment, now works in harness with Communists. The N.U.F. includes the Khmer Rouge, which has 'pro-Vietminh' elements, 'pro-Chinese' elements (younger men), and 'pro-Russian' elements'. These last, oddly enough, are substantially represented among the ten ministers in Peking. 'They are discreet, knowing the realities in China,' Sihanouk observed, 'but they like Russia.' The crucial line of division within the N.U.F., however, is not within the Khmer Rouge but between the Khmer Rouge and the 'Sihanoukists'.

The Prince willingly entered this alliance with the Communists. The Lon Nol *coup*, he says, forced an unwelcome choice between the 'Free World' (his phrase) and the 'Socialist Camp'. But he knows he will not necessarily like the ultimate outcome. Even now his control is slipping. He calls the Communists 'my red Khmers' and there is evidently a strong nationalistic bond between Khmer Rouge and 'Sihanoukist'. Yet the Prince sees that the Cambodian Communists will draw further away from him so long as the tragic polarization in Indo-China continues.

I knew Chou En-lai had discouraged Sihanouk from travelling outside the triangle of China, North Vietnam, and North Korea. But the Prince put a new complexion on the matter. 'My own Prime Minister [Penn Nouth] does not want me to travel outside these three countries.' Sihanouk did not hide the trend of things within the N.U.F. 'After Liberation perhaps there will be a Marxist Cambodia. Frankly, the ministers who are leading the struggle are all extreme leftists. My Sihanoukists are administered by the extremists.' He had been mixing English with bits of French, but now he went on in his preferred French. 'My red Khmers don't want me to go back to Cambodia. So in the long run the Sihanoukists may also become leftists. I don't criticize them for it...'

His exposition I found moving. He does not like the idea of a Communist Cambodia ('Cambodians have no vocation to be Spartan'). But seeing no alternative other than U.S.-sponsored endless war, he has nodded in this direction. At the same time he retains his beliefs and dignity as a Buddhist socialist. He will not become a red Khmer just because that is the trend of events. And he is able to detach – how painful it must be for this ball of patriotism! – his own future from that of Cambodia. He is serving as midwife of a new Marxist alignment for tomorrow's Cambodia. But he himself will go back to France as Cambodia enters the Communist camp.

On the question of Vietnamese in Cambodia, Sihanouk showed his regret, but coped with it in a philosophic way. The problem, he pointed out, is that as the Saigon armies pushed toward Phnom Penh, Cambodian peasants fled to the capital and were largely replaced by Vietnamese. Said

Sihanouk, 'We'll have to let them stay. We can't treat the Vietnamese worse than Lon Nol has treated them.' He paused and sighed, and one hand stretched out to adjust a daffodil in the bowl before him. 'So we will have Vietnamese living in our country. It is an insoluble problem.'

What are Norodom Sihanouk's impressions from his rich contacts with the Peking leadership? He reviewed his fall off the tightrope of non-alignment in March 1970. When word reached him in Russia of the *coup* by Lon Nol, he did not return immediately to Cambodia because he would have been killed. He learned in Moscow, from two colonels loyal to himself, of a plan hatched by the Lon Nol group. Should he arrive at Pochentong airport, he was to be driven not into Phnom Penh but along Route 4 to Kirirom and there shot like a dog. So he did not return. Kosygin promised support. Sihanouk said he must go to China and get support there also. On the plane to Peking he drafted his appeal to the Cambodian people. Moscow went back on its promise. But Sihanouk found himself taken seriously by the Chinese leaders. Several days in a row he talked with Chou En-lai.

What was China to do in this situation pregnant with implications for both the war and relations within the Communist camp? At first Chou did not commit himself. He mainly quizzed Sihanouk on his views and plans. The Prince — he told me — said to Chou that there was no choice but to mount immediate struggle against Lon Nol. The Chinese Premier noted this but struck a note of caution. 'We must warn you. We have experience. Wars like this are not easy; they are hard and long. Reflect upon it.' Sihanouk in his emotional state wanted no delay. It seemed that the reflection was more on the Chinese side.

Between this session and the next, Chou consulted the (then) Vice-President, Lin Piao. This was not the last time the number three man referred to the (then) number two man during that week of Sihanouk's destiny. On 'all important questions,' the Prince recalled, 'Chou En-lai went

to talk with Lin Piao.' On some of these important questions Chairman Mao himself adjudicated. Sihanouk did
not himself deal directly with Lin Piao. Apart from Chou,
the Chinese leader he saw most frequently (through the
summer of 1971) was Huang Yung-sheng, Chief of the
General Staff. Of Lin Piao's position at that time the
Prince remarked, 'Lin is kept free from most day-to-day
responsibility in order to prevent him becoming vulner-
able to criticism. It is Chou who takes the responsibility.'

The Chinese decided to ask Hanoi's Premier, Pham
Van Dong, to come straightaway to Peking. Sihanouk was
a little wary of the Vietnamese leader – Cambodians
generally are of Vietnamese. The two of them did not
meet immediately. Chou met with Pham Van Dong, then
Chou and Sihanouk met again. At these meetings the out-
lines of a bargain crystallized. By now Mao had laid down
that Sihanouk was a crucial figure and must be backed to
the hilt at all cost. Indeed, the Chinese now urged upon
Sihanouk that he personally must head any struggle that
was to unfold. The Prince had opted for struggle. But not
necessarily with himself at its head, for he may have had
in mind to go very soon to France. The Chinese opted
for the Prince, for a kind of struggle in which the Prince
would be indispensable.

Whether Pham Van Dong was as keen as Mao to put all
eggs in the Prince's basket is unclear. At any rate, Chou
En-lai brought Sihanouk and Pham Van Dong together
in a compact of which China was the initiator and
guarantor. This was reflected in the pattern of meetings.
Once the Chinese position was firm, and Chou had held
separate sessions with Sihanouk and Pham Van Dong,
the latter two met with each other. Chou had paved the
way to this agreement.

The Prince was to join the 'front of the three Indo-
Chinese peoples in full solidarity against imperialism'.
Pham Van Dong said to Sihanouk, 'We are happy to
have you as comrade-in-arms.' Hanoi promised that after
the war Cambodia would be 'independent, neutral, and

free of any Vietnamese military presence'. Sihanouk was highly satisfied to have Pham Van Dong declare, 'After Liberation, we'll go together to the Vietnam-Cambodia border and plant frontier marks, at the existing borders, with the international press present, to indicate the complete integrity and independence of each country.'

Apparently the Chinese as well as Sihanouk were eager to get it clear that Vietnamese forces would not stay in Cambodia any longer than was necessary. Chou said to Sihanouk, 'We do not support the so-called Maoists in Cambodia. China is one country, Cambodia is quite another – you should remain neutral.' Such a statement, given the angled complexities of Chinese foreign policy, can be construed different ways. But Peking certainly backed Sihanouk handsomely, despite all the odds against exile governments doing anything but wither on the vine. Enormous and open-ended sums of money were promised him, to cover all military and political expenses. 'To respect our dignity,' Sihanouk explained, 'they called it a loan.' But the question of paying it back will not be opened until thirty years after the war has ended.

I asked him if China may under any circumstances send troops into Cambodia or other parts of Indo-China. 'They have told me,' the Prince replied, 'that they will send volunteers to Cambodia if I request it, but that, in their opinion, it is better not to have any Chinese soldiers in Cambodia.'

Sihanouk eventually had a 'long and cordial' session with Chairman Mao. China, Mao made clear, was going to take Cambodia seriously on its own terms, not just as ideological potential for international communism. Said the Chairman to the Prince, 'You know, I like princes when they're not reactionary, but with their people, and against imperialism as you are. I'm not only in favour of the people, I'm in favour of princes, too, if they're good.' It was vintage Mao, if unconventional by Leninist norms. Sihanouk was convinced the backing from China was a personal enthusiasm of the old rebel who 'liked princes'.

Mao said to him at the end, 'You can have anything you want from China.'

But how to account for the difficulties – beyond the normal frustrations of being in exile – Sihanouk has had since that spring of 1970? Are they due only to developments within the N.U.F., and to the differences of interests between Hanoi and the Sihanoukists? Or has Peking edged back from its support for Sihanouk's nationalist and neutral position? The Prince's hand seems to have weakened on certain issues. The Khmer Rouge (Communist) influence within the N.U.F. rises while the Sihanoukist (neutralist) influence wanes. The Prince did not say how strong the tie-up now is between Hanoi and the Khmer Rouge (through its pro-Vietminh elements). But he does not believe the Chinese are actively trying to undermine the Sihanoukists within the N.U.F.

On the matter of the Prince's travels, however, the Chinese do seem to be clipping his presently folded wings of neutralism. He has said to Chou En-lai, 'You should help me travel outside the triangle of China, North Vietnam, and North Korea. Some people say I'm a prisoner. It's not good to have this believed.' The Chinese Premier said he feared for Sihanouk's safety if he should venture to additional countries. 'The C.I.A. may kidnap you,' he warned. Sihanouk not long ago asked Chou straight out to put a plane at his disposal for wider travels. According to the Prince the answer was furry. 'The Premier says he is preparing a plane. But he does not seem keen, I don't know why . . .'

Toward the end of our morning together I asked Sihanouk about the future. What ground can there be to hope Cambodia will regain the independence he so ardently believes in? 'Marxist or not,' the Prince said with some feeling, 'Cambodia will always be independent-minded. Hanoi is independent-minded – that is the important thing. Cambodia has no borders with China. So long as Hanoi is independent-minded, Cambodia will not be dominated.' He presented a second line of argument.

'It is not in China's *interests* to make Cambodia a satellite. First, because it is a poor country, and would be a burden. Second, because if China subjected Cambodia, it would no longer be able to convince Afro-Asians that China respects small nations.'

Prince Sihanouk left me with a summary of China's present strategic outlook as he understands it. 'In their view,' he said, *'Russia is China's biggest problem,* and *Japan is Asia's biggest problem.'* On 15 July, I later learned, Chou En-lai visited Sihanouk late at night to brief him personally on the announcement (due ten hours thence) of Kissinger's trip to Peking and Nixon's impending trip. (China's allies got a little more advance notice than America's allies!) The Chinese Premier assured the Cambodian of 'total solidarity'. An anti-Russian theme quickly entered. 'We are not like the leaders in Moscow; we will not sacrifice our friendships and principles for the sake of détente.'

Then Chou added, 'Even if we get the necessary concessions out of the Americans, we will not be finished with imperialism in our region. *For the Japanese are ready to take over.'* For his part, Sihanouk welcomed the news of the impending Mao–Nixon meeting. He thought it a 'stroke of genius' by the Chinese leaders. It would, he judged, 'isolate and disconcert' America's allies in Asia – above all Lon Nol.

16   Barbarians in the Middle Kingdom

I found myself wearing two hats in China. That of an Australian accompanying Mr Whitlam; and that of a scholar from the United States. Peking was aware that I work at Harvard. But 1971 political developments – especially in China–Australia relations – explain the timing of my China visa. By the time the phone rang on Memorial Day with word from Peking of a visa, much had happened in the political sphere which gave my visit its context (every visit to China has its context in Peking's eyes).

Australia had no diplomatic relations with Peking. But China was a major buyer of Australian products, especially wheat, on which over the past decade she had spent a yearly average of £46 million (sometimes 25 per cent or more of the entire Australian wheat crop). The China trade is vital to many Australian farmers, and important to the political party – named without embellishment 'Country party' – based on their support. A blind eye is turned by the Country party to matters of ideology, for trade's sake. It also suited Peking, Canberra's embassy in Taipei notwithstanding, to buy heavily in Australia. (One reason is hardly flattering. Australian wheat, a trade official explained to me in Peking, suits China more than some other foreign wheat because its 'quality is not so high.' This makes it suitable to mix with the even lower quality Chinese wheat!)

In 1970 the wheat order from Peking had been especially large (2·2 million metric tons). But in 1971 no order was placed. Consternation among the farmers 'down under'. Political rumblings, too, because the large opposition Labour party charged the government with having lost business for farmers due to rigid political hostility to China. The Country party sat on the horns of a dilemma. Many of its members and leaders have wanted to recognize Peking for some time. But the party is in coalition with the right-wing Liberal party, which insults Peking at every opportunity and embraces Taipei with a zealot's persistence. The Labour party has long had a policy of recognizing Peking, dropping Taipei, and voting for Peking's seating in the China seat of the U.N. It stood to gain in the situation which developed in the spring of 1971. And gain it did.

It is interesting to see how Peking proceeded. It blew no trumpets, spoke in whispers. At a Peking dinner in mid-March, a Director of the Chinese Ministry of Foreign Trade casually remarked to the British chargé that China didn't want Australian wheat this year. When it needed wheat, purred the official, it would turn to countries more friendly than Australia. China, after all, had 'friends all over the world'. Canberra officials, it had to be remembered, have said 'foolish things' about China. Specific scorn was heaped by the Chinese trade official on a statement of a former Australian Foreign Minister. This self-righteous fellow had spoken of 'serious questionings of conscience in Australia about how far we're justified in trading with China.'

Of course the British passed on this offhand bombshell to Canberra. In late March, the Chinese Natural Resources authorities in Hong Kong did agree to meet Australian wheat men. But the message was the same. In the first weeks of April, Canberra got a report of this meeting that confirmed what the British had heard in Peking. Meanwhile, Chinese officials told an influential Australian-born journalist that China would transfer whatever imports it conveniently could from Australia to West Germany. The reasons given were, first, that West Germany was not involved in Indo-China; second, that West Germany was less involved than Australia with Taiwan.

Of this bleak news the Australian government dared say nothing in public. Friends of Mr Whitlam, however, got hold of it. The Labour party went onto the offensive. The complacent moguls of the government said politics had nothing to do with China's failure to order Australian wheat. The Chinese are just 'carpetbaggers', explained the Prime Minister, Mr McMahon. Another minister dismissed as 'cocktail party gossip in Hong Kong' the alleged message from Peking. Mr Whitlam, now privy to the message, was able to shoot down the prevarications about cocktail party gossip. The Labour party decided to publicly put to the test the government's argument that politics had nothing to do with Australia–China trade. It took a spectacular step. On 14 April it cabled Chou En-lai. Would China receive a delegation from the Labour party to talk things over?

The Prime Minister exploded, in a speech on 15 April, about this political delegation 'going to China, to Peking China'. His majestic scorn for a hopeless venture was strangely mixed with a troubled fury at it. He reaffirmed his support for Taipei. Before Peking could ever become a 'member' of the U.N., he declared, 'there must be some kind of assurances that they will live up to their international obligations.' It was vintage Liberal party myopia, emitted with a rare smugness that only conservatism and insularity joined together can produce.

Meanwhile Peking was considering the Labour party's request. Friends of Mr Whitlam were interceding with the Chinese to interpret it and urge a favourable response. Within Australian politics, the issue blew up to one of the biggest foreign policy issues Australia has had. Was Mr Whitlam out on a limb? Or was he positioned for a big *coup*? It was easier to be pessimistic than optimistic. Especially since the Labour party needed an *early* reply. Also, it was known that the Australian 'Maoists' were vigorously urging Peking *not* to invite Labour party people. Would Peking see eye to eye with their left arm in Australia?

No. On 10 May came a cable from the People's Institute for Foreign Affairs in Peking. A delegation from the Labour party was invited 'for discussions on questions concerning relations between the two countries'. Mr Whitlam was elated. The Prime Minister did a somersault – letting his policies, it seemed, be determined by Peking's actions – and on 11 May and 13 May came out for détente with China. He put aside his rich collection of veiled titles for China: 'Continental China', 'Mainland China', 'Peking China', 'Communist China'. Panic lent him boldness. He now said he sought 'normal bilateral relations with the People's Republic of China'. He now felt 'contacts' with China were highly desirable. His government quickly moved to make its own diplomatic contacts. At Australian request, the Chinese and Australian Ambassadors at Paris soon held two (unfruitful) meetings. Meanwhile, Mr Whitlam reached China on 2 July for a twelve-day visit.

The Whitlam mission was the most important Australian visit to China ever, and one of the few visits made to China by the leader of a social democratic party. E. Gough Whitlam revelled in the opportunity. A tall man of boundless energy, he took a gruelling schedule in his stride. Up and down China, his intellectual curiosity never flagged. Peering at machines; sitting at a child's school desk reading the Red Book; making humorous and well-informed after-banquet speeches; downing the explosive rice wine, *mao-t'ai*.

On a flight from Peking to Shanghai, an Australian journalist asked Whitlam what the previous evening's film show had been about. The Labour party leader explained that it dealt with the unearthing of cultural treasures during the Cultural Revolution, 'some of them Han bronzes'. The reporter inquired, 'How old are these treasures?' Whitlam instructed him patiently: 'Well, as you know, the Han dynasty ran from 206 B.C. to A.D. 220 ...' Typically, Whitlam was better informed than the journalist. Typically, too, he had attended the film, which was a special screening for the Australian group; most of the press corps had skipped it out of fatigue.

What did the Chinese have in mind with these initiatives toward Australia? Was this a typical example of the new foreign policy line which has followed the distractions of the Cultural Revolution? A pattern behind the invitation was borne out by events during the visit itself. The starting points were two. China was trying to get the U.N. and Taiwan issues fixed up to its satisfaction. Australia could help here. But not, it seemed, the present Australian government, given its present approach. Second, China's need for imported wheat had shrunk. The Foreign Trade Minister explained, 'China has had several good seasons and this year's has been reasonable.' Grain reserves above the commune level stood at 40 million tons late in 1970. (True, China bought in 1971 from Canada ten per cent more wheat than she had bought in 1970. But this was a gesture in response to Canada's recognition of China, and Peking has already conveyed to Canada that there will be no similar increase in 1972.) China could therefore be choosy about Australian wheat. It could tie economic issues to political issues.

So in the spring of 1971 there unfolded a sequence of events not without its logic. The wheat order was omitted. Word passed that political attitudes played a part in this omission. Then the invitation to Whitlam (whose party has the 'correct' position on Taiwan and the U.N.). At the same time a few mild slaps in the face were administered by Peking to Australian Maoists.

The Chinese by early summer were actually relating to Australia on three political levels. Contact at Paris with the McMahon government; the Labour party mission; continuing fraternal ties with the Maoists. But the Labour party was getting most of the smiles, for, given Peking's current aims, its role was crucial. This is not to say Peking was certain Mr Whitlam would soon be Prime Minister. But in any event the way to prod McMahon, as events so eloquently proved, was to smile upon Whitlam.

And if this tactic involved a little bitterness for the Mao-ists? Well, any Maoist should know that tactics (flexible, short-term) are not to be confused with strategy (unwavering, long-term). To satisfy immediate needs is not, for Peking any more than for Rome, to prejudice ultimate visions.

Within China, it was absorbing to compare Chinese attitudes toward Australia and toward America. While Mr Whitlam was there, Peking saw me as an Australian, accredited correspondent for a Sydney publication. Before and after the Whitlam mission I was a 'scholar and writer' from the United States, who was going to write for American readers. The Chinese liked to keep the two aspects distinct. (One day a Scandinavian head of mission, pondering this Chinese insistence on keeping national categories crystal clear, told me this story. Sweden was planning the biggest trade exhibition it had ever held outside Sweden for April 1972 in Peking. Air France, with an eye to filling acres of empty seats on its Europe to Shanghai service, sent an employee who is a Swedish citizen to Peking to get a foot in the door for some of the air traffic. This Air France official was told that nothing is known about the planning for the exhibition. In fact, the Chinese had already been dealing with S.A.S. (Scandinavian Airlines) about flights to and from the exhibition. An S.A.S. official had visited Peking and made preliminary arrangements. The Chinese considered it a matter of principle: a Swedish exhibition should be serviced by S.A.S., not Air France or any other airline.)

I found that the U.S. liberal approaches China more idealistically than the Australian labourite (the same is true of journalists from the two countries). The American tends to be very well informed, excited to be in China, and concerned with large questions of value about Chinese society. U.S.–China relations are something of personal importance to him. He carries himself – even if he's a newspaperman – like an unofficial ambassador for

America. What his President does or doesn't do about China matters to him, and seems tied intimately to what he feels he ought to do in China. He is acutely conscious of the ambiguity of past U.S.–China relations, but optimistic that if the two peoples' leaders can sit down with each other, intimacies can quickly start afresh.

The Australian is casual, detached, and pragmatic. He goes without awe to China. Australia, of course, has never been in passionate embrace with China, as the U.S. government and public once were. Nor does anything of moment for the world hang on China–Australia relations. A steady if small traffic of Australian visitors has been going to China ever since Liberation. There is less excitement for the Antipodean than for the U.S. visitor, because the fruit of the Middle Kingdom has never been absolutely forbidden to Australians. If the Australian journalist is pragmatic about China, it only reflects the ties between the two nations. Say 'China' in Australia and (until recently) you have said little more than 'wheat'.

In the factories, on the farms, the Aussie's comparative lack of idealism is marked. His questions betray no overriding awareness that this society is Communist. He thinks not of systems but looks for performance. If a thing seems to work – as it sometimes but not always does – he waves aside the categories. The typical question of the U.S. liberal in a factory concerns freedom of choice in work and living patterns. The Australian labourite typically asks where are the trade unions, and why on earth do workers put up with military men on the factory floor.

The Australian does not take the Chinese leaders with any more seriousness than he takes his own leaders. That means he treats them bluntly, yet with a touch of naïveté that bluntness sometimes masks. All in all, it is quite a contrast. The Chinese try to accommodate these differences which they hardly expect. They cannot always hide their shock at Australian insular pragmatism. Nor their discomfort when American moralism exceeds their own. When it comes to language, the Chinese much prefer

Americans. Radio and, in the case of older people, pre-Liberation encounters, make them familiar with the American accent. But the Australian accent is a thing of terror to any Chinese who thinks he knows the English language.

To watch the Chinese dealing with Mr Whitlam was to glimpse their hand on several issues. On diplomatic ties, Whitlam sought and obtained Chinese assurance that Peking and Canberra could exchange ambassadors on the 'Canadian formula'; that is, recognizing the Peking government of China, and taking note of, without necessarily endorsing, Peking's claim to Taiwan. However, Canada had no embassy in Taipei, as Australia has had since 1966. What, asked Chi P'eng-fei, wreathed in his enigmatic smile, will you do about that? 'I will not send an ambassador to Taipei,' replied Whitlam.

It seemed a crab-like approach, since an Australian envoy is already there, warmly nesting with the government of the 'Republic of China'. To further Chinese questions, Whitlam said a Labour government would, as recognition arrangements proceed, 'withdraw' the embassy from Taipei. In private remarks, Whitlam restated this intention vigorously. He does not bother to hide his non-regard for Chiang's régime (which he has taken pains never to visit – other than one airport stop). In Shanghai on 11 July, he publicly put the matter beyond doubt: 'When we propose to establish diplomatic relations with Peking as the sole legal government of China, we will close the embassy in Taipei . . .'

The Labour leader wondered about Peking's attitude toward Australian Maoists, tightly grouped under Comrade Ted Hill in the Australian Communist party (Marxist-Leninist). What kind of backing would Hill enjoy from China when a Labour government got the reins of power in Canberra? The Chinese Foreign Minister said 'non-interference' was the policy. 'We do not know what is best for Australia.'

The answer remained general, but light shines on the

matter from other sources. There is in Sweden a group similar to Hill's in Australia. A man in a position to know says the only aid Peking gives these Swedish Maoists is mass purchase of their publications – a form of subsidy – for distribution in China's airports and hotels. After Mr Whitlam had left China, Peking made a gesture which signified not only 'non-interference' in Australian affairs, but a quiet effort to clip Comrade Hill's wings.

Richard Hughes of the London *Sunday Times* wrote from Hong Kong that Australian Maoists had urged Peking not to receive Mr Whitlam (also not to give me a visa). This had been suspected in Australia. The startling thing was that 'official Communist sources', according to Hughes, made a 'deliberate disclosure' to him of these fruitless interventions. These sources added for Hughes's information the fact that Comrade Hill had cabled Peking with his Party's recommendations. Maybe Peking is irritated that Hill should claim a 'monopoly' on channels between China and Australia, and a veto power on China's behalf over who from Australia may visit China. Frankly, I believed the Chinese when they said they have little possibility and less interest in making revolution in Australia.

Foreign Minister Chi was generally practical and to the point. The only time Chairman Mao's name came up, through a morning of talk between him and the Australians, was when Mr Whitlam asked to have his respects passed on to Mr Mao. For some reason, Mr Chi during this private talk was less harsh on the present Australian government than was Chou En-lai in a semi-public dialogue the next day. Chi did not burn his bridges, as Mr Chou seemed to do, for any serious dealings with Mr McMahon. On one issue Mr Whitlam got essentially no more satisfaction than the Australian government (through intermediaries): the fate of the eccentric Australian journalist and adventurer, Francis James, who is held by the Chinese for having used forged travel papers in China. Despite careful and persistent efforts, Mr Whitlam found out no more than that Mr James is alive and well.

When the topic of U.S.–China relations came up, Mr Chi said frankly that 'Taiwan is the crux.' On Japan he was tough as everyone in Peking is tough. He hammered at three outrages on Tokyo's part. The 'illegal peace treaty between Japan and the so-called Republic of China'; the plans to acquire nuclear weapons; the Japan–Taiwan–South Korea liaison committee for exploiting resources on the continental shelf near China. It seemed from what Chi and other Chinese said to Whitlam that Peking's hostility toward Japan nearly always boils down to Japan's involvement with two specific areas vital to China: Taiwan and Korea.

Broaching the U.N., the Foreign Minister put unexpected stress on its specialized agencies. He accepted that an Australian Labour government would vote for Peking's seating in the China seat. But he wanted to be clear that Whitlam would vote the right way to ensure the 'removal of the Chiang group from every part of the specialized agencies of the U.N.' He was after a 'U.N. solution' which not only gets Peking to New York, but shoots down every vestige of Taipei's claim to be a separate state.

The trade talks with the Australians showed that Chinese interest in foreign trade – now aimed far more toward the non-Communist world than toward China's fellow Communist states – is expanding in a number of directions. Politics, we came to believe, is brought into trade when Peking has wide options open to it, but kept out when such options do not exist.

This resembles the relation in old China between the 'tribute system' and trade. The tribute system expressed the Chinese view of the world. The Chinese emperor was not just ruler of China but Son of Heaven. He reigned over all known civilization and all activities theoretically fell within his preserve. But Peking did not always have the capacity to make its authority operative. Sometimes theory and practice did not mesh. Thus in the first half of the eighteenth century, Russia traded much with China but only once made the respectful mission of tribute. It is this way with trade today. China cannot always maintain the politics–trade connection. But it does so when it is able to.

Peking could put pressure on Australia this year because of China's favourable overall grain situation. Pai Hsiang-kuo, the Chinese Minister for Foreign Trade, told Whitlam that China–Australia trade 'cannot but be affected' by political ties or the lack of them. He and his aides laid down principles for such trade with Australia as involved Japanese and American companies. China will have nothing to do with any company in Australia that is a hundred per cent owned by Americans. The door was not specifically closed, however, to dealings with companies *almost* totally American owned.

Regarding Australian–Japanese companies, the Foreign Trade Minister applied in an extended way the 'four principles' which Chou En-lai gave for China–Japan trade in April 1970. China will not trade with any company in Australia linked with a Japanese company which is disqualified by the Four Principles from trading with China. Curiously, the Chinese showed no great concern about the lopsided character (in Australia's favour) of China–Australia trade. In 1970, for example, China bought from Australia £61 million worth of goods, and sold to Australia only £17 million worth of goods. Yet Pai Hsiang-kuo talked with Whitlam far more about what extra goods China might *buy* than about what extra goods it might *sell*.

The Chinese did not say, as some had expected, that Peking would baulk at Australian companies continuing to trade with Taiwan. It was understood that Australia (under Whitlam) would not trade with Taiwan *through governmental agencies*. But private companies may trade with the island. The Australians had wheat uppermost in their minds when they entered the Hall on Number 42 Anti-Imperialist Road for trade talks. But the Chinese indicated that the major prospects for Chinese purchases in Australia were iron, steel, and bauxite. Wheat will still be needed, though in smaller quantities. Dairy products (powdered) and wool will also be sought.

As important as wheat, Chinese officials said, will be sugar. China's increased desire for sugar reflects a stress on consumer needs; it goes into cakes and ice cream. China produces 2·8 million tons of sugar and imports some as well (notably 500,000 tons each year from Cuba). When 'prices are favourable', China re-exports sugar to Hong Kong, Malaysia, and other places. 'As living standards rise,' the Australians were told, 'and given our annual population increase of 15 million,' more extra sugar will be needed than China can produce from land available for additional cultivation. So Peking will consider Australia if Canberra mends its political fences with China. The trade official summed up: 'When normal relations between China and Australia have been established, China will be very interested to buy Australian sugar, within the framework of the International Sugar Agreement.'

Lights burn late in the new cream-brick block which houses China's Ministry of Foreign Affairs. After the Cultural Revolution, the number of personnel at the Ministry was slashed by almost half. Those who remain must work fantastic hours to cope with a swelling volume of business. Some work who are too tired and ill to work, like Vice-Minister Ch'iao Kuan-hua this past summer. Some who speak a Western tongue fluently must punctuate policy work with translating tasks. 'Peking wives' – it occurred to me – must have even more to put up with than 'Washington wives'. (I say 'wife', but in fact the Chinese no longer use the established word for wife, *t'ai-t'ai*; they use *ai-jen*, 'lover', for spouse or amorous friend alike.)

Yet morale is high. Officials are naturally encouraged that their Ministry has become as much a focus of attention as any foreign ministry in the world. The more so because it firmly relegates to an unlamented past the period of 1966–7 when the Chinese foreign-policy establishment was very nearly derailed by a hot avalanche of ultra-leftism. Ch'en Yi, the Foreign Minister at that time, was harassed and 'supervised' so unrelentingly by Red Guards that Mao eventually declared: 'How can Ch'en be struck down? He has been with us forty years and has so many achievements. He has lost twenty-seven pounds in weight. I cannot show him to foreign guests in this condition.'

Ch'en Yi no longer works on foreign policy, but it does not seem that he has been purged. A senior Chinese military man, when it was remarked to him by a European ambassador that Ch'en's going was a 'loss', replied with a broad smile: 'Your loss is our gain.' One of China's true military experts, Ch'en Yi, though seriously ill, was probably working on high military matters. He resurfaced as a vice-chairman of the top Military Affairs Committee.* Of other high officials in the Ministry, it is remarkable how few were blown away by the storms of the Cultural Revolution. In 1967, the two Vice-Ministers most assailed by the zealots were Chi P'eng-fei and Ch'iao Kuan-hua. Yet how little the huffing and puffing availed. Today, Chi is Acting Foreign Minister, and Ch'iao is the Vice-Minister in charge of Western affairs and top man at the U.N. for the 1971 session.

At one point in the struggle of the Cultural Revolution, ninety-one senior men in the Ministry put up a manifesto backing Ch'en Yi against those who reviled him as 'poison' and classified him as 'bourgeois'. Almost every responsible man one meets in the Ministry today is one of the ninety-one, as are most of the ambassadors who have been flying out to occupy new posts and dust down old ones. I often talked with one official, of middle age, as much a scholar as a diplomat. Like his wife, he is a graduate of Yenching University. His home is as well furnished with books as his mind is with ideas. I asked if the zealots (in conversation they were always called *chi-tso fen-tzu*, 'ultra-leftists') had tried to get at his books. For there was a bit of 'book burning' in 1967. Self-appointed maestros passed the wand of ideology over certain works, and pronounced even gold to be dross. 'No,' he answered with an expression that gave nothing away. And if they had come? 'If they had quoted Chairman Mao to me, I would have quoted other parts of Chairman Mao to them – and I would have won.' (Remarkable was the diplomat's belief in the power of persuasion, in the importance of the correct Word. But you find it everywhere in China. The Chinese apparently have not, like many in the West, from the greatest philosophers to the hippie at the corner, lost confidence that reason and conduct are related.)

*Ch'en Yi died of cancer in early January 1972.

We find continuities in the history of new China's foreign-policy community that rival Andrei Gromyko and J. Edgar Hoover. There have been only two regular Foreign Ministers in the years 1949–71. Most of China's senior diplomats come from a small circle of negotiators and propagandists who cut their teeth on four diplomatic operations prior to Liberation. First, a liaison group headed by Chou En-lai at the Nationalist capital of Hankow (and, after Hankow fell to the Japanese, at Chungking); second, a branch outfit at Kweilin which put out a news service. A third knot worked out of Hong Kong; Ch'iao Kuan-hua distinguished himself there. Fourth, the Chinese Communist party was represented on the 'truce teams' which the Marshall Mission operated in North China and Manchuria. Huang Hua, the ambassador to the U.N., was an active part of the Marshall Mission machinery. He ran the information work at the Mission's Executive Headquarters in Peking. Many of China's senior diplomats are Averell Harrimans of the East, their resilient careers interlaced with decades of their country's (or Party's) foreign policy.

What does the Chinese foreign-policy machine consist of? It is small by U.S. standards – the Foreign Ministry has no more than a thousand people – but not simple. Chou En-lai as Premier heads the State Council. It is a kind of cabinet at the pinnacle of the state administration. Its well-staffed corridors include a Staff Office for Foreign Affairs. The Foreign Minister feeds to this office – for the benefit of Chou and his staff – papers from his Ministry. Into the Staff Office also goes material from the 'international liaison' section of the Party Secretariat of the Chinese Communist party. This section may well be extremely important, especially for relations with Communist countries, but the visitor learns nothing about it.

The Ministry itself seems in some ways a very conventional place. You cannot altogether wonder that the zealots of 1966–7 considered it a 'bourgeois' island cut adrift from the seething Maoist mainland. Diplomatic procedures are much as in a European foreign ministry. There are ambassadors, and there are third secretaries; commercial counsellors and military attachés. Very few become ambassadors who have not been career diplomats for many years. Secret files exist. Zealots briefly challenged this practice in 1967, one crying out as he rifled the files on 13 May, 'What's so terrific about secrets? To hell with them.' Yet the attempt in the middle of the Cultural Revolution to transform the style of Chinese foreign policy in the end went little further than frills like what clothes to wear and how many courses to serve at diplomatic dinners.

One important change in organization did occur (beyond the cutting down in size). A Revolutionary Committee now runs the Ministry, and several sources style it a quite effective example of this new kind of organ. It is chaired by Chi P'eng-fei, top man among the Vice-Ministers, and Acting Foreign Minister. But the second and third figures in the Revolutionary Committee are not Vice-Ministers. They are People's Liberation Army men (Li Yao-wen, Ma Wen-po). At a banquet given late in June by the diplomatic corps, to thank the Ministry for the recent diplomatic tour of various provinces, it was made clear in the ways the Chinese make these things clear that Mr Li and Mr Ma ranked above Ch'iao Kuan-hua and other Vice-Ministers. So the army has found its way to the highest levels of the Foreign Ministry. What looks like genuine collective leadership has been set up in the Revolutionary Committee. It is quite different from the days when Ch'en Yi ran the Ministry with brusque authority. P.L.A. men and Vice-Ministers work things out together. The amiable and somewhat reticent Chi is no strong man. Having set this new pattern and found it good, China may not appoint a really strong successor to Ch'en Yi for some time.

Geographic groupings within the Ministry have altered interestingly over the years. The original tendency in 1949 to divide the world into 'socialist countries' and 'the rest' has totally gone. In those days one Vice-Minister, Wang Chia-hsiang, looked after the Communist bloc and another, Chang Han-fu, spanned everything else. Gone, too, is the inclusion of the Asian Communist states in the same department as the European Communist states. Later they formed a separate and important department of their own. Preferring to salute the future rather than reflect the present, Peking included the affairs of Laos and Cambodia with 'Asian Communist states'.

Since the Cultural Revolution brought a severe pruning of the Ministry, there is now a single department for 'Asia', Communist and non-Communist states together. The other geographic departments are West Asia and Africa (this starts west of Afghanistan); East Europe (including the U.S.S.R.); the West. This last department takes in not only the United States, but West Europe and Australia and New Zealand. But it has a quite powerful Deputy Director heading an America–Australasia sub-department (Mr Ling Ching) and another (Mr T'ang Hai-kuang) heading a West Europe sub-department. In addition to these geographic departments, the Foreign Ministry contains five functional departments: Information, Protocol, Personnel, Treaty and Legal, and General Affairs.

Outside Peking are officials who work in the 'foreign affairs section' of each province's Revolutionary Committee. These people, twenty or thirty strong in the provinces I visited, deferred on all non-local points to the Foreign Ministry people who travelled with me from Peking. They have no policy role, and concentrate on receiving foreign visitors with charm and informed conversation. One in Canton had dug up a fact about Australia that few Australians know. 'Oh, you are from Melbourne,' he remarked the morning he met me at the Canton train station. 'It is, of course, the former capital, in the days before Canberra was built.' There is little point in talking foreign affairs to most of these provincial foreign-affairs officials. They seem to specialize in what might be called the 'kangaroo' or 'fauna and flora' aspects of foreign lands. ('China has never had a Prime Minister drown in the sea, as your Prime Minister did in 1967.') But they can give the visitor data about their province.

Officially separate from the Foreign Ministry are a number of 'people's organizations' essential to the conduct of Chinese foreign policy. Their personnel circulate like satellites in the outer orbit of the Ministry. One of these bodies is the People's Institute for Foreign Affairs. It was for years a mysterious body until it surfaced last summer. It receives ex-statesmen, such as Clement Attlee in 1954 or the ex-President of Mexico some years later, and it receives people 'who are not governmental but too distinguished to come to China in an ordinary way.' Its former research function has in recent years been 'neglected'. Only a dozen people work full time at its offices now. Its directors are mostly former ambassadors or distinguished professors, many of them extremely able, most of them fairly old.

The Chairman of the Institute, Chang Hsi-jo, is a former Minister of Education and one of China's most prominent non-Party intellectuals. Chatting with him at banquets and receptions, I found myself in yesterday's spacious, languid world. The patrician head of well-groomed white hair, the silk clothes, the polished walking stick which he wields with authority, suggest an Oriental aristocrat from the pages of Somerset Maugham. Here is a man who participated in the 1911 revolution and went soon after to study in London, yet who is part of Mao's foreign-policy establishment in the post-Red Guard era. The elegance and cultivation are matched by a certain strength reserved for occasions of need. During the Hundred Flowers period in the spring of 1957, Professor Chang assailed the Chinese Communist party for having 'contempt for the past' and a 'blind belief in the future'. He is still capable of caustic comment on bureaucrats, and gentle irony about ideologists who talk as if they had history's agenda tucked in an inside pocket.

We discussed political science, which he studied at Columbia University and the London School of Economics, and taught for many years at Tsinghua and other leading Chinese universities. This meant neither the Thought of Mao nor computerized social science. In the warm Peking afternoon, banners of Mao's quotations above us, we talked about the ideas of Harold Laski, Graham Wallas, and A. L. Lowell! Required by the occasion one evening to allude to Australia, Professor Chang managed to recall two famous Australian tennis players he had once watched play in New York. It was 'people's diplomacy' of a casual and catholic kind. You could mistake Chang for a retired professor presiding over a lawn tennis association, rather than a retired professor presiding over Chinese Communist semi-official diplomacy.

Another finger on the hand of Chinese diplomacy is the Association for Friendship with Foreign Countries. It deals with notable foreigners who seem well-disposed toward China. I never found out where its offices are. Its leaders are like a heavenly host making appearances but having no known abode. You can sometimes get from them illuminating, informal explanations of Peking's foreign-policy line. Edgar Snow had given me a letter of introduction to an Association figure. One morning I got into a taxi at the Hsin Ch'iao Hotel to deliver it. The driver said he did not know where the offices of this body were. He went into the staff booth to inquire. Sitting in the taxi, I watched a series of consultations in the staff booth. Twenty minutes later a Luxingshe aide came out of the hotel and said I was wanted on the phone. It was the Foreign Ministry. Could I come immediately? Postponing the delivery of the letter, I drove instead to the Ministry. We had a 'business meeting' about my programme, none of it of an immediate character. Eventually the subject of Snow's letter of introduction to a leader of the Association was broached. Just what was this letter? I explained its harmless nature. 'We will deliver it for you.' So I handed it over. Three days later when the

Association figure gave a lunch for me at the Peking Hotel, a Foreign Ministry official was present throughout our four hours of conversation. Liaison between the Ministry and the Association is clearly close. Maybe the Ministry would like it to be even closer.

These semi-official agencies of the Chinese foreign-policy establishment – others include the Overseas Chinese Commission, the Friendship Associations between China and various nations, the Council for the Promotion of International Trade – are led by a fascinating array of able and experienced diplomats. You find they are finely tuned to the Foreign Ministry. Yet they have a flexibility which makes them better gatherers of information on the world, and better defenders of the Chinese position, than many diplomats in the formal structure of the Ministry.

Wang Kuo-chuan, ambassador to Poland in the mid-1960s, now does important work on Japan questions from a base in the China-Japan Friendship Association. Li Shu-teh, an economist on the Council for the Promotion of International Trade, played a key role in talks with Mr Whitlam about trade between China and Australia. When the Trade Minister had a session with Whitlam, he was accompanied by a deputy director of his Ministry, and by Mr Li. Similarly, in the session with the Foreign Minister there was present one senior Ministry aide and also one aide from the world of semi-official diplomacy: Ling Ching, head of American–Australian affairs in the Ministry, together with Chou Chiu-yeh, a former ambassador now prominent in the People's Institute of Foreign Affairs.

In short, the Chinese foreign-policy machine is like an orchestra of diverse instruments. Now a drum is used; now a violin for a mellow effect; now a flute to achieve a delicate and modest melody line; now a trumpet such as Radio Peking to sound the major theme in unmistakable fashion. The musicians are highly professional even when they are packaged as amateurs, and most of them have been at the job, with a change of instruments, for many years.

Of the training of new diplomats the visitor discovers little except that it is done not by a single method but by many. A few have a background in the Institute of International Relations of the Academy of Sciences. But this has been suspended since the Cultural Revolution. Its members have gone off to communes to exchange the care of nations for the care of pigs. The Foreign Language Institutes are an important source. They began the path back to regular work late in 1971 (with even more emphasis than before on Western tongues). There used to be an Institute of International Relations in Peking, which taught at the graduate-student level. But some of its former students (who include foreigners) told me that it no longer functions.

In the next few years, diplomats with an army training will emerge in China's embassies. Just how they are being trained is not known, but two interesting points surround the army's role in the foreign-policy corps. One is that a number of able men were sent into the army, some at Chou En-lai's own instigation, to 'hide' from the furies of the Cultural Revolution which might otherwise have cut them down. This is one more case of the Premier running the Cultural Revolution with his left hand while limiting its destructiveness with his right. It is also one more case of the army extending its role beyond military tasks. The result is that there are many diplomats (and other professionals) in the army who are not ordinary army men, but whose career patterns are now bound up with the army.

The second point can be put simply. Watch out for the navy and the air force. After Lin Piao took over Defence from the less 'Maoist' P'eng Teh-huai, the army swelled up with prestige as a 'model' and a 'school' for the whole nation. A little resentment stirred in the other two services. They felt that the colossal stress upon politics left the more professional and more technical aspects of military work enfeebled. The navy and the air force were the natural repositories of these neglected aspects. There was pressure to give more prominence than Lin Piao's policies had done to air and naval work and weapons. Already in the autumn of 1971, it became one of several issues surrounding the eclipse of Lin Piao, and accompanying changes in the relation of the army to politics.

In the leading universities, teaching of international relations was resumed in the autumn of 1970. One place I glimpsed it was Peking University. The seven subjects taught in the Department of International Politics are not designed to tease an idle imagination: Philosophy of Marxism; History of the C.C.P.; History of the International Communist Movement (starting with the First International); Anti-Imperialism (starting in 1945); Anti-Revisionism (from the Third International or 'Comintern'); National Liberation; Foreign Languages. Yet into these austere categories some teachers manage to fit interesting material.

Liu Shao-ch'i seems more famous since his fall than before it. Three of the courses (Anti-Imperialism and National Liberation as well as Anti-Revisionism) make him a prime target. The slogan for him is *san-ho i-shao* ('three reconciliations, one reduction'). He was, it is now said, on good terms with three enemies: reactionaries, revisionists, imperialists. He reduced support for glorious national liberation struggles. Some of the students from this department were doing their practical work on map-making at a Peking publishing house. Others were labouring on the construction of a new harbour near Tientsin.

I will not soon forget the teaching of the Korean War in Chinese schools. Few events are better known to Chinese students of society than this one. There is a double stress (beyond the themes of patriotism and Chinese–Korean solidarity). It was one episode in the long story of the United States trying to 'get at' China. Three paths to China's heartland, it is said, were mapped out by Washington: via Taiwan, Korea, and Vietnam. And over twenty-three years the U.S. has trodden each path. The second stress is upon Russian selfishness. It is not asserted, though it is hinted, that Moscow cooked the whole adventure up. At any rate, China had to bear the burden. Every gun and bullet China got from Russia she paid for at 'the highest prices'.

It is odd to hear the Korean War taught this way. You have heard American students taught that Russia and China, composing a 'monolithic Communist conspiracy', together hatched the whole thing. You have been told that the United States could never have wished to 'get at' China. Actually, the version I heard in Chinese schools is nearer the truth than that taught in the United States. China did *not* push North Korea into war. General Mac-Arthur *did* get at China – by the time Peking entered the war, he had bombed bridges touching Chinese territory.

But beyond the soundness of what was being taught, the seriousness of the tone in these classes on Korea was haunting. In Western classes, students take up this political topic or that, but how few topics really grip them. Fewer still if we think only of international politics. But these Chinese students talked about the Korean War with a clear and immediate sense of its connection to their own lives. A threat to China stirred in them deep personal feelings. If some will tomorrow be diplomats, the Chinese Foreign Ministry – whatever it may lack in experience of the world – will not lack conviction and purpose.

18 Foreign Residents in Peking

The diplomatic community in Peking is marked by irony and by a sense of brotherhood rare in the bitchy world of diplomacy. Irony because of a gap between repute and reality. The image: diplomats in Peking are intimate monitors of Chinese foreign policy, agog at each fresh twist of Middle Kingdom intrigue. The reality: diplomats in Peking often sit around and drink, and some are so cut off from the Chinese that they wonder if they mightn't be better off in Hong Kong. Brotherhood because this state of affairs binds the diplomats together in the furtive secret of their shared dilemma, and because Peking has few distractions, and diplomats are thrown relentlessly into each other's company.

I have caricatured, yet no one could deny a leisured manner and signs of boredom within the embassies of the Chinese capital. It is a delightful world for the scholar-diplomat, and ideal for those who like to bring up their children by paying much attention to them. There is no superfluity of paper to read. Much of what there is cannot be read by most ambassadors, for it is written in Chinese. In the summer, few chancelleries work after lunch. Parties begin early and end late. They are lavish because there is time to make them so. It comes as a shock to find Chinese servants of an older breed, schooled in deference and discretion before Liberation, when you walk off the street into certain European legations. A silver-haired, impassive butler clips cigars in the Dutch residence as he has been doing for decades. A waiter at the French Embassy walks with Gallic lightness (no resemblance to the Chinese shamble). He handles a capacious wine cellar with informed calm and the French language without disaster.

At embassy functions, there is a tendency for stories and rumours to bounce back repeatedly like ping-pong balls in a very small room. Yet the absence of 'news' has a good side. Long-range reflection germinates in those with a taste for it. Some ambassadors will stroll on their verandas, and talk very well about the larger trends concerning China and the world. If Peking is seldom a good place for an ambassador to report from, it is not a bad place for him to think in.

There is little travel outside Peking, for the Chinese government seldom permits it. This is one reason why diplomats envy the visitor. The only place they can go to automatically is the holiday town of Peitaiho. Well known to old China hands, it is on the coast east of Peking. Many ambassadors were lolling there in sun-baked peace when Kissinger came in and out of Peking in July. Diplomats do not go to and from their nation's consulates in other cities. For the only operating consulates I know of in this country of 800,000,000 people are a Polish and a Vietnamese consulate in Canton and a Nepalese consulate in Lhasa (Tibet). If a diplomat leaves Peking, he is likely bound either for Hong Kong or for his home capital.

Almost daily the Chinese Foreign Ministry issues a bulletin in English of 'News from Foreign Agencies and Press'. It is comprehensive, unbiased, unedited. Most of its material comes from wire services and newspapers of the West. The bulletin was unavailable during most of the Cultural Revolution. Only last June did it appear again for its select audience of diplomats and journalists (there is a Chinese version, similar but not identical, sent to high officials, and to lower officials who work with foreigners). Though the bulletin did not appear during the Cultural Revolution, it is clear from its numbering sequence that it never stopped production for any length of time. Moreover, inquiries revealed that at least the Albanians and Romanians continued to receive it. The Chinese version also kept coming out. This bulletin is extremely valuable to the foreigner in Peking. Of international news and commentary it has as much as any daily newspaper in the world.

There are really two diplomatic quarters in Peking. The old Legation Quarter lies just east of the Tien An Men square. Architecturally it is a hodge-podge of nineteenth-century European turrets and gargoyles and pillars. But it is picturesque and not without charm, and some of Peking's most splendid villas sit among its trees. In this area, only nations which are (or recently were) friendly toward China remain. The Burmese are in the former Belgian mission. Prince Sihanouk has the old French Embassy. The Romanians are busily here. The Hungarians occupy the superb mansion built in the days of colonial largesse by the Empire of Austria-Hungary.

The other diplomatic quarter is bland and remote. North-east of the city, it accommodates all the countries which recognized China substantially later than 1950, and all those which wished to put up new buildings. Not far away is a forest of new apartment blocks for Chinese workers. This section is almost like Manhattan, with its soaring heights and geometric regularity. On a summer evening you catch the smell of cooking, and the shouts of children playing. Older people sit and smoke, on chairs or *tatami* under carefully planted trees that line the streets.

But the new diplomatic area itself is flat and placid. Pink mimosas line the dusty yellow streets. A pale blue sky above fits the delicate and understated colour tones of the scene. Noise, too, is muted, and with virtually no traffic the cicadas have the airwaves all to themselves. P.L.A. soldiers guard each embassy gate without martial fuss. They will chat and laugh freely with a passer-by. The tensions of 1967 – when these streets rang with the sounds of demonstration and sometimes of battle – have totally gone.

Arriving a little early one evening for a British dinner, I stroll from gate to gate. The Pakistanis are out in the grounds of their vast brown monolith, playing badminton. They are in crisp white shirts hanging long outside dark trousers, and they talk at each other loudly and rapidly. In front of the Egyptian Embassy, Arabs clamber out of cars with bundles. The Finnish Embassy looks like a country cottage that has not been lived in with any vigour for some time.

At the British office the man on duty is a cockney for whom Peking seems to offer too few listeners. He keeps himself and others amused by offering commentaries on the B.B.C. news bulletin which is transcribed each afternoon. 'Learie Constantine is dead,' he begins with a long face. A whole bag of anecdotes tumble out about this West Indian cricket champion. As I leave him he does not stop: 'A great fast bowler, Constantine, one of the very greatest ...'

Many embassies contain one or two younger China specialists poring over documents. The Russian, French, and East German offices have quite a lot of them. These Sinologues do not often see responsible Chinese officials. Yet they pick things up from living in Peking with a knowledge of Chinese. They can sift the bookshops; they chat with people in the street. Ambassadors vary enormously from the brilliant to the bovine. Effectiveness depends on how Peking at any point of time regards their country, and what background and interest they have for the job. Peking is a post that can make a poor diplomat worse and a good one very good. If he is cut off from the country and the leadership, and cannot overcome this, he withers into a clerk. If he can get an angle on events in this vast nation, and a foot in the door with officials, the challenges to mind and spirit (and digestion) are limitless.

Observing the foreign policies of China from a Peking chancellery is quite different from reading Chinese foreign policy documents in Washington or Paris or Hong

Kong. First, you realize that China's political language loses point and freshness on the printed English page. Breathing the air of China, where the cryptic, earthy Chinese language has constant spoken life, and where you hear political language as debate and exchange as well as read it as pontification, the whole effect seems more serious and lively.

Second, you are better placed to see that the practice of Chinese foreign policy is not a mechanical reflection of its theory. In Hong Kong you have the ideological documents, and you have the reports of what Peking actually does. Relating the two is not always easy. In Peking you may discern the 'middle ground' – those sinews of reason and judgement which link ideology with day-to-day decision. Third, the diplomat in the Chinese capital can supplement public statements with private talks. This is the crucial superiority of Peking as a vantage point. For it is in these talks that the thought processes of the Chinese reach the non-Chinese world.

The printed page cannot ask a question, yet the questions Chinese officials ask tell as much as the answers they give. I found this true in the weeks preceding Kissinger's July visit to China. One ambassador furnished me with a recent instance of his own.

He had just been talking with a department deputy director at the Foreign Ministry. Persistently the Chinese officials questioned him about the office of Secretary-General at the U.N. Who were the candidates to replace U Thant? What of the so-called troika system? Meanwhile, it became quite clear not only that the Chinese are interested in all current details about the office, but that they scorn any 'troika' arrangement and favour a 'strong' office with power to act quickly and effectively.

Ambassadors at Peking generally praise the competence of the Chinese Foreign Ministry. A Scandinavian ambassador about to return after four and a half years in his post looked back: 'Going to the Foreign Ministry here has been just the same as going to the Quai d'Orsay.

The level of knowledge is similar. You have the same kind of free, frank exchange about world affairs. Of course, it's not as close as when we talk to Washington or London – for with these two my country has a special tie. But it's about like talking with the French.'

Sometimes – I am not referring to the Scandinavian – there is effusive praise that rings a little oddly. It is streaked with condescension, as if the foreigner did not expect anything but a sub-European level of competence from the Chinese, and over-reacts when he is surprised.

In the areas I could observe, the Chinese seem as well-informed as the foreign ministries of medium-rank nations. But their political shrewdness, their sense of the volatile nature of power, is outstanding. Often they get hold of angles quite absent in Western thinking. You could not find cooler practitioners of the science of power anywhere. This does not mean they have shrunk back from revolutionary aims and values. It is just that they are clear-headed about the distinction between means and ends. And – an even more important point – they have relatively few illusions about themselves.

How the mountain looks, of course, depends on what path you approach it by. Some ambassadors have excellent access to the Chinese leadership. Others are like fish upon the sand. Here are three cases:

France. Étienne Manac'h is perhaps the outstanding ambassador in Peking today. This stems both from the cordial Paris–Peking relationship and from Manac'h's acuteness and long background in Asian affairs. A precise, modest man, he has long been a socialist. Enjoying a good relationship with de Gaulle, he was chosen personally by the General for the Peking Embassy. Trade between France and China did not leap after diplomatic ties were set up in 1964, though many Frenchmen expected it would. Indeed, it is smaller than Chinese trade with West Germany, which has no diplomatic relations with Peking. In 1970, for instance, total French–Chinese trade turnover was $151 million. Total West German–Chinese trade turnover was $253 million.

But there is a similar way of thinking about 'independence' and 'super-powers' in Peking and Paris. Both are sticklers for 'national sovereignty'. Both suspect that Russia and America would like to divide and order the world on their own terms. Both lack a little bit in power what they think they have in status. Both berate super-powers. Yet this prevents neither from thinking of itself as a *super-civilization*. These modes France and China share.

France is busy as intermediary between Peking and certain hesitant nations. Thus, during 1971, China and Thailand nibbled at each other through the grille of French diplomacy. Paris has been China's major diplomatic base in Europe and a site for wider activities. New agreements to establish relations – such as that with Turkey last summer – have been hammered out in Paris.

Manac'h sees the Chinese leadership regularly. More than once Chou En-lai, inveterate night owl that he is, has drawn Manac'h aside after a reception and started (at midnight) a two- or three-hour chat in a side room in the Great Hall of the People. The Frenchman sees Chairman Mao from time to time. He has found Mao an eager student of French history: fascinated by Napoleon and the Paris Commune, avid for details on the siege of Toulouse, impressed by de Gaulle.

The Chinese statesman, it seems, admired both de Gaulle's realism about the world of nations and his poised style and tendency to take a lofty view of politics. (The visitor to China often hears praise of de Gaulle. Chou En-lai invoked him – in scorn of S.E.A.T.O. – when debating with Mr Whitlam. Officials more than once drew to my attention the fact that Mao took the unusual step of sending a message on the death of a foreign leader when de Gaulle died in 1970.)

Laos is an opposite case. Not because Laos is unimportant to China. But China supports the Pathet Lao, which is in rebellion against the Vientiane government that is represented in Peking. So Kienthong Keorajvong-say, the polite and stoic Laotian chargé, in his neat villa on a quiet street of the new diplomatic quarter, is truly a fish upon the sand. He might as well be on the planet Mars. It is a minor miracle, of course, that Vientiane has a diplomat in Peking at all. Mr Kienthong watches the Pathet Lao leaders trip to Peking for talks with Chou and Huang Yung-sheng (Chief of the General Staff). Yet he himself from one year's end to the next sees no one higher than a desk officer at the Foreign Ministry. No one in his tranquil little embassy speaks or reads Chinese.

This charming man knows in full measure what Chinese aloofness can be like. All he can do is talk with other foreigners and make detached social observations. 'How hard the Chinese work,' he said with a certain awe as we sipped a morning cognac. 'Not like Laotians.' He gestured outside to the street where P.L.A. men were on duty. 'You don't see them drinking as they work. They eat frugally. They come home from a meeting, and you ask them what happened. They tell you not a word. In Laos people will chat about it: this man was criticized, that man was amusing. But here the discipline is so strong. Oh, no, not like Laos at all ...' He took more cognac, and said I really ought to visit Laos some time.

Britain. John Bull is something else again. He is not stranded like the Laotian, but he does not enjoy Manac'h's entrée. Britain was one of the first countries to recognize the Chinese Communist government (January 1950). But, in their usual manner, the British did not make a clean sweep of things; they tried to have a shilling each way. They kept a consulate on Taiwan (accredited not to the Republic of China but to the provincial government of Taiwan, which Chiang Kai-shek pretends has a separate life of its own). London also supported (until 1971) America's 'important question' resolution in the U.N., a procedural device to make it more difficult than it would otherwise have been for Peking to take its seat.

These two points China has held against Britain. For twenty-one years Peking declined to exchange ambassadors with London. Each country had in the other only a chargé d'affaires office, not an embassy. In Peking, the Chinese maintained the distinction fastidiously. Even the taximen are schooled. If in haste you ask to go to 'the British Embassy', they correct you and say they are prepared to take you to 'the British chargé's office'.

Before ambassadors were exchanged late in 1971, the British had an able staff of a dozen or so in Peking – a lot smaller than the French. Face red and suit white, the chargé, John Denson, looked a colonial type but was not. He purred with pleasure that relations between the two countries had been improving ever since he crossed the bridge at Lo Wu in 1969. The dark days of 1967, when the British office was burned and its staff imperilled, are altogether gone. London abandoned the 'important question' device at the U.N. in 1971. It overcame Conservative party hesitations and made the decision to remove the offending consulate from Taiwan. Even if trade with Taiwan suffers, the loss cannot be great. Britain's trade with China is worth some ten times its trade with Taiwan. A Chinese order for six Trident aircraft nicely boosted the late 1971 trading lists.

Meanwhile, sweetness and light prevail in Hong Kong. Dealings between the Hong Kong government and Chinese Communists in the colony and in Canton have been smooth, at least since the attempted hijacking to China of a Philippines plane in March 1971. A senior British official in Hong Kong recalled: 'The Chinese hate hijacking. They're totally against it. When the Filipino incident occurred, an official at our Hong Kong airport just picked up the phone and called White Cloud Airport in Canton. Immediately, matters were fixed up. The Canton people gave the details: how much fuel, how many passengers, what time the plane would take off. Very businesslike; no problems; no politics.'

The British in Peking do not enjoy easy access to the

Chinese leadership. Until Denson saw Chou En-lai during 1971, there had been very little access at all. But they feel the trend is upward. With a new ambassador to China arriving every couple of weeks, the British frankly confess that they do not want to be left paddling in the shallows as the new diplomatic wave surges upward. However, the Chinese are not giving the British an easy road, and since the summer of 1971 a new obstacle has loomed large: London's insistence that the status of Taiwan remain 'undetermined'. Peking says the British wish to retain this formula as a basis – should future developments make it convenient – to recognize an independent Taiwan. So the feud still simmers, despite the resolution of the U.N. issue and London's readiness to remove its consulate from Taiwan.

A few score foreigners other than diplomats live in Peking. Of various nationalities – including American – they have thrown in their lot with China. Some work on China's foreign-language publications (scattering idioms like 'jackals of the same lair' through the pages of *Peking Review*). Others who are especially well regarded, such as the American Saul Adler, work in the 'international liaison' section of the C.C.P. A few, of whom the New Zealander Rewi Alley is the most notable, work as independent writers and publicists. They have been called '300-per-centers' because of their fulsome support for Peking's policies.

These ardent exiles are often marvellously well informed about China. They are helped by wider travel possibilities than are open to visitors not committed to the Chinese government or the Chinese line. Rewi Alley made my mouth water with details of his visits to Sinkiang, Hainan Island, and Tibet. These are three of China's most sensitive spots. Sinkiang because of problems on the border with the U.S.S.R., Hainan Island because it is so close to the Vietnam war, Tibet because of smouldering social and political tensions.

At the same time there can be a stiffness about these

'300-per-centers'. A poignant paradox attends their 'pro-Chinese' stance. Their eager orthodoxy sometimes hides an alienation from the sheer 'Chineseness' of the life they have chosen to share. The result is occasionally a brittleness from which disillusionment is not far removed.

In the Cultural Revolution a number of '300-per-centers' fell from grace with a bang. Sidney Rittenberg and his wife (an American couple) were among several who backed 'ultra-leftism' with a vigour that betrayed a touch of insecurity. The Rittenbergs worked zealously in the May 16 organization which is now so much under attack. They sought to be as Maoist as the Maoists. In the process they misjudged the nuances of the situation. They became more Maoist than the Maoists, and got into trouble. Many others did the same and have now left China. At the border, the luggage of '300-per-centers' was often closely searched by Chinese officials. This proved disastrous for one man who was not only taking *ta tzu pao* (wall posters) out of China illegally, but had actually secreted them behind a framed portrait of Mao! He was detained for more than a year before finally being allowed to leave China.

Among those who remain, the Cultural Revolution has cast a shadow hard to dodge. I went to see Rewi Alley in his apartment in the Peace Committee Compound. The enormous high-ceilinged rooms are shabby but comfortable in the nineteenth-century manner. Vast couches, embroidered cushions, bits of old China, and a silent old Manchu servant recall an earlier era. Shelves are stuffed with books in Chinese and English. Manuscripts are piled here and there (Alley has written far more than he has published). He shows me a photo of his friend Lu Hsun. It is the last photo ever taken of the writer, at an exhibition from which he went home and died. Downstairs used to be the apartment of Anna Louise Strong, the American journalist who died in 1970. Alley used to eat dinner with her and misses her bubbling talk. Now she is gone he is in a way the dean of the '300-per-centers'.

Alley has lived in China for the past forty-five years. He knows physical China like the palm of his hand. But his craggy looks and dry voice and the gentle irony of his style place him as a New Zealander. His Chinese is perfect and he loves China. Yet he seems to feel his separateness from the Chinese more than before. He is sharp on ultra-leftism. I mentioned I was going next day to Peking University. 'I haven't been out there for quite a while,' he said quietly, 'not since they were killing each other with spears.' Of recent creative writing in China he was critical. 'They have just sent me some poems to translate.' He screwed up his face. 'But they are untranslatable – just a string of slogans.' One more disappointing fruit of ultra-leftism. A boy comes in with the mail which includes *Time*, *Newsweek*, and the *Economist*. 'I have a secretary now,' Alley remarks with a very faint smile. 'During the fiery years [the Cultural Revolution] I had a guard instead.'

Rewi Alley had an explanation for ultra-leftism. 'You notice they were mostly from middle-class families. Yao Teng-shan (the "Red Diplomat") was a product of a mission school. ["X" and "Y"] who were so mixed up with May 16, are from a New Zealand family with big financial connections.' He also saw an element of the generation gap in the Cultural Revolution. 'Many cadres were summarily pushed out by inexperienced youth who didn't know what the revolution was about.' Then he added, not without a trace of satisfaction, 'Now it seems the old cadres are coming back from the correctional schools, and young ultra-leftists are going in their place.'

The New Zealander saw things in the cities during 1966–8 which he did not like. But he said – and he knows the countryside well – that work on the communes was not interrupted by the goings-on. 'The Chinese peasant got used to working through flood and famine and war. He worked through the Cultural Revolution too.' For his part, Alley goes on reporting the life and struggles and achievements of the Chinese. 'I do not try to pontificate any more.' He is gazing into the distance. 'I just write what I see. There are others to pontificate.' If he is still an alien in an unfathomable land, Alley is also one of the very few true China hands.

19　How Do the Chinese See the World?

What in the world does China want? How do the Chinese see the rest of the nations with which their own destiny is now intertwined? With China more than with most countries, what she *is* and how she *understands herself* weigh as much as what she explicitly *seeks*. A visit puts a light on some territory behind China's approach to the world. It is four shades of this subsoil of Peking's foreign policy that I sift in the following pages.

1. Sense of place

Stray from Peking and the gateway cities of Canton and Shanghai, and it is easy to forget that the world beyond China exists. You meet no foreigners, see no foreign products, hear little foreign news. You observe in the Chinese mentality such a strong 'sense of place' that China seems by nature isolationist. A Chinese word for landscape is made up of two characters meaning 'mountains' and 'waters'. One day in Yenan, I recalled with amusement a phrase used to me at the U.S. State Department in 1966: 'the China that exists on the mainland'! (And where are the others?) Of no country on earth could it be more absurd to separate the *location* from the *essence of the nation*. There is nothing abstract about China's view of itself (as perhaps there was of Gaullist France's view of itself).

It is not only that the Chinese have dwelt for four thousand years amidst these incomparable mountains and rivers. The rounded mountains and yellow rivers *are* China, the soil and the nation are almost one. In Chinese literature you find natural features given personalities. So it is said that, when Mao sent his telegram to Yenan in 1949, 'even the mountains and rivers rejoiced' to receive it. Chinese towns and provinces are often geographically named. Hunan, Mao's province, means 'south of the lake'. Yunnan, the hilly province near Vietnam, means 'south of the clouds'. Peking translates as 'northern capital', Shanghai as 'to the sea'. China seldom names towns after a great man (as Washington, San Francisco). Or after a place in another country (as New York).

In China's heartland, the cliché of China as 'Middle Kingdom' (which is the literal translation of the Chinese word for 'China') does not seem absurd. Here is a superior people, you reflect, but whose sense of their superiority is rooted in contentment with their own mountains and rivers. Not an active sense of superiority which pants to convert the world to its excellence. A passive sense of superiority, which basks, inward-turned, within its own possessed excellence.

At a banquet given for Mr Whitlam, the head of the Institute for Foreign Affairs, Chang Hsi-jo, spoke about relations between China and Australia. Despite the 'vast oceans that separate us', Chang pointed out, there is a 'tradition of rich contacts'. He illustrated the tradition, mentioning sportsmen, scientists, writers, and others. But he spoke only of Australians who have gone to China. Not a single example did he give of a Chinese visiting Australia. I don't think this lop-sidedness was mere chance. Professor Chang was expressing a widespread Chinese attitude when he spoke of relations between China and another country in terms only of the foreigners coming *to* China. The Middle Kingdom receives; less often does it stir itself to send. And when it does send, it is not often with any high sense of mission or expectation, but with entirely practical goals in mind.

Of course, a nation's foreign policy is a stew of many morsels. It refracts much more than cultural attitudes. Yet this 'sense of place' deeply affects every Chinese's view

of the world. It underlies China's lack of interest in con-
quering, subverting, or even understanding other countries. True, Marxism has brought to one level of the
Chinese official mind a global sense and global concerns.
Communism has 'internationalized' China to a degree. No
less true, there is in China today an impulse to 'catch up'
with advanced countries. Many factories display a poignant quotation from Mao: 'The Chinese people have will
and ability. In the not-too-distant future they will certainly catch up and surpass advanced world levels.' Yet
my abiding impression is of cultural self-confidence, out-
weighing national insecurity.

The Chinese are a rooted and a continental people
(they have emigrated only when their own country was
in chaos). Their cultural memories run the length of the
dynasties. They possess effortless assurance of their own
cultural identity. This does not negate the fact that
Peking sees the world through the spectacles of Communist ideology. But something in the Chinese way damps
down the lust and swagger of Marxism. The Chinese
frequently take a long view of things. Dwelling amidst
the mountains and waters of ancestors ten times as ancient
as the Pilgrim Fathers has given the Chinese a patience of
the ages. They do not, in fact, go around the world lighting fires of revolution, for they are genuinely sceptical
that one nation can ignite another. And they believe in
their hearts that few others, if any, can follow the epic
Chinese way to revolution and socialism.

Most Americans would be surprised, I believe, by the
tranquil confidence of China today. It is not a restless
nation keen to prove itself in ambitious world-wide
schemes. A fundamental contentment springs from cultural security. China seems less dismayed than amused
that the chief of super-powers should fear them. Most
Chinese do not *care* enough about the world to want to
uplift others. Nor did they fret terribly when other
nations kept China from its seat at the U.N. They are
secure and content in their habitation.

I watch lovers strolling around the Monument to the People's Heroes in Peking at sunset. Little boys pissing peacefully under a tree of the Tien An Men Square, then mounting the solemn stone lions beside the Forbidden City to play at riding and hunting. P.L.A. men during a lunchtime break at Sian, talking with nostalgia and absorption of their home counties: what they eat there, how the accent varies, who the local folk heroes from antiquity are. Students in Canton, reading *Dream of the Red Chamber* under a tree, asking me not about Australia but about the way of life of Chinese in Australia. These people, it seemed to me, are not missionaries to the world but gardeners of their own heritage.

2. Independence

Five roots sit under China's insistence on complete independence (and associated principles such as 'self-reliance').

First, the cultural particularity which I have illustrated by the deep Chinese 'sense of place'.

Second, the simple geographic fact that China is a continental nation cut off by sea or mountains from other major world centres. Except for receiving Buddhism from India, China drew little on other cultures. It had no experience of allying with a second nation in order to counter a third nation. China's isolation was its independence.

Third, China's buffeting by foreign powers since the Opium War has made it acutely sensitive to any pressures which- qualify its total independence. Having known dependence so recently, China is daily conscious of the quality of the air of independence it now breathes.

Fourth, the Chinese Communist party did not win power in China by following Soviet models or by virtue of Soviet help but by turning inward to tap China's own resources of sinew, mind, and will. In the Chinese Communist party's experience, the evening cup of alliance turned sour by morning. The Chinese made their revolution by self-reliance. The experience has convinced them that no one – not even China – can make another nation's revolution for it.

Fifth, the aggravating presence of two super-powers makes it natural for Peking to stand up for the principle of independence. Super-power hegemony threatens independence, whether it is the Russians in Eastern Europe or the Americans in Central America. China is incommoded by the 'blocs' orchestrated by each super-power. It is the card of independence that it can best play amidst the power realities of today's world. Independence is the logical banner for a self-respecting major power which has no bloc of its own and could only be 'number two' in another bloc.

Always I found the principle of independence echoing in foreign policy talks with Chinese. It accounts for their sensitivity to the pretensions of super-powers. It is the basis of their intimacy with Rumania and France. It justifies (to themselves) support for Pakistan. They were against any sympathy for Bangladesh which implied questioning of the Pakistan government's right to run its own affairs. Chou En-lai gave the principle of independence extraordinary stress. 'Why is it,' he asked, 'that there is a lack of any ability in the Eastern part of Europe?' Politicians rarely say such astonishing things in public. For his gasping listeners, the Premier supplied an answer. Because the biggest country there [in Eastern Europe] wants to control the others.' It was a lavish assertion of the fruits of independence (and the costs of dependence) in the husbandry of nations.

During the same conversation, Mr Chou underlined that China likes to pay debts promptly and owes nothing to anybody. He referred to the painful period in 1960 when the U.S.S.R. suddenly took back all its aid and its experts. 'But in those years of our greatest difficulty we paid back all our debts to the Soviet Union.' The Premier was not finished with the theme. He recalled how China has always paid quickly and in cash for Australian wheat. He inquired with a broad smile and a gesture of both hands, 'Do we still owe you anything?' Mr Whitlam shot back with an allusion to the lack of a wheat order from China, 'I wish you did.' Mr Chou laughed. The Foreign Trade Minister smiled faintly. Chou En-lai wanted us to understand that China is beholden to nobody.

Chinese military strategy likewise enshrines the principle of independence. 'People's war' – one of Mao's central notions – is a formula for a nation standing alone. Not allies but 'the people' play the decisive role. The enemy is lured in deep. He is invited to over-extend himself. Then he is met by a people's struggle. By definition, it can be mounted only by the inhabitants of the territory which is resisting.

Perhaps if China had had allies in the 1930s, 'people's war' would never have entered Chinese Communist party military theory. But China did not. Neither Britain, the United States, Russia, nor yet the League of Nations was prepared to help China stop Japan at a time when Japan could have been stopped. So the Chinese Communist party – which did a lot of the fighting in China's Anti-Japanese War – had no choice but to turn inwards to the resourcefulness of the Chinese people. Mao said the soldiers of the Red Armies were 'fish' depending entirely on the peasant masses of China, who were 'water'.

The same ideas prevailed in the military controversies of the 1960s. This time the threat came not from Japan but from the United States. How to resist a possible attack? Some military professionals took a conventional view. Rely on Russia and its advanced weapons. Go outside China if necessary (perhaps into Vietnam) to stop the enemy before he gets to China.

Mao took a different view. Rely on nothing else but the Chinese people. Prepare them politically. That is more important than lining up allies and fancy weapons. Wait for the enemy. Lure him in. Go onto the 'strategic defensive' at first; then when the enemy gets bogged down, seize the moment to go over to the 'counter-offensive'. Get your arms the way the P.L.A. has always got its arms: from the enemy. Mao won this debate over how to fight a war. His theories are complex and I have done them no justice. But the heart of them is 'people's war' based on *self-reliance* in order to preserve *independence*.

Mao supports his military ideas by citing ancient Chinese strategists, including Sun Tzu who wrote a treatise, *The Art of War*, some 2,500 years ago. To the lay eye, 'flexibility' is the keynote of Chinese military tradition. To maintain flexibility, to keep the initiative in your own hands, you must hold on to your independence. In 1928, Mao set down a formula which is close to Sun Tzu: 'The enemy advances, we retreat; the enemy camps, we harass; the enemy tires, we attack; the enemy retreats, we pursue.' It is the motto of an army that puts 'mind' over 'mechanization'. Of an army which knows itself weaker than the enemy at the start of the struggle. An army patient and steady-nerved enough to turn aside at times from confrontation, wait for a mistake by the enemy, then spring back selectively at a moment of its own choosing.

Above all, it is the motto of an army which can switch and turn because it keeps in its hands full independence of action. The Chinese *think* this way about war and diplomacy because they have always had to *act* this way. It is a method of coping with weakness. Independence, and the stratagems that fit with it, have often been the only strength the Chinese Communist party had in the face of a superior foe.

3. Unlike the Russians, the Chinese reject 'bloc thinking'

The point touches both Chinese insistence on independence and the Chinese view of power's fluidity. One terrible error about China from the 1930s to the 1960s was
the view of the C.C.P. as a mere appendage of Bolshevism.
Shrewd men (George Kennan; numerous U.S. diplomats
in China) saw from the start that the Sino–Soviet tie was
not tight or enduring. Among many reasons for this are
the divergent ways of thinking in Moscow and Peking
about the relation between communism and the nation-
state. Through the 1960s, the divergence grew. In the two
Communist giants' attitudes towards Prince Sihanouk
of Cambodia after his fall in March 1970 it is displayed
in a pure form.

Moscow thinks – Stalin taught it how to – in terms of
a Communist bloc. The land of the October Revolution
naturally heads the bloc. National sovereignty within the
bloc is not total (as Prague recalls). Should one lamb in
the flock stray from the proper path of socialism, the shepherd has the right to reach into his life and set him right.
It is all-important to Moscow whether a nation is inside
or outside the bloc. In Indo-China, to choose an instance,
only Hanoi really counts to the Russians. Hanoi is
(Moscow hopes) part of the bloc. Everything in Soviet–
Vietnamese relations follows from that. The rest of Indo-
China seems to be viewed from the Kremlin mainly by
the yardstick of its 'Leninist potential'.

While I was in Peking, President Ceausescu of Rom-
ania visited China, and the fury of the Russians at his
flirting with the Chinese was richly evident. Moscow
reproaches Ceausescu with not being a loyal member of
the 'socialist camp'. The Romanians actually stand between the Russians and the Chinese in their attitude to
the socialist camp. They accept a notion of a 'bloc' (which
China no longer does), but they insist on the complete

independence and sovereignty of each country within the bloc (which Russia no longer permits).

The Chinese are altogether more flexible. They reject 'bloc thinking'. First, it does not fit in with independence. Second, it tends to go against China's experience that socialism can only be won from within a nation. Third, Mao has a view of power too volatile to be accommodated by 'bloc thinking'.

Mao scandalizes the Russians by asserting that even a bloc has 'contradictions'. The Leninist fold may be divided against itself. One of its members may be 'chauvinist' and seek 'hegemony' over the rest. It comes as no surprise that Peking tosses around the term 'super-power'. In no sense is it a Marxist term. It describes not a class reality but a power reality. The Chinese have started no Comintern of their own. It is by no means only Communist parties which interest them. So we confront a paradox. The Chinese are more rigid about national sovereignty than bloc-thinking allows. Yet they have a more flexible notion of power than bloc-thinking permits.

On this visit to China, I heard several echoes of how the experience of the Korean War soured China's view of the 'bloc' (and the Sino–Soviet tie generally). It seems that the Chinese group at the Twenty-second Congress of the Communist party of the U.S.S.R., in 1961, had some disagreement within it about how far China should commit itself in Vietnam. Under Russian pressure – Moscow derided the idea of any socialist country 'going it alone' – certain Chinese (maybe P'eng Chen among them) were ready to commit China further than Mao Tse-tung wished. (Chou En-lai flew back to Peking early, leaving P'eng Chen in charge at the Congress.) Mao stated: 'We don't want another Korean War!' He feared that he might again be led into a war situation created by Moscow, and then have to do the fighting himself. He apparently suspected that Moscow might 'do another Korea' on China, in the case of Vietnam and adjacent areas. According to my sources, the phrase 'We don't want another Korean War' surfaced again in 1965. Mao used it against Liu Shao-ch'i and Lo Jui-ch'ing, who were both ready for bolder action in support of Vietnam than Mao was. The Korean War, it seems, may have taught Mao a bitter lesson about the open-ended commitments which entanglement in a 'bloc' can entail.

Today, the key unit of Chinese thinking about strategy in the world is not the *bloc* but the *united front*. What is the difference? The bloc is a phalanx of the faithful. The united front is a loose partnership set up for a specific task. The partners do not come together out of agreement on socialism. Partners change as circumstances change. A new target calls for new partners. So in the 1930s when Japan became the chief target, the Chinese Communist party linked arms with the Kuomintang, which had in recent years been steadily murdering C.C.P. forces. No less suddenly, a power shift may render today's partner unnecessary for tomorrow's struggle. He is tossed aside like a used Kleenex. This is the Chinese way of politics. They can be tough as a pine or as bending as a willow. But they simply do not think in terms of blocs.

Why has Peking embraced Sihanouk while Moscow continues to recognize the Lon Nol régime? Here the difference between the two capitals over bloc thinking is illustrated. Chou En-lai spoke a lot of this 'extraordinary man' Sihanouk. 'A Prince, a Buddhist, a pacifist,' he remarked to us, 'has now become a fighter against American imperialism.' It seemed less than vital to the Premier that Sihanouk is not Marxist. Crucial was the Cambodian's membership in the united front against the United States.

One of Mao's maxims runs: 'Learn to play the piano.' In playing the piano, all ten fingers should be used to get maximum effect. But not all at once. The art is to use the right finger for the right task: to have a wide range; to be flexible in utilizing the range. Sihanouk is one of those ten fingers. He is not suitable for all purposes, but for some purposes he is ideal.

The Russians are more rigid. They do not trust Sihanouk, and have given him no support (though Kosygin remarked to the Prince when he [Sihanouk] reached Moscow Airport from Paris just after the coup against him: 'We will support you to the end'). Sihanouk explained the Soviet attitude to me. 'Their chief concern is their particular brand of Communism. One reason they stay in Phnom Penh is to propagandize among young Cambodians for anti-Maoist Communism. The same with the East Germans. They have mounted a vast effort to educate Cambodians in revisionism.' Sihanouk was not Moscow's kind of socialist, so they dropped him.

The Chinese were more supple. Their view of the flux of power in Indo-China is not bound in a straitjacket of ideology. The Chinese never use the term 'Maoism'. They never refer – except in embarrassed caricature – to 'Maoists' outside China. Sihanouk made this point at length. It is plain to any visitor to China or reader of China's press. Peking refers a lot to foreign 'friends of China', but never to foreign 'Maoists'.

Here they have stepped out of Communist tradition. Moscow is proud to point to 'Leninists' in foreign lands. But the Chinese – I feel – do not really believe in 'international ideology'. Sihanouk is weighed on another scale entirely. He is part of the united front against Washington. He is a welcome barrier to any ambitions Hanoi may cherish for a Cambodia made in Vietnam's image. (Chou En-lai remarked to a European ambassador while I was in Peking, 'We do not want to see any one country of Indo-China dominate the others.') These are notions within reach of Lenin but within even closer reach of the ancient strategist Sun Tzu.

James Reston wondered why Chou En-lai, when speaking of Soviet policies toward China, used the word 'lasso'. A story around Peking during July 1971 gives an answer. Mr Chou himself recounted the story to a French visitor. In a herd of Mongolian horses, when the leader bolts, the herdsman has but one recourse. He must lasso the leading horse. Otherwise he will lose his herd forever. The Premier likened the herdsman to the Soviet Union. It fears for its herd. China has bolted away, and many 'horses' go with her. Moscow sees only one recourse. *It tries to lasso China.* Chou En-lai laughed for his French visitor and quipped: 'But the Chinese horse is still bolting!' China will not be lassoed. And she continues to disrupt the tidy 'herd', which is Russia's best vision of the world of nations.

4. The Chinese have not abandoned their Communist theory, but Realpolitik is built into the very heart of Chinese Communist theory

Am I trying to suggest the Chinese leaders are Bismarckian pragmatists? No, they are Communists. They believe capitalism is in decline, that the world will one day be Communist. They take their theory of the world as seriously as any government does. Cadres in China believe as much in the Thought of Mao as lawyers in the United States believe in the American Constitution. But what is often missed is that Mao's theory is no armchair speculation. It is distilled from practice. 'If you want to know the taste of a pear,' wrote Mao in *On Practice*, 'you must change the pear by eating it yourself ... All genuine knowledge originates in direct experience.'

And what has the Chinese experience been? It consists among other things of two broad yet vital ingredients: Chinese cultural history, and China's collapse before the impact of the West after 1840. From both sources an apparent pragmatism has entered Chinese Communism. Fifty years in the land of Confucius has stripped Marxism in China of the vaporous clouds of German metaphysics. As for one hundred years of pressure from superior outside forces, it has mercilessly confronted China with the fact of her own weakness. She has had to learn how to 'pit one against ten' and still win. This has led her to stitch many a practical patch on the splendid but unserviceable garment of Marxism.

Consider the two basic Maoist ideas of 'contradiction' and 'united front'. Mao's method of analysis is, first, to identify the principal contradiction in a situation. After 1937 it was between China and Japan. Today it is between the revolutionary peoples of the world and U.S. imperialism. Then Mao builds a united front against the target. You 'unite with all whom you can unite with.' We see that pure power considerations are intrinsic to united-front thinking. Get with you whomever you can get! After 1937 Mao was even prepared to go into a united front with Chiang Kai-shek.

But there comes a fresh stage. You go over to the offensive. Press for your goals in sharper form. Mao has a theory for this transition. Each contradiction, he submits, has a principal aspect (the stronger side) and a non-principal aspect (the weaker side). When do the scales tip? When does the non-principal aspect of a contradiction turn into the principal aspect? Mao puts it simply. When the 'overall balance of forces' alters. *When we become stronger than the enemy*. Then one can be more choosy about allies, no longer having to link up with just anyone.

Again, power factors are found at the heart of Chinese strategy. 'Contradiction' and 'united front' are sacred vessels in the church of Chinese Communist theory. But the way they work is prosaic. The oil in the vessels is no holier than that in any other vessels of political theory. It is power. Considerations of power are not exactly in *tension* with considerations of ideology. They are the operative means of getting to the ideology's goals.

So it is not 'un-Maoist' (whatever else it may be) for China to ally with Pakistan. Pakistan is an ideal member of the united front that Peking maintains against several adversaries. It is neither 'un-Maoist' nor inconsistent to let Britain keep Hong Kong while loudly protesting U.S. occupation of Taiwan. The United States, not Britain, is

China's main target. Certainly Peking wants Hong Kong back. But there is no hurry. Toothless Britain presents small challenge to the emerging future Mao sees over history's horizon. Meanwhile, letting Hong Kong stay in British hands brings Peking some £250 million a year in foreign currency.

Taiwan is another kettle of fish. Peking makes it a number one issue, not just because it wants Taiwan back, but because the issue of Taiwan has involved a U.S. military challenge to China. To be sure, national emotions stir over Taiwan. But that does not explain Peking's stress upon it. The Chinese are always patient when there is no reason to be impatient. It was as the United States step by step installed itself on the island that Peking step by step elevated the Taiwan issue to top priority.

So China's policies toward these two lost bits of her territory – Hong Kong and Taiwan – are not a case of random *ad hoc* pragmatism. The methods bend like a bamboo. Transcending methods, however, fixed and firm as a pine, is the Chinese Communist vision of tomorrow's world and China's role in it.

I am not discounting ideology or Peking's belief in its ideology. The issue is more oblique. How does ideology sway day-to-day practice? And here one more point arises. *Realpolitik* is not a science like physics. Its practice rests on how you first see the conditions around you. The perceptions of the crudest pragmatist are filtered through a honeycomb of prejudices. It is *as Marxists* that the Chinese leaders weigh and reason about international affairs.

They study a situation. What they see is not separable from the Marxist spectacles through which they peer. Take the Ceylon rebellion of 1971. Mr Y told me why Peking did not support the rebels. 'You see, there were two things wrong with them.' He sounded like a mechanic accounting for a stalled motor. 'They put the gun above the Party. And they did not practise the mass line.' Mr Y summed them up as 'Guevarist'.

Now, is this really why Peking would not back the

Ceylonese rebels? China's position had two inseparable roots. Peking felt the rebels would lose. Here were grounds for keeping clear of them. But the *reasons* which convinced Peking the rebels would lose were ideological. As Mr Y detailed, the youthful Ceylonese had fallen into two errors which Peking believes fundamental.

The 'reality' which the exponent of *realpolitik* reveres cannot be measured by thermometer or scale. What you see is not unaffected by what you believe. Mao thought the Ceylon rebels were wrong – and calculated accordingly. Che Guevara might have thought them correct – and calculated accordingly.

To sum up. The Chinese are certainly among the Realists of history, not the Zealots or the Romantics. Yet their realism is at once an aspect and an application of their (China-tested) Communist convictions. The Chinese are not Communists with the left hand and Bismarckians with the right. To an extent remarkable for men of ideology, they see the world with a single eye.

While watching a ping-pong exhibition at a Physical Training Institute near Peking, it occurred to me that the game of ping-pong illustrates Chinese foreign policy. Ping-pong is almost *premised on adversity*. Light as a feather, the ball is incredibly wayward. Now it hangs in the air on a tiny gust; now it sulkily falls short of its expected destination. One recalls the chances and trials of the C.C.P. Seldom could it make common-sense projections; often it was blown off course.

The bat is modest. A frail wand hardly larger than the muscular hand which grips it. Yet it must guard thirty feet of space. I thought of the C.C.P. pitted against Japan. Sometimes its weapons were poor enough to make a peasant blush. Always it had to make up for with timing what it lacked in brute force.

The table is frustratingly small. Can that floating ball be delivered from twenty feet to such suburban confinement? The groping athletes in blue shorts and red shirts turn into P.L.A. guerrillas before the eyes. Mao's rule of guerrilla war comes to mind: 'Our strategy is "pit one against ten" and our tactics are "pit ten against one."' What did he mean? Dare the impossible in the long run (one against ten). But calculate to the last detail in the short run (ten against one). The ping-pong player has feeble tools at his command. His task – to work his will on that feather of a ball – seems more than you can expect him to fulfil. Even now a cross-breeze wafts by to upset all calculation.

But what is long odds *strategically* he makes short odds *tactically*. He divides the job into its several aspects. Is the ball far to the left? He leaps like a tiger to get near it. Then he abandons vigour and goes limp. The fingers twitch imperceptibly and he caresses the celluloid in a mini-lob. It grazes the net from the sharpest of angles. His rushing opponent is confounded by the surprise of it. He has met the challenge of one against ten by finding the moment to pit ten against one. Mao wrote of the uphill fight against Chiang in the early 1930s: 'We generally spend more time in moving than in fighting.' So with the sharp-eyed player and his mini-lob. Position was vital, the blow itself almost incidental.

The plotting minds of the players are an almost tangible force in the stadium. You see that the human beings are everything, the 'weapons' nothing. Did not Mao say of the struggle for China's destiny that ultimately men always count more than weapons? It is in ping-pong as in guerrilla war. *Human resourcefulness in adversity* is the theme. The name of China's game has been to turn weakness into strength. To transform defence into offence. To snatch mastery from the jaws of necessity.

Leaving China by train through the technicolour lush-
ness of Kwangtung's rounded hills, I felt a complex emotion. Fazed by South China's beauty on a summer morning, I could not yet untangle its two conflicting strands.
First there was a feeling that rubs off from the buoyancy
of corporate aspiration in China. The people seemed like
Rousseau's 'Spartan mother', putting country before self,
living as lambs of Shepherd Mao – and that is ennobling.
But – here was the second current – also a feeling of painful separation from the high pitch of collective spirit. I
could not live like that– how can others do so?

Behind the pain and separation lies anxiety at the
'mental unity'. Mao rules them, Nixon rules us, I said before; yet the systems of government have almost nothing
in common. We have no mental unity, we have 'freedom',
and of our kind of freedom China has none. Peking has a
parliament, but it has no more power in China than
Queen Elizabeth has in England. The individual in
China, insofar as he reaches beyond the practicalities of
life – I don't know how many do – is enveloped by an
Idea, the Thought of Mao Tse-tung. The myth of Mao
Thought has reached into homes and even spirits (which
Leninism or Stalinism hardly did in Russia).

This near-total control is not by police terror. The tech-
niques of Stalinist terror – armed police everywhere, mass
killings, murder of political opponents, knocks on the
door at 3 a.m., then a shot – are not evident in China today. Though force remains the ultimate basis of any state,
control of the people in China is more nearly psychological than by physical coercion. Its extent would be

hard to overstate. As this book records, politics reaches into almost every corner. Yet the method of control is amazingly light-handed by Communist standards. The informal way P.L.A. men mingle and work with the population is remarkable to see. Peking trusts its citizens in their millions with rifles at home (members of the militia). What it does not trust them with – for the Dictatorship is by Idea – is their own minds.

There is paradox in the impression, got especially in rural parts, that people proceed with their daily lives in a relatively unpressured way. On one hand, Mao Thought pervades. On the other, the family (for instance) is extremely important to the Chinese I met on this trip. The bridge is the age-old social discipline of the Chinese. The C.C.P. has *used* the traditional bonds. An instance is reverence for ancestors. The Party does not stop the girls at the Nanking factory from visiting ancestors' graves, but it tries through propaganda to turn ancestor-reverence as much as possible toward *revolutionary martyrs*. In the environs of Nanking, I saw roadside ancestral altars turned into little shrines of Mao Tse-tung Thought; the central tablet was re-done in red, featuring the star of the C.C.P., and quotations from the Chairman ran in strips from top to bottom down each side.

It is no longer simply 'Communists' on one hand and 'Chinese society' on the other. A merger has occurred at many points – a new kind of *tao* (way) emerges. This makes possible a Dictatorship by Idea (rather than by force). It is not like Poland or Hungary, where the Communists are a blanket spread over the body social. This may be what gave me an impression in China of pervasive yet light-handed control.

Is it not worse in China than Poland or Hungary, in that the people seem to cooperate in their own unfreedom? No, because the Idea fits the experience of most Chinese. At the Peking Chinese-Medicine Hospital, I met a railway worker who'd been hit by a train, and the resulting spine disorder paralysed him from the waist down.

His legs had shrunk, his hope had dwindled, and he had lain in bed like a vegetable for eighteen years. In the Cultural Revolution, when doctors were urged to tackle 'even the impossible', a team at the hospital began acupuncture treatment on 151 such half-paralysed people. Most had lain in bed so long that the marks of bedsores were on them like burns. One hundred and twenty-four can now walk with a stick; fifteen can walk without a stick; and eight of these are at work again.

The railway worker hobbled across the room on crutches to greet me, and said: 'I am out of bed because of Chairman Mao's Thought. Soon I will go back to work for the sake of the revolution.' At that moment the remark seemed embarrassing, yet the Myth of Mao is functional to medicine and to much endeavour in China. Was the schoolgirl really studying French to 'further world revolution'? No, but the myth of revolution gives her the zeal to study French well. 'Myth' is not falsehood but dramatization with a kernel of truth. The Myth of Mao sums up bitter Chinese experience and lends hope. It seemed to give the railway worker a mental picture of a world he could rejoin, and his doctors a vital extra ounce of resourcefulness.

For the nation, it gives a recognizable (if distorted) summary of past struggles against landlords and foreigners, and an impulse to keep going further in the collective drama of China 'standing up'.

When Professor P'u at Sun Yat Sen University said his new research was aimed to serve 'workers, peasants, and soldiers', he invoked a myth. This 'Blessed Trinity' suffuses China today. Everything is weighed against its service to these three groups. I sometimes found that what this Trinity put out the front door it let slip in the back (a violinist in the Red Guard Art Troupe in Sian said his father had been a 'peasant', but he'd been a landlord who later corrected his ideas; a cadre's daughter at Peking University contrived to call her father a 'worker'). But though not a full portrayal of reality, the 'Blessed Trinity' has meaning as an alchemy of fact and hope which suggests what the collective drama of China's revolution is about.

Workers stands for industrialization. They come first, since, according to Marx, workers make the revolution. Workers didn't in China, but modernizing China is a good part of the revolution's aims. Mao has not made an idol of industrialization as some Marxists have in Russia. But ever since the impact of the materially superior West shattered the Ch'ing dynasty, China's opinion leaders have defined the national power they seek partly in terms of large-scale production. Here Marxist theory and national aspiration and the instinct of the 'modern' Chinese mind all coincide.

Peasants stands for the reality of a China still eighty per cent rural. The revolution came from the villages. It had to; there was no other adequate source. Mao became its leader by grasping this, and he still resists notions of development (perhaps Liu Shao-ch'i's) which would leave rural China lagging behind the industrial sector. Producing enough food for 800,000,000 people is *the* great daily task of the Chinese nation; three quarters of the Chinese spend their time growing their own food; the industrial and service sectors are tiny beside the food-producing sector. To keep the country ticking over and hold it together, peasants are the key. To pursue equality, as Mao is doing, the peasants are also, of course, the key.

Soldiers stands for the international defence of the revolution, and also for a crucial fact about the politics of the revolution. Peking's leaders won power by the gun. They have always felt threatened by U.S. encirclement. At any moment it might have been necessary once more, as against Japan, to mount 'people's war'. Soldiers are in this way central to China's revolutionary drama.

But the People's Liberation Army is also the linchpin of China's politics today. For it is the *bridge between the peasant reality of China and the modernizing tasks*. It is a peasant army. As such it is the national institution which best represents the political reality of China. Better than the Party, better than the state administration. That is why Mao used it in the Cultural Revolution for a political task – as he had used it before. It is his weapon against 'revisionists' (but perhaps they are China's most orthodox Marxists!) who put their socialist faith in historical process propelled by transformation of the material base, and would leave the peasants behind. It is his weapon against 'ultra-leftists' (but perhaps they are China's purest Maoists!) who took Mao's idea of uninterrupted revolution all too seriously, and spiralled into the factionalism of 1967.

Workers, peasants, soldiers. Like so many slogans in China, it has a practical kernel. It ties together aims, methods, and resources. It is a myth with roots in reality.

I cannot say in blanket fashion whether this Mao Myth is 'good' or 'bad'. For the ordinary Chinese it seems to give meaning to things. He can see such spectacular benefits from this present government that the collective drama – which the Mao Myth expresses – seems an acceptable way to try and get the further improvements in his life that he would like. It also stirs his national pride.

Recall, too, that the individualistic or 'privatistic' alternative, in a country with *per capita* income perhaps one twentieth of America's, is not a glittering one for the ordinary Chinese. And China simply could not afford to encourage the privatistic alternative. At today's economic levels, Peking could hardly permit its 800,000,000 people to build their separate individual worlds, to carve out separate career patterns and philosophies, to surround themselves with their separate sets of possessions.

It is the intellectual who pays the big price. A scholar in a Chinese city, at the end of an evening's conversation, said three big things have happened since Liberation. China has 'stood up'. Class exploitation has gone. The nation is being 'proletarianized'. The first two he elaborated effectively, but he didn't convey much of the third. Either the idea seemed forced, elusive to him, or he had regrets about the way it has worked out.

Was he thinking of how the Mao Myth had 'proletarianized' his field of study, twisting it to fit the needs of the collective drama? I thought of his daughter, a bright graduate of a major university now working as a farm labourer. He had said of her in a rather flat way: 'We hope that later she may be given a job that will make use of her abilities.' For this man, the Mao Myth leaves high and dry his own concerns (and those of his children, and many of his colleagues). Whether the spoiling of these 'careers' is worthwhile for the sake of the Chinese millions whose interests are put first – it is a question of values, in Peking as in Boston. In a new way, each man still has his China, as he has his Rousseau.

Remembering what I saw in China – and the feeling of painful separation on the train from Canton – I venture to say that it must be terribly hard for Chinese intellectuals to accept the Mao Myth. Of course they can and do support the revolution's nationalism. That China has 'stood up' puts a flash of pride in any Chinese eye. Yet they can hardly approve – especially since the Cultural Revolution, which several seemed embarrassed to talk about – of Dictatorship by Idea.

People ask, 'Is China free?', but there is no objective measure of the freedom of a whole society. Observation in China, as study of China, suggests that the revolution has been good for workers and peasants but problematic for intellectuals. It is hard to go on from there and make overall value judgements that are honest.

First, there are so many gaps in our knowledge of China that it can be like judging America on the basis of the Kent State and Attica events (I know this because I used, before I came here, to judge the United States mainly by its spectacular lapses). Second, our experience has been so different from China's. Not having plumbed the depths of brokenness and humiliation that China did in the century following the Opium War, we cannot know the corporate emotion that comes with the recovery. Third – a related point – the relatively powerful should judge the less powerful with caution. It is easy for the rich man to scorn the loose morals of the poor man who steals his dinner. Easy for pluralist America, which has 6 per cent of world population and about 35 per cent of its wealth, to attack the regimentation of China, which has about 25 per cent of world population and 4 per cent of its wealth. Easy, too, for tired America to shake its head at the psychological simplicities of China's nation-building mood, and forget that America was itself once in a proud, naïve stage of nation-building, bristling with a sense of innocence and mission.

Yet at one point we and China face the same value judgement. Which gets priority: the individual's freedom or the relationships of the whole society? Which *unit* is to be taken for policy and moral judgement alike: the nation, trade union, our class, my cronies, me? This is the hinge on which the whole issue turns. Professor P'u at S.Y.S.U. did not make his own decision to take up the problem of insect pests – it was handed him. Is that wrong? The writer, Kuo Mo-jo recalled, cannot now do books for three thousand or at most eight thousand readers, as Kuo used to in Shanghai in the 1930s, but must write for the mass millions – and he's judged by whether he can do that well or not. Is that wrong?

I am not a good guide here. I felt the double emotion on the train from Canton because I am both moved by the collective priorities of China's new order *and* sad at the lack of individuality and choice. As a democratic socialist (Australian variety) I am – to use caricatures – against both the 'jungle' of capitalism and the 'prison' of communism. This is not a popular position today, when revolution and reaction snarl a *pas de deux*. I criticize the Dictatorship by Idea in China, but not with capitalism's yardstick. To put a big matter in three sentences, I criticize China not for lacking capitalism's freedom, but for distrusting the creative personality. The yardstick used – the dignity of each person, the fellowship of all persons – is the same one I use against capitalism. Capitalism opens the door to tyranny of wealth; Chinese Communism opens the door to the tyranny of a corporate design.

After leaving China, I met in Hong Kong a young man caught between 'jungle' and 'prison'. Chu – as I shall call him – swam from Kwangtung province to Hong Kong, ten hours by night in the water, mainly to get better educational opportunities. (In 1971 some twenty thousand left China for Hong Kong, many of them young people who wanted to go to college and got sent to a village instead.) But his father, a teacher of Japanese in Hong Kong, would not or could not pay the big sum of money needed to educate him, so Chu went to work in a factory. Now he is disillusioned with Hong Kong. 'I work hard – and for nothing. To work hard for my country, that's all right. But here, it's not for China; it's not for anything. All you can do in Hong Kong is spend.' Chu is capable, and left China because he wasn't using his abilities there. Now the lack of social purpose and the jumbled priorities of Hong Kong weigh on him. As we parted he asked my advice – should he go back?

I am not going to end with moral judgements, because history is just now scrambling up our moral categories rather drastically, not least those used between Americans and Chinese. A symbol catches the change. In Taiwan today you watch Chinese boys play baseball – America's game. In Hong Kong you watch Chinese boys play cricket – Britain's game. In 1971 Peking launched its new America policy with table tennis – China's game.*

The point is that China, so long the object of our policies and our judgements, is no longer a passive but an active factor in the world. Moral judgements are inescapable, but the formulation of the issues is often at history's mercy. The flux of 1971 may turn out to have

* Not in point of origin – it came from Britain – but in the sense that Chinese are especially skilful at it.

been a watershed in the way people look at China. What we think of China will matter a little less. What China thinks of us will matter a little more.

This happens by delicate nuance; yet it adds up to a major historical mutation. The Chinese are going to start asking some questions of us. No doubt they will be just as odd as some of our questions about China. A Chinese official who follows American affairs, unable even to conceive that Daniel Ellsberg may have acted alone in divulging the Pentagon Papers, inquired of me one day in a confidential tone, 'Is it the Morgans, or the Rocke-fellers, who are behind him?'

Afterword to the Reader

Let me sketch some changes in China since I wrote this book three years ago. The military has had its wings clipped. With the fall of Lin Piao, the P.L.A. soon became less prominent in non-military affairs than I had found it in 1971. No chance is now missed to say that the army is under the Party's leadership.

Economic growth has been steady enough to allow wages and purchasing power to rise. Oil is a great new star on the horizon, as China exports increasing amounts to Japan and plans to produce 300–400 million tons by 1980.

The political temperature is generally a bit lower than in 1971 – the disappearance of the Mao badge is a symbol of it – though a campaign surges now and then, such as that against the influence of Confucius and Lin Piao in 1974.

The experimental organs which arose from the Cultural Revolution have tended to be eclipsed by a strong re-assertion of Communist party authority. Red Guards are no longer important; trade unions and the Communist Youth League have a new lease of life. On the other hand, the experiments in education to which the Cultural Revolution gave rise have been strongly sustained.

Views on Japan expressed by Chou En-lai (chapter 12) have been sharply modified since Tokyo and Peking normalized relations in September 1972. No more talk of 'militarism' in Japan; mutual trade and visits are on the rise. The worst thing said is that Japan is at the 'cross-roads', as between the paths of peace and militarism.

The issue of America has come out from the shadows,

where it was in 1971, to a clear and central place in China's foreign policy. Pushing the U.S. back from Asia is no longer Peking's main concern; the U.S.A. is useful as a lever against Russia and also as a trading partner. Since Richard Nixon met Mao Tse-tung in 1972, and a Peace Accord on Vietnam was signed in 1973, China and America have exchanged semi-embassies and a steady stream of delegations.

And being an Australian visitor to Peking is now different from in 1971. Mr Whitlam's bold trip to China bore quick fruit, in 1972, when as Prime Minister he abandoned the Chiang Kai-shek régime and set up full and cordial ties with Peking. Regular diplomacy has replaced an illusion-breeding vacuum.

Of smaller changes I note these few: China's air services have expanded (cf. pp. 16, 47). Eight major air routes now link China with other countries; China's own airline flies to Europe, as well as non-stop to Moscow and Tokyo; Boeing jets have also improved domestic services. The Foreign Ministry has seen much growth and change (cf. p. 204) to cope with China's deepening involvement in world politics. A few churches and mosques are open again (cf. p. 87); cosmetics can be seen (cf. p. 90) and Western music has had a certain exposure since 1973 (cf. p. 112).

March 1975 R.T.

Index

Index

books, 71–2. *See also* textbooks
bookshops, 29, 38, 42, 83, 86; restrictions on foreigners, 86
Botany Institute, Academy of Sciences, 82
Britain, 27; and Hong Kong, 120, 237–8; and displomatic relations with Peking, 151; office in Peking, 215, 217, 219–21; trade with China, 221
British Customs House, Shanghai, 30, 40
Burma, 214
Bush, George, 169

Cambodia, 25, 180–88, 205; Vietnamese in, 183–4; Chinese in, 186, 188; in Soviet strategy, 234–5
Canada, 193
Canton, 11, 14, 16, 24, 28, 31–3, 86–7, 123–9, 225, 228, 246, 247; dress, 36; temperament, 43; political gaudiness in, 48–9; and leftism, 77–8; daily life, 107–8; birthrate, 113; cuisine, 118, 120, 126–7; sights and sounds of, 124–6; and educational experimentation, 139–40; Polish and Vietnamese consulates in, 213
Canton Fair, 49
Canton Institute of Foreign Languages, 107
cars, 30, 31, 55, 56
cassava, 128
Ceausescu, Nicolae, 72–3, 163, 232
Ceylon, 239
Ch'angan boulevard, Peking, 34
Chang Han-fu, 205
Chang Hsi-jo, 206–7, 226
Changsha, 31, 36, 108, 116–17, 123, 139; birthrate, 113; Guest House, 117; and Mao, 123; education, 134

Chao Fu-san, 48
Chengtu, 69
Ch'en Li-fu, 87
Ch'en Yi, 201–2, 204; death of, 202n
chess, 62
Chiang Kai-shek 32, 37, 46, 64, 95, 168, 171, 174, 237; and Chou En-lai, 143; and Sian Incident, 170–71; and U.S. support, 171; and Australia, 195; and the British, 219–20. *See also* Taiwan
Chiehtse River, 64
Ch'iao Kuan-hua, 151, 156, 201, 202, 203, 204
Chia Tao, 56
Ch'ien Men gate, Peking, 34
children, 28–9, 61
China, 23–30; U.S. image of, 12, 26, 246; international influence of, 15; major routes into, 16; visa acquisition, 16–18; channels for tourists, 17–19; restraints on author, 44–5; and U.N. issue, 166–8, 193, 198; and Taiwan issue, 170–9; 193, 237–8; view of U.S., 176; and U.S. internal affairs, 178; and Cambodia, 180–88; world view, 225–40; and repayment of foreign debts, 229–30; rejection of bloc thinking, 232–4; 'united front' strategy, 234; and myth of Mao, 241–8. *See also* Peking
China Airlines, 16, 116; hostesses,32; political slogans, 48
China-Japan Friendship Association, 208
China Travel Service, *see* Luxingshe
Chinese Communist party (C.C.P.), 28, 30, 53, 206, 219, 232; and Yenan, 64–7, 68; Political Bureau, 64, 66, 143,

254

Index

Index

More about Penguins
and Pelicans

Penguinews, which appears every month, contains details of all the new books issued by Penguins as they are published. From time to time it is supplemented by *Penguins in Print*, which is a complete list of all titles available. (There are some five thousand of these.)

A specimen copy of *Penguinews* will be sent to you free on request. For a year's issues (including the complete lists) please send 50p if you live in the British Isles, or 75p if you live elsewhere. Just write to Dept EP, Penguin Books Ltd, Harmondsworth, Middlesex, enclosing a cheque or postal order, and your name will be added to the mailing list.

In the U.S.A.: For a complete list of books available from Penguin in the United States write to Dept CS, Penguin Books Inc., 7110 Ambassador Road, Baltimore, Maryland 21207.

In Canada: For a complete list of books available from Penguin in Canada write to Penguin Books Canada Ltd, 41 Steelcase Road West, Markham, Ontario.

China Readings

Volume 1

Imperial China

Volume 1, *Imperial China*, shows the growth, influence and eventual chaotic decline of the great Manchu dynasty. It analyses the nature of Confucian society in the eighteenth and nineteenth centuries and pinpoints its weakness when confronted with the expansive psychology and technological superiority of the West. The undercurrents of resentment and popular revolution which erupted in the Taiping and Boxer rebellions are considered, with the more constructive, self-strengthening movements, in the context of Chinese responses to the West. Amongst other material this volume contains extracts fom the ancient Chinese philosopher Mencius, the Imperial Decree to Lord Macartney's mission in 1793, and famous accounts of Imperial China by Quesnay and the Abbé Huc.

Not for sale in the U.S.A. or Canada

China Readings

Volumes 2 and 3

Volume 2, *Republican China*, describes the
tumultuous period between 1911 and 1949, a time of
terrible hardship which witnessed the disintegration
of Confucian society and, after two brutal wars (one
national, against Japan, and one civil), the victory
of Communist forces under Mao Tse-tung. This
selection of material by Sun Yat-sen, Chiang
Kai-shek, Mao Tse-tung, and Western experts
demonstrates how after Mao's epic Long March the
Communist strategy of peasant revolution succeeded
where the Nationalists failed – in making the people
a political weapon. In this, the formative period of
the new China's relations with both the Soviet Union
and the U.S.A., two fundamental questions emerge:
Was the rise of Chinese Communism inevitable, and
how are present-day Chinese thought and action
influenced by the domestic and international
experiences of Republican China?

Volume 3, *Communist China*, brings the story from
the triumph of Communism in 1949 up to the present
day and the latest, still unresolved, upheavals.
Although their ultimate aim remains the
establishment of a Communist society, Chinese leaders
have alternated between visionary and practical
approaches to this ideal. Extravagant attempts at
violent change, such as the Great Leap Forward and
the Cultural Revolution, have been interspersed with
periods of patient planning and even an interlude of
liberalism (the Hundred Flowers campaign). This
volume, which includes material by Mao Tse-tung,
Lin Piao, Chou En-lai, Dean Rusk, and Edgar Snow,
provides much of the evidence necessary for
interpreting Chinese ideology and policy in the age
of the Sino-Soviet split and the Cultural Revolution.

Not for sale in the U.S.A. or Canada